There is no place that the hypocrisy of ruling classes exposes itself more explicitly than in the law. It is here that they must spell out their intentions with the greatest precision. It was Anatole France who noted that the law forbids rich as well as poor from stealing bread and sleeping under bridges. And it is in the body of law where the elites have been forced by popular pressure to include all in the liberatory language that they needed for only themselves: the Rights of Man and so on. In these interstices, slavery was brought under critical scrutiny using the language that slave-owners crafted, and out of the struggle against slavery, the struggle for women's emancipation took strength, then civil rights and labor, and one after another the precision of legal language was turned on privilege and power.

This process has created a special class of litigators and legal scholars who have set aside the practice of the legal profession for personal gain and committed themselves to the powerful flanking tactics of liberatory-law: law that has been a pivotal contribution to all of the great liberation struggles of the past two centuries. These juris doctors have taken the central documents of ruling class law and converted them into weapons for the people, like the guerrillas who must recover the enemy's weapons from the battlefield. The Constitution of the United States falls most decisively into this category.

Jennifer Van Bergen is one of those legal scholars, and "The Twilight of Democracy" is one of those flanking attacks. It is coming at a time when our own ruling class is exposing both its ruthlessness and its hubristic stupidity, and this book is a special contribution to describing that brutality and folly, as well as the danger it represents to a dumbed-down, complacent society.

—Stan Goff, Master Sgt.
Special Forces, retired
author of
Full Spectrum Disorder:
The Military in the
New American Century

The Twilight of Democracy

The Bush Plan for America

Jennifer Van Bergen

The masses are prone to exchange an age of freedom for an hour of welfare.

—R. Carter Pittman,
Our Bill of Rights: How it Came to Be[1]

Common Courage Press   Monroe, Maine

ISBN 1-56751-292-5 paper
ISBN 1-56751- 293-3 cloth

**Library of Congress Cataloging-in-Publication Data is
available on request from the publisher**

Common Courage Press
121 Red Barn Road
Monroe, ME 04951
800-497-3207

FAX (207) 525-3068
orders-info@commoncouragepress.com

See our website for e versions of this book.
www.commoncouragepress.com

Printed in Canada
First Printing

For my daughters, Sarah & Giselle,
who are my inspiration and my strength

Acknowlegments

This book would not have been written without others' faith in me and my writing: Greg Bates, who asked me to write this book in April 2002 after seeing my PATRIOT Act series on Truthout, has guided me and waited patiently and faithfully for almost two years for the manuscript. Henry Gluckstern, my friend and attorney, who has been there for me when no one else was and helped me through more than one disaster.

My many activist colleagues in Florida and elsewhere, including the Broward Anti-War Coalition, Broward Bill of Rights Defense Coalition, South Florida Peace & Justice Network, the ACLU, Miami Indymedia, and the National Lawyers Guild. Ray Del Papa, Paul Lefrak, Paul C. Namphy, Jeff Keating, Bill Houser, Kwame Afoh, Jim Sanders, Bruce Glaser, Jeanne Baker, Keith Kessler, and Matthew Stanton have all supported my work in more ways than one. Thanks to Stan Goff and Lynne Stewart for their courage, and to all the amazing people in the Haitian community, from attorneys Brian Concannon and Judy DaCruz, to all the people fighting for democracy in Haiti. Further thanks to Ali Amir Abdul-Aziz for his work in fighting oppression on all levels.

I also want to give special thanks to E. Nathaniel ("El") Gates, who was my American Legal History Professor at Benjamin N. Cardozo School of Law. Without the gentle help of El's great mind and spirit, I would not be writing.

To all those who have had me come speak against the PATRIOT Act: Chicago Media Watch, the Georgia Bar Association & the African-American Georgia Bar, Cardozo Law School, the National Lawyers Guild, American Voices Abroad, the League of Women Voters, the ACLU, and numerous other groups and associations. To all those U.S. Attorneys and FBI agents I have debated (or who have tagged or shadowed me), who are working hard to keep us safe.

To the students and faculty at the *Cardozo Public, Law, Policy & Ethics Journal*, who published my obscure but groundbreaking article on the electoral tie of 1801 between Thomas Jefferson and Aaron Burr (Spring 2003), and my lengthy and detailed article on the material support and designation provisions of the PATRIOT Act (Spring 2004).

Further thanks to Charles B. Gittings for his work on the Project to Enforce the Geneva Convention (PEGC) and his contribution to Chapter Ten, *Global Dominance in Action*, and to Bruce Glaser for his work on the data-mining program, MATRIX, particularly for insisting that the ACLU look into it more thoroughly, and for his contributions to the MATRIX section in Chapter Six and bits and pieces to other chapters. To Keith Kessler for his brilliance and for understanding my disability. To Ray Del Papa, for keeping me afloat and for not forgetting I'm a human being.

To John "Splitting the Sky" Boncore for confirming what I wrote about torture, long before Abu Ghraib, for his amazing book *The Autobiography of Splitting the Sky*, and for his equally amazing mind and heart. And to the nation of all the First Peoples who are still the keepers of the Great Spirit and to whom my soul most deeply belongs.

Marc Ash, the master-publisher of Truthout, holds a special place here, too, for it was Marc who hired me to write, had a mysterious link to my writing self, got great work out of me, and called me all hours of the day and night to keep me under the whip. I had deep disagreements with Marc, but I owe a lot to him.

Finally, I would like to thank those who *didn't* help me, who might rather have silenced me, whom I won't name, but who are many. I write to them and hope this book can open some doors in their minds.

Note on Sources

While I am grateful for the help I've received from others on this book, I am solely responsible for all the research and conclusions. Because I feel it is helpful for readers to have sources they can easily verify and explore, I have footnoted abundantly and used internet sources extensively. All line editing was done by me and while I have done my best to double-check every sentence and every web site address and citation, some errors are bound to creep in and web pages will expire in time.

Every reference is cited in full when first used in a chapter, even if it has been cited previously. Thereafter, I have used a short citation form for subsequent citations within a chapter.

This book was not funded by any person, company, organization or foundation.

Contents

Acknowledgements   vi

Note on Sources   viii

BOOK I:
DECIPHERING THE DEMOCRATIC CODE

Preface: 2
Tertium Quid

Introduction: 5
Crossing the Rubicon: The End of the American Era?

1. Down the Road to Fascism   8
Fascism & Empire
The National Security State, the PATRIOT Act, and Parallel
Legal Systems
Faith, Terrorism, and the Rule of Law
Principles of Democracy

2. The Law is King   20
The Constitution of the United States
Statutes and Regulations
Case Law or Common Law
Treaties and Customary International Law

3. Our Individual Rights   30
Balancing Tests
Due Process
First Amendment Freedoms
The Fourth Amendment
The Sixth Amendment Right to Counsel

4. The Constitutional Code 43
Separation of Powers
Judicial Review
Court Stripping
Probable Cause

5. Types of Courts & Standards of Review 52
Civil Courts
The FISA Court
Immigration Court
Military Courts & Military Tribunals

BOOK II:
THE BUSH PLAN

6. The Demise of Democracy: Fascism in America 66
Part One: Is America Becoming Fascist?
　　　Britt's List

Part Two: The Bush Plan
　　　The PATRIOT Act
　　　Guantanamo, Enemy Combatants, & Abu Ghraib
　　　Iraq: Preemptive War & International Law
　　　Withdrawal from the International Criminal Court
　　　"Free Trade" and Corporate Dominance
　　　Prosecutions & Proceedings
　　　　　The Prosecution of Greenpeace
　　　　　The Prosecution of Lynne Stewart
　　　　　Grand Juries & Actions Against Activists
　　　MATRIX
　　　Environmental Laws
　　　The 2000 Election
　　　Secrecy
　　　Enron & the Cheney Energy Task Force
　　　September 11th
　　　Doublespeak
　　　Summary

7. The PATRIOT Act—   110
The Mainstay of Oppressive Power
on the Homefront
     The Threats to Civil Liberties
         The Threats to Due Process
             Indefinite Detentions
             Designation
         The Threat to Freedom of Association
         The Fourth Amendment Threat: Surveillance
     & Privacy

8. Ashcroft's Way: 121
A Closer Look at the PATRIOT Act
   I. The PATRIOT Act allows investigators to use the tools that
     were already available to investigate organized crime and
     drug trafficking.
         (a) Surveillance for More Crimes of Terror
         (b) Roving Wiretaps
         (c) Sneak & Peek (Delayed Notice)
         (d) Third-Party Records
  II. Information sharing

9. The Cheney Plan for Global Dominance   147

10. Global Dominance in Action: 153
Military Necessity or War Crimes—
Violating the Geneva and Hague Conventions
     The Geneva & Hague Conventions
     The War Crimes Act of 1996
     Military Necessity
     The Truth About Bush's Wars

11. Conclusion   162

Epilogue: Detainees and Torture   166

Appendix   193
The Bill of Rights

Notes   196

About the Author   227

BOOK I

*Deciphering the
Democratic Code*

~Preface~
Tertium Quid

"Tertium Quid"—"a third Something—the supercilious, contemptuous … man who takes pride in his unsympathy, and who plays with judgment trivially, smartly, and sneeringly, even in the face of … violent crime—who found nothing in human life worthy of serious consideration save the etiquette and intrigue of his own polite circle."[1]

Robert Browning, the restive 19th century British poet, in his dramatic poem, *The Ring and the Book*, about an actual marriage and murder in 14th century Rome, invented an archetypal character whom he called "Tertium Quid." This "third Something" was created in contrast to "two purely, typical, anonymous personages," "Half-Rome" and "Other Half-Rome," whom Browning made represent the "two prejudiced camps of opinion which made up 'reasonless, unreasoning Rome.'"[2]

Tertium Quid, that contemptuous man who plays with judgment trivially, smartly, and sneeringly, even in the face of violent crime, reminds me of George W. Bush, Jr.

This is what I see in Bush: contempt for fellow humans and for the rule of law. And I am not the only one who sees it. Mark Crispin Miller wrote a deeply disturbing portrait of Bush based on Bush's own public words in Miller's brilliant and devastating book, *The Bush Dyslexicon: Observations on a National Disorder.* Bush's sick humor about the death penalty, for example: "A jury found them guilty and—it's going to be hard to punish them any worse after they get put to death." And his mocking parody of convicted and repented murderer Karla Faye Tucker, just before her execution: "Please …. don't kill me!"[3] Renata Brooks wrote about Bush's "language of contempt and intimidation to shame others into submission and desperate admiration."[4] Anthony

Lewis writes: "The Bush Administration is really attacking a basic premise of the American system: that we have a government under law."[5]

This book is a response to the contemptuous man who takes pride in his unsympathy that I see in Bush and his cabinet. I would be grateful to Bush for inspiring me, but my concern is too great. Freedom and democracy in America are in grave danger.

I relate Browning's "two prejudiced camps of opinion" to the proverbial telling of both sides of the story. Unlike Browning, however (but acknowledging the general acceptance of the idea that all stories have two sides—whatever they may be: left wing versus right wing, Democrat versus Republican, good versus evil, wronged versus wrongdoer, rich versus poor, or some other set of polarities), I have no intention of attempting to present either camp. For the most part I attempt to present only one view: what I consider to be the constitutional one. This means, simply, that I advocate the principles of the United States Constitution. This book, therefore, ferrets out principles of constitutional law and juxtaposes them with a variety of other things: statutes, regulations, international laws, legal strategies, and actions of the Bush Administration, and asks the question: are they consistent with the principles of the U.S. Constitution?

With this in mind, I address two main topics: the Constitution and "The Bush Plan." While the book is an indictment of the Bush Plan, as I see it,[6] I intend the book to be more than the story of what's wrong. Rather, I intend that it also be an exposition and affirmation of some fundamental principles of democracy. I have tried to take the negatives of the Bush administration and turn them into an opportunity for Americans to reclaim lost knowledge. In my opinion, the defensive response to civil liberties incursions and human rights violations is wholly inadequate. A mere defensive response is hardly better than not acting at all, as it gives the human rights abusers a continual head-start. I believe we must talk and act with an affirmative construct of human rights in our minds. To do so requires that we understand certain principles of domestic and international law.

This time, the time we live in now, during which civil liberties have been broadly violated to an unprecedented degree, and—with the increase in technological capabilities—privacy has been increasing invaded, Americans have the opportunity to experience anew the process of reconstructing the meaning of democracy. My goal is to lay bare what the government does and is doing, and why it is so profoundly anti-democratic.

However, because I believe in letting people decide for themselves what is what, and what to do about it, and because I also believe that prescriptions make people complacent and that change comes from a degree of discomfort that allows for and spurs thought and action, I do not offer a prescription for fixing what's wrong. If pressed, I will tell you that I believe that Bush must not be re-(s)elected. I think that corporations and corporate-government trade agreements should be abolished. I think capitalism is inherently exploitative and destructive. I believe the electoral college should be done away with, and clean election systems and direct, popular voting should be instituted. And, although our Constitution is imperfect, I believe we must adhere closely to it, to the Bill of Rights, to the U.N. Declaration of Human Rights, and to international law. However, more important than my opinions on these matters is that the simple facts and elementary deductions I present here themselves be absorbed, discussed, disseminated, and debated so that people can decide among themselves what needs to be done. This is, after all, supposed to be a democracy. People must hear their own voices.

~Introduction ~

Crossing the Rubicon:
The End of the American Era?

> America under George W. Bush appears to be the
> new Rome.
>
> —Charles A. Kupchan,
> *The End of the American Era*[1]

> Here I abandon peace and sacred law; fortune, it is you I follow.
> Farewell to treaties from now on; now war must be our judge.
> Hail Caesar! We who are about to die salute you.
>
> —Caesar's troops about to cross the
> Rubicon River, from Marcus
> Lucanus, Pharsalia

There has always been a tension in the halls of our government since the beginning of the Republic over the exact balance of powers between the three branches: executive, legislative, judicial. However, never before in history has a president been put into office by fiat of the Supreme Court of the United States. Never before has that Court invaded the election process, stopped a vote recount, and implicitly declared a candidate a winner.[2]

Never before now has anyone crossed over the line to overt empire as the Bush administration has.

Bush has declared war—not on terrorism, for that was never his intention until he was forced to it[3]—but on the Republic of the United States. Since his election, viewed by many in the first instance as illegitimate, he has curtailed civil liberties, invaded privacies, and, indifferent to due process, detained people indefinitely. He has disregarded treaties, human rights, and constitutional law.[4] He has violated international law and custom and has alienated many of our oldest and staunchest allies. Even moderate conservative analysts like Charles A. Kupchan realize that "American unilateralism ... has been tearing away at the fabric of the international community."[5]

Is history repeating itself? In 49 B.C., the Senate of the Republic of Rome, threatened by the increasing popularity and power of General Julius Caesar, ordered him to disband the armies he had commanded as governor in Gaul. At the time, Caesar was staying in the northern Italian city of Ravenna. Ancient Roman law forbade any general from crossing the Rubicon River (which was the frontier of his province), and entering Italy proper with a standing army. To do so was treason. This tiny stream would reveal Caesar's intentions and mark the point of no return. After purportedly having a vision which prompted him forward, Caesar cried out, 'Let us go where the omens of the Gods and the crimes of our enemies summon us! The die is now cast!'[6]

By crossing the Rubicon, Caesar in effect declared civil war on the Roman Republic. He marched on Rome while the consul and most of the Senate fled to Greece. Caesar then assumed the office of emperor for life. This was the end of the Roman Republic and the beginning of the Roman Empire. Although the Roman Empire lasted hundreds of years, civil rule did not return. Caesar's opinion of the Roman Republic is captured in his words: "The Republic is merely a name, without form or substance."

The actions of George W. Bush, Jr. echo Caesar's words. Bush has treated the principles of our American Republic as words without form or substance. Once, like the Republic of Rome, the Republic of the United States of America was considered the strongest in the world. Alexander Hamilton wrote:

> It has been frequently remarked that it seems to have been reserved to the people of this country, by their conduct and example, to decide the important question,

whether societies of men are really capable or not of estab-
lishing good government from reflection and choice, or
whether they are forever destined to depend for their
political constitutions on accident and force.[7]

The Bush regime has no qualms about using force, but its
political and legal approaches do not appear to be accidents.[8]

Clearly our government is obligated to protect its citizens
against terrorists, but violating human rights and laws is neither
necessary nor wise. Caesar's dictatorship was violently ended
with his murder by some of his own men and Rome never
returned to republican law. Hopefully, Bush's term will have a
more peaceful and happy end.

But, if America has crossed the Rubicon, there may be no
going back. Ed Djerejian, former U.S. Ambassador to Syria and
Israel, says: "The bottom has fallen out of support for the United
States around the world." Margaret Tutwiler, former
Ambassador to Morocco and presently under-secretary of State
for public diplomacy, echoed that view when she emphasized
while testifying before Congress that "it will take us many years
of hard, focused work" to restore America's standing abroad.[9]

Kupchan concludes:

America under George W. Bush appears to be the
new Rome. There is, however, an alternative view of the
long-term consequences of the U.S. war against Iraq, one
that puts the future of American primacy in a different
light. Far from opening a new American century,
Washington has embarked on a course that is precipitat-
ing the end of the American era.[10]

CHAPTER ONE

Down the Road to Fascism

This year we are witnessing not just a series of brutal but fundamentally independent human rights violations committed by disparate governments around the globe. This year we are witnessing the orchestrated destruction by the United States of the fragile scaffolding on which international human rights have been built, painstakingly, bit by bit by bit, since World War II.

—Bill Schultz, Exec. Dir.,
Amnesty International
Amnesty NOW, Summer 2003

We must sacrifice some liberties in order to have greater security.

—Popular Saying, ca. 2002

Americans may not realize it yet, but the United States is already more than three-quarters of the way down the road to fascism. The 2000 electoral coup, the enactment of the PATRIOT Act and other privacy-invading laws, the unlawful detentions at Guantanamo, the invasion of Iraq, the abuses at Abu Ghraib prison in Iraq and other violations of international laws, the withdrawal from the International Criminal Court (ICC), the promotion of the Free Trade of Americas Agreement (FTAA), legal actions against Greenpeace and Lynne Stewart and other activists, the subversion of environmental protections, corporate invasion of the environment, and a broad policy of secrecy. All these are signs on the road America is traveling of something gone terribly wrong.

There are certainly other disturbing government measures, but these signs mark the foundational components of what I call "The Bush Plan."[1] The Bush Plan is nothing more nor less than what I see the Bush Administration doing. (I discuss the Plan at length in Book II: The Bush Plan.) The Plan leads, at minimum, to anti-democratic results and the creation of a fascist infrastructure. At most, it is an intentional plan to subvert and overthrow democratic systems.

Whether there is intentional subversion of democracy or not, the subversion and the damage are real ... and the effects, if not yet felt by Americans, will be felt eventually, painfully, and for a long time into the future, most likely by our children and children's children.

However, the Bush Plan is not the doing of one man or perhaps even a group of men. On the shoulders of those currently in office, those before, and those who will follow rests the responsibility for these doings and for the consequences. The Plan grew out of an anti-democratic culture that in turn grew out of the capitalist, corporate culture. It operates like a shadow government, parallel to and independent of our government and its moral values. While it is separate from government, it not only influences but controls government.[2]

However, we all share the burden of this and it is up to us to keep our country in the hands of the people. It is important, then, before getting into the Bush Plan, to take a brief look at some important concepts: the U.S. Constitution and the rule of law, fascism, empire, the national security state, and the three major parallel legal systems found in the U.S. Following this brief overview will be several chapters of more in-depth discussion of the sources of law, our individual rights, some constitutional principles, and the types of courts we have here. These chapters will show the stark contrast between the Bush Plan and the way of a democracy.

Fascism & Empire

My dictionary defines fascism as "a system of government marked by centralization of authority under a dictator, stringent socioeconomic controls, suppression of the opposition through terror and censorship, and typically a policy of belligerent nationalism and racism." Stan Goff, a retired military officer[3] who has spoken out eloquently against the invasion of Iraq, says:

> I think we already have a fascist executive branch, but that does not translate into systemic fascism yet. Fascism is a middle class phenomenon, which means it is something that happens in countries that have achieved a level of development. Right now we are seeing a preparatory phase by the fascist executive branch, putting in place the legal infrastructure to impose a distinctly American fascism if the opportunity arrives. Guantanamo, PATRIOT Act, the FTAA demonstrations, all of it."[4]

Laurence W. Britt, writing in *Free Inquiry Magazine*, delineated fourteen "common threads" of fascism:

1. Powerful and continuing expressions of nationalism.
2. Disdain for the importance of human rights.
3. Identification of enemies/scapegoats as a unifying cause.
4. The supremacy of the military/avid militarism.
5. Rampant sexism.
6. A controlled mass media.
7. Obsession with national security.
8. Religion and ruling elite tied together.
9. Power of corporations protected.
10. Power of labor suppressed or eliminated.
11. Disdain and suppression of intellectuals and the arts.
12. Obsession with crime and punishment.

13.   Rampant cronyism and corruption.

14.   Fraudulent elections.[5]

If Britt's list rings alarm bells, there is something more alarming, something beyond the raw fascist elements now growing in America, one large, looming idea: EMPIRE.

Empire in Caesar's time meant the extension of Roman rule as far as England. Empire now means *global domination*. The plan for global dominance is blatantly manifest in the policy planning documents of the Cheney Plan, articulated in detail by John Armstrong in Harper's Magazine in 2002[6] and discussed in Chapter Nine, *The Cheney Plan for Global Dominance*. Policy planning documents, however, set forth ideals and show intent, but they do not prove a plan. Actions speak louder than words. As Dante wrote: "I make no other answer than the act … the only fit reply to a fit request is silence and the fact."[7] We must look at Bush's actions.

Judging someone by his deeds does not mean ignoring his (or anyone else's) words, but it does mean remembering some basic principles. This seems to me to require three different strategies in one: (1) looking at key doings of key players (namely Bush, his cabinet and department heads) and properly naming those actions,[8] (2) recalling fundamental principles of law and democracy, and (3) drawing the logical conclusion. This is more or less the method of this book.

The National Security State, the PATRIOT Act, & Parallel Legal Systems

America is not yet fully fascist. It can, however, be characterized as something just short of fascist: a "national security state."[9] National security is certainly one of Bush's main themes, his mantra. Increasingly, the Executive has justified itself by declaring it acts in the interests of national security.

Under the PATRIOT Act, the term "national security" is

synonymous with "foreign intelligence." The reason for this is that foreign intelligence is used to protect national security. Thus, what used to be called "foreign intelligence investigations" are now somewhat misleadingly called "national security investigations" by the Department of Justice. They are also sometimes called "terrorist investigations," for the obvious reason that such investigations are meant to protect against terrorist attacks.

However, the mixing of the terms national security, terrorist, and foreign intelligence has unfortunate ramifications for people both inside and outside the U.S. Calling an investigation a national security investigation masks the fact that such investigations increasingly result in criminal prosecutions. What's wrong with that? Well, a warrant to do a search or surveillance for foreign intelligence purposes does not require probable cause of criminal activity. When material from a foreign intelligence investigation is gathered without probable cause and used in a criminal trial, what happens to Fourth Amendment protections? Suddenly you have nothing preventing the government from tapping the phones of innocent people and using a "mosaic" of pieces based on speculative and third-hand testimony to convict them of crimes that are increasingly vague and broad.[10]

The USA PATRIOT Act is the primary mechanism that our government is using to create this dilution of constitutional standards. It amends and combines three areas of law: (1) criminal laws and procedures, (2) foreign intelligence law, and (3) immigration law. Each of these types of law have valid separate uses and purposes. In fact, immigration law and foreign intelligence law each make up separate, parallel legal systems. They even use different courts. But, the PATRIOT Act merges and exploits these systems.

Immigration law involves primarily the laws that apply to the admission and removal of aliens into the United States. These cases are heard in Immigration Courts, which are part of the executive branch, not the judicial branch. Courts have determined that admission and removal of aliens do not require the same constitutional protections as suspects in a criminal prosecution, despite the fact that aliens may be deprived of liberty (and, under the PATRIOT Act, deprived of liberty indefinitely). The PATRIOT Act exploits these constitutional dilutions by applying immigration laws and definitions in criminal prosecutions.[11]

Foreign intelligence law (which falls under the Foreign Intelligence Surveillance Act of 1978, or FISA) involves the investigation of foreign powers and their agents. No cases are actually brought under foreign intelligence law directly. Only requests for foreign intelligence warrants are brought and these are brought before a special secret federal court (the FISA court). The purpose of such warrants is, of course, to obtain foreign intelligence.[12] However, the PATRIOT Act amends foreign intelligence laws to allow them to be applied to ordinary law-abiding persons without the constitutional privacy protections of the Fourth Amendment. Information under foreign intelligence law may also now be more easily used in criminal prosecutions, even when that information was obtained without probable cause of criminal activity.

Criminal law, of course, involves investigation and prosecution of criminal suspects. These cases are prosecuted in regular courts in the judicial branch, with full constitutional protections. Criminal law is where you find the Fourth, Fifth, Sixth and Eighth Amendment protections. It's also where you'll find substantial Supreme Court case law about First Amendment and Fourteenth Amendment protections.

The PATRIOT Act allows surveillance and searches to be conducted without probable cause, by resorting to foreign intelligence law. The Act circumvents First Amendment protections by permitting convictions on the basis of mere association or financial support, without any requirement of knowledge or participation in crime.

The dilution of constitutional protections ties back into the notion of the rise of an American national security state, where security, not individual rights, is what we fight for and protect. We have forgotten, then, what America is about and what our ancestors fought and died for. Patrick Henry said "Give me liberty, or give me death!" Fortunately, we do not need to make the choice between liberty and death. As the ACLU declares, we can be both safe *and* free.

Justice Ahron Barak, the president of the Israeli Supreme Court, wrote in 2002:

> Terrorism does not justify the neglect of accepted legal norms. This is how we distinguish ourselves from the terrorists themselves. They act against the law, by violating and trampling it, while in its war against terrorism, a democratic state acts within the framework of the law and according to the law. It is, therefore, not merely a war of the state against its enemies; it is also a war of the Law against its enemies.[13]

Faith, Terrorism, & the Rule of Law

Terrorists do not attack without reason. Nor are reprisals by regularly-constituted state military forces carried out without justification. Many people in the world are willing to die for their country, their faith, or their moral causes. However, no matter what the reason, violations of fundamental rights are human rights abuses and terrorism is a crime against humanity. Two wrongs don't make a right.

Terrorism has multiple causes, but American arrogance and intrusiveness have a lot to do with it. Neoconservatives believe that forcing religion into government and courts will cure the moral problems in this country.[14] But, faith cannot be forced and the First Amendment requires separation of church and state—which means religion or expressions of religious faith do not belong either in the courtroom or in government.[15]

In this regard, the religious right is not unlike fundamentalist Islam. Both believe that their faith must control the way the world works. As Bernard Lewis puts it, both Christians and Muslims "shared the conviction that there was only one true faith, theirs, which it was their duty to bring to all humankind."[16] Lewis says: "Today we in the West are engaged in what we see as a war against terrorism, and what the terrorists present as a war against unbelief."[17]

I am not anti-law enforcement, anti-military, or anti-intelligence, despite my critiques. I have the greatest respect for those who put their lives on the line to uphold the rule of law. But I am not for American global dominance.

Whether we are fighting terrorism or unbelief, and while laws must address and punish acts of terrorism and government must use and listen to intelligence, violations of human rights and the rule of law do more to hurt than help humanity. The fallout from the Abu Ghraib prison abuse scandal has illustrated this point vividly.

Principles of Democracy

We must choose between freedom and fear—we cannot have both. If the citizens of the United States persist in being afraid, the real rulers of this country will be the fanatics fired with a zeal to save grown men from objectionable ideas by putting them under the care of official nursemaids.

—Zechariah Chafee, Jr.,
The Blessings of Liberty (1956)

The actions of the Bush Administration are only half of the equation. The other half is principle. In other words, it is not just the actions of this Administration but the precepts of our entire culture that we need to question. To put it simply, we need to release the hold of corporate opportunism on us and rediscover the principles of democracy.[18]

If we are marching so steadily towards fascism, why do a great number of Americans continue to believe America is still a democracy? In my view, the answer is that many Americans no longer have a clear feel for what democracy is.

For example: a man emailed me protesting against the American Civil Liberties Union (ACLU). He said that he believed *Ashcroft* was supposed to determine what was constitutional, but that the ACLU and the courts kept overturning Ashcroft's determinations.

This is a fundamental misunderstanding of how the U.S. system works (or why it is so structured). Ashcroft may very well do what this man suggests, but it is not Ashcroft's constitutional duty. On the contrary, it would be unconstitutional for Ashcroft to be the determiner of constitutionality. Ashcroft is part of the executive arm of the government. His job is to execute the laws: to bring prosecutions against those who break the laws. If Ashcroft were the final arbiter of what is constitutional, the executive branch, of which he is an employee, would be prosecutor, judge, and jury (and maybe even executioner). The job of judge is a function reserved to courts. Neither courts nor certainly the ACLU can "overturn" or overthrow Ashcroft's determinations of constitutional law, since Ashcroft does not have the constitutional power to make such determinations. To be sure, the ACLU can challenge Ashcroft's views of the Constitution, as Ashcroft can challenge theirs, both in and out of court. And equally for sure, courts can decide whether they agree or disagree with those views.

If Ashcroft were the final determiner of what was constitutional, it would also violate the "separation of powers" doctrine under our constitutional structure. Each branch is separate. "Again, there is no liberty, if the power of judging be not separated from the legislative and executive powers," wrote one member of the Constitutional Convention in 1787.[19] Thus, it would be unconstitutional if Ashcroft had this role.

On the other hand, the function of the courts is not to

simply throw out what Ashcroft thinks. The function of the courts is, in fact, to do what this man thinks Ashcroft is supposed to do: determine what is constitutional. Unfortunately, as a journalist who writes on civil liberties, I have received all too many emails like this man's.

The Founders understood the tendency of people to form cabals, to make intrigue, and to try to subvert legitimate processes and ideals. They attempted to create a system of checks and balances in government and in the federal election processes. In fact, our Founders' knowledge of the human tendency to plot and subvert is what prompted them to express their principles in the Constitution and Bill of Rights.

But, unfortunately, constitutional principles have become largely the province of theoreticians. After all, what does the Constitution have to do with getting ahead in life, with making money? The answer for most is: *nothing.* What can free speech possibly mean to people who have to repress their real thoughts in order to kowtow to a corporate boss? What does freedom of association mean to someone who has to look good in the eyes of the Old Boys Network? What can privacy mean to those who must submit to having all their emails monitored by some CEO or operations manager? And if they keep quiet and don't bother anybody, what do they care about the right to silence, right to counsel, and right to a fair trial? They want their kids to attend a good college. The words—Liberty, Freedom, Democracy—that once roused people to revolt now go in one ear and out the other.

In 1809, a woman wrote to her sister: "What sacrifice would not an American...at the earliest age have made for so desirable an end [as liberty]—young as I was (twelve years old when the war began) the word Liberty so continually sounding in my ears seemed to convey an idea of everything that was desirable on earth—true that in attaining it, I was to see every present comfort abandoned."[20] No longer in America will you find such fervent responses to the language of liberty.

A second reason for the demise of public understanding of democracy seems to be that people believe that constitutional law is hard to understand. They believe that you have to major in political science in college or go to law school to learn it. To an extent, this is justified, as even many lawyers won't touch a constitutional claim. But, two hundred years ago, Thomas Paine's books, *Common Sense* and *The Rights of Man*, swept the country, were carried on horseback, passed hand to hand, house to house. Alexander Hamilton, John Madison, and John Jay published articles every week in the papers that discussed constitutional principles and argued for ratification of the nascent United States Constitution. These articles were read widely and later compiled into what is now known as *The Federalist Papers*.

Many ordinary folks also contributed essays to the debate.[21] A politically-minded farmer named Jonathan Smith of Lanesboro in the western part of Massachusetts declared:

> I am a plain man and get my living by the plow. I am not used to speak in public, but I beg your leave to say a few words to my brother plow joggers in this house. I have lived in a part of the country where I have known the worth of good government by the want of it. ... Now ... when I saw this Constitution, I got a copy of it and read it over and over. I had been a member of the Convention to form our own state constitution, and had learnt something of the checks and balances of power, and I found them all there. I did not go to any lawyer to ask his opinion. We have no lawyers in our town, and we do well enough without. I formed my own opinion, and was pleased with this Constitution.[22]

Basic constitutional principles, thus, are *not* out of the reach of ordinary citizens. Constitutional principles take some thought, but they are mostly common sense. WE, the people, are the ones who must finally decide what we believe in.

Still, for the average person to absorb constitutional precepts, she must make a positive effort to set aside the precepts of corporate and consumer life with which she is bombarded all day long. We need to let go momentarily of the mandate to make money above all else, to buy, to exploit things and people in order to get ahead, to repress our morals in favor of business policy, and to promote impossibly unlimited growth and profit. We must let these things go long enough to think about the logical consequences of corporate rule and the beauty of basic civil rights and liberties. And remember that we are not just talking about our standard of living. We are talking about sustainable life on earth.

It is crucial Americans return our attention to understanding basic constitutional principles if we are to discern and deter actions that subvert human rights and if we are to retain the delicate balance of international relationships we have labored long to develop.

CHAPTER TWO

The Law is King

[I]n America, the law is king. For as in absolute governments the King is law, so in free countries the law ought to be king; and there ought to be no other.
—Thomas Paine, *Common Sense*[1]

If this were a dictatorship, it'd be a heck of a lot easier, just so long as I'm the dictator.
—George W. Bush, Jr.,
December 18, 2000[2]

In America, the law is king. George W. Bush, Jr., would reverse the American way and revert to the way of absolute governments. While Bush seemed just to be joking in December 2000, we shall see later when we discuss the Bush Plan, that there is every reason to believe he was serious. Every measure he has taken has been a step towards despotism and away from democracy.

There is a saying that we are a country governed by laws not men. In this sense, the rule of law means that the government, not just the people, must be law-abiding. Which means a government has to follow its own laws, can't break the rules, must pay a penalty if it does so.

The Bush Administration would exempt themselves—the government—from being held accountable to the law. They have purposely refused to adhere to the Geneva Conventions (which itself is a war crime under 18 U.S.C. section 2441), pulled out of the International Criminal Court (ICC), and have gotten 89 nations to agree to exempt Americans from being prosecuted under the ICC, while at the same time abuses and homicides have been carried out at Abu Ghraib prison in Iraq and apparently in Guantanamo and prisons in Afghanistan by our servicemen under orders from their commanders, leading all the way up to Secretary of Defense Donald Rumsfeld and White House Counsel Alberto Gonzales.

In times like these, it's important, then, to go back to the beginning, to look at the fundamentals.

An articulation of the individual rights that the Founders believed were natural rights, is found in the Bill of Rights, the first ten amendments to the U.S. Constitution.[3] Certain constitutional rights in criminal proceedings, such as the right to counsel, to a trial by jury, to not be compelled to testify against oneself at trial (also called loosely the right to silence), to confront one's accuser, and the right to obtain a writ of habeas corpus (that preserves the right to be taken before a court of law when you are under arrest or in prison), are central to our form of representative democracy, and to what our forefathers called Liberty, with a capital L.

Other fundamental rights are freedom of speech and the press, the right to redress of grievances, to peaceable assembly, and to the free exercise of religion. The individual rights I have found at issue most often since 2000 are the rights to due process (to be heard in a court of law), free speech and association, and freedom from unreasonable searches and seizures (also sometimes identified as the right to privacy). The right to counsel (which gives you the right to the assistance of an attorney in a criminal prosecution) has also arisen under the Justice Department attorney/client monitoring regulations and the case of Lynne Stewart who was prosecuted for supporting terrorism, which will be discussed in Chapter Six. These rights mentioned here are what I will discuss most in this volume.

The issue of equal protection was raised by Bush in the 2000 election, albeit wrongly, as we shall see, but it is worth mentioning here that the right to equal protection of the laws, which means that whatever laws are made, every person has the right to equal protection under them, while obviously an individual right of great importance, falls under the 14th

Amendment, not the Bill of Rights. Equal protection will be discussed in the section on the 2000 election in Chapter Six.

The Constitution of the United States

The important ideas here are that (1) the Constitution creates the basic structure of our government and contains an enumeration of powers and rights, (2) the Constitution was meant to keep people secure from oppression by our own government, (3) laws can be declared unconstitutional in several ways, and (4) constitutional questions are determined by a variety of different "balancing tests."

On the National Archives and Records Administration website, it says:

> The Constitution was formed, among other purposes, to make the people's liberties secure—secure not only as against foreign attack but against oppression by their own government. They [the people] set specific limits upon their national government and upon the States, and reserved to themselves all powers that they did not grant.[4]

On the same page, it asks: "What is meant by the term 'constitution'?" and answers:

> A constitution embodies the fundamental principles of a government. Our constitution, adopted by the sovereign power [ie., the people], is amendable by that power only. To the constitution all laws, executive actions, and, judicial decisions must conform, as it is the creator of the powers exercised by the departments of government.[5]

The Constitution is considered the bottom line. If a law is constitutional, it is acceptable. If it is unconstitutional, it is not. A law can be constitutional in one way and not in another. A court may declare a law "facially" unconstitutional, meaning the entire law is struck down and may no longer be used in any application. Or it may declare it unconstitutional "as applied," meaning it is unconstitutional only in a certain context or application. (It is harder to prove facial unconstitutionality.)

What is or is not constitutional, however, has grown into a huge body of case law, with a variety of different tests applied depending on what area of constitutional law is involved. For example, a law could be unconstitutional because it violates due process. To determine whether due process has been violated, a court will employ a "balancing test," in which it will weigh three factors: (1) the private interest affected by what the government does, (2) the risk that a particular procedure will erroneously deprive the individual of his interest, and the value of any additional procedures in minimizing that risk, and (3) the government's interest, including the administrative burden and cost, in having to comply with the additional procedures.[6]

Another example: unreasonable searches and seizures are prohibited by the Fourth Amendment. This implies that *reasonable* searches are all right. Thus, a court would have to determine what is reasonable by "balancing the need to search … against the invasion which the search entails."[7]

Thus, constitutional rights are not absolute and courts will always need to engage in some sort of balancing test. However, as we shall see in the next chapter, balancing tests are also a slippery slope, and where a "national security" issue is raised, balancing tests can be (and increasingly are) applied to literally balance away constitutional rights.

Statutes and Regulations

Statutes are laws that are enacted by Congress. Regulations are laws that are promulgated by administrative agencies. Statutes override regulations, although in the absence of a statute, regulations are the law (as long as they are not unconstitutional).

The USA PATRIOT Act is a statute.[8] The Foreign Intelligence Surveillance Act (FISA) is a statute. The

Racketeering & Influencing Corrupt Organizations (RICO) is a statute. The Classified Intelligence Protection Act (CIPA) is a statute. The Immigration and Naturalization Act (INA) is a statute. The Antiterrorism & Effective Death Penalty Act of 1996 (AEDPA) is a statute. All of these laws come into play in the war on terrorism. All of them are subject to the U.S. Constitution. In other words, statutes are the law, unless they are challenged and struck down as unconstitutional by a court, or repealed by another statute. There are, of course, federal laws, state laws, and local laws (county, city, etc.). Here we are only considering federal laws: the ones that apply in all parts of the country. All of the laws mentioned above are federal laws.

An example of a regulation is Ashcroft's order for monitoring attorney/client communications.[9] The Center for National Security Studies (CNSS) describes this regulation:

> In October [2001], the Attorney General issued an order authorizing the Justice Department to monitor conversations between certain individuals being detained by the government and their lawyers. 66 FED. REG. 55062 (Oct 31, 2001). While the number of detainees so far affected by the order may be small, the effect on those detainees is dramatic and damaging. The monitoring scheme authorized by this order radically undermines the confidential lawyer-client relationship of those affected, so much so that it violates the detainees' First Amendment right to access the courts and their Sixth Amendment right to effective assistance of counsel. The monitoring scheme lacks the strict procedural protections for the attorney-client relationship required by the common law and the Constitution. In addition, it violates federal wiretapping statutes and the Fourth Amendment."[10]

The CNSS, therefore, claims that this regulation is unconstitutional, but no court so far has decided the question.

Regulations are published in the Federal Register. Another regulation is the so-called "Creppy Memo," a memo put out by the Director of the Immigration and Naturalization Service (INS) in 2001 that authorized closing some immigration hearings.[11] This regulation was challenged in several law suits in two different circuits, one of which struck it down (declared it unconstitutional), the other of which upheld it. The Supreme Court refused to hear the case, so the circuit split remains.[12] This means that in one area of the country, the Memo is *not* the law, while in another area, it is.

It is clear that what IS the law can be very difficult to know, and officials with executive or administrative powers can unilaterally declare laws that thus become the law, unless and until injured parties challenge them.[13]

Case Law or Common Law

Case law used to be called "the common law." It is judge-made law. There is less and less actual case law—law that has developed purely through cases. Most cases resolve statutory issues. Nonetheless, reading cases—which contain the interpretation of statutes and development of law through prior cases— is the only way in this country to determine what the law actually is. So, when someone (including judges, who do this often) says "The Constitution requires....," they are usually talking about what Supreme Court or other federal court case law has said, sometimes over the course of centuries.

Case law is complex, because the Supreme Court might say one thing and state cases can say something else, and district and circuit federal courts can differ from each other, as well, as we saw above. An example of a federal/state difference: the Supreme Court decided that the right to counsel attaches only upon indictment. This is therefore the authority for all federal courts. Under Florida state case law, however, the right to counsel attaches upon arrest or custody. Depending upon whether the person is brought up on federal or state charges, the difference can have very real consequences for a suspect who makes admissions to police after asking to see his attorney. However, when we are talking about federal statutes, like the PATRIOT Act, FISA, RICO, etc., we are only considering federal law and the federal court system.

Because federal districts and circuits can also differ in their interpretations, case law will vary from district to district and circuit to circuit. District courts are contained within the thirteen federal circuits. District courts are the federal trial courts. Circuit courts are the federal courts of appeal. In other words, if your case is tried in federal district court and you want to appeal the verdict, you go to the circuit court, also called the Court of Appeal. After that, there is only the Supreme Court, which does not have to take an appeal if it doesn't want to.

So, although for all these reasons, case law is complex, what is important to know is that *you cannot know what the law is,* even if you've read the Constitution and studied the statutes, *unless you read the highest cases on the question.* (And make sure you read the most recent ones, as well!) That means that if there is a Supreme Court case that resolves the issue, that's the law. If not, you must look at the circuit courts. If they agree, the law is easy to determine. If they don't, well, the question is still open in a broad sense, but, from your own personal perspective, the law of the circuit you're in is what the law is for you. (Of course, a decision in one circuit court may be persuasive in another circuit that hasn't ruled on the issue yet.) If the circuits haven't ruled, you have to look at district court rulings, and these can vary tremendously across the country. (District Court rulings generally are not cited in districts from other circuits. They are sometimes cited by neighboring districts as persuasive.)

Treaties and Customary International Law

Many people, including judges, do not know that treaties and "the law of nations" (also known as customary international law) are the "supreme law of the land" of the United States.[14] In other words, treaties and customary international law are THE LAW, as much as constitutional, statutory, or regularly laws are. This means that if we violate a treaty or customary international law, we are breaking the law of our own country.

According to constitutional professor Jethro Lieberman:

> International law governs the relations between nations and between the subjects and citizens of those nations. Because there is no universally recognized final authority for adjudicating international legal disputes, international law sometimes seems to be a particularly obscure blend of diplomacy and politics. But the Supreme Court has said that "[i]nternational law is a part of our law and must be ascertained and administered by the courts of justice."[15]

Lieberman adds that:

> The body of international law is not spelled out in or dictated by the Constitution. It is a composite of international customs and practice, judicial decisions, and treaty obligations. One of the principal modern sources of international law is the United Nations Charter, a multilateral treaty that the United States ratified in 1945. The Court has never ruled on whether its provisions are automatically binding on the United States and the states in the absence of implementing congressional legislation.[16]

There are basically two types of international law that apply domestically in the United States: (1) treaties, and (2) customary international law. Treaties are in force only once the President signs them and the Senate ratifies them. Customary international law, on the other hand, is operable by dint of customary international recognition. For example, prior to the promulgation of the international Convention Against Torture, torture was nonetheless universally abhorred and prohibited by customary international law. Customary international law, then, may also be specifically adopted by a judicial decision.

Another important element of international law domestically is that case law has come to distinguish between self-executing and non-self-executing treaties. Those that are self-executing do not need Congress to pass any additional "implementing legislation" to put them into effect. Those that are non-self-executing require Congress to pass implementing legislation before courts will enforce them in specific cases. One frustration that individual complainants have in the application of international laws to a specific case is that courts frequently decide that they apply only between nations and not between a nation and an individual. These distinctions have great significance in the Guantanamo and unlawful enemy combatant complaints. The Fourth Circuit decided that Guantanamo detainees may not raise the claim that their detention violates the Geneva Convention, since that treaty applies only to nations, not individuals.[17]

As Lieberman pointed out, too, there is no universal enforcement mechanism for international law violations. The United Nations has no enforcement power without moment-to-moment agreement by the parties involved in a conflict. There are a variety of permanent and *ad hoc* international courts where complaints can be brought, but, again, their jurisdiction only applies where the parties agree. The International Criminal Court (ICC), which came into existence only recently, is the first permanent international tribunal for war crimes, crimes against humanity, and so on. Shortly after Bush came into office, he pulled the United States out of the enabling treaty, the Rome Statute. We'll see that this is one card in the house of cards which Bush has built in his plan for global dominance and subversion of democracy.

In Conclusion

Do we want a country of laws and not of power-mongering men? I think this is the real question. If we want a country of laws, then we need to get a grasp of how our legal systems work. Similarly, if we want to know what's gone wrong, we'd better find out the right way, or at least take a look at what we've got and think about how we want it to be. Law may or may not be difficult on its face to understand, but the sources of the law are many and complex. Most importantly, the U.S. Constitution is the benchmark for judging the propriety of our laws. Where the Constitution does not answer, it is appropriate to turn to international legal norms, for at bottom all laws are about consensus, and international consensus is at least as powerful and meaningful as the consensus of all Americans. Where laws are proper and just, they will remain long on the books. Where they are not, they deserve to be overturned or repealed, and it is finally the province of the populace to make this determination.

Courts have, over the years, fashioned laws their own ways. Sometimes this is good, sometimes bad. While courts exist to hear cases, they will almost without exception dismiss any case or any cause the judges do not strongly feel *must* be determined in deciding the case. This is why courts will also avoid constitutional questions where they can. Such questions should not be decided frivolously or lightly, but only where necessary. This means that the development of law is slow.

Over the last century, courts appear to have increasingly ruled more in favor of government interests and less in favor of individual rights. This is, in my opinion, not a good trend. While government interests are supposed to consider the "good of the many" over the "good of the one," more often these interests serve only to protect the wealthy who pay for the campaigns of those in office, or conversely, the bureaucracy of government itself. Corporations now dominate government. The concept that corporations are "persons" in any sense is anathema to a society of *people*. Individual rights are for *individuals*, not corporations. The Constitution was formulated to protect *people*. All laws are subject to that fundamental precept.

CHAPTER THREE

Our Individual Rights

> There are certain unalienable and fundamental rights, which in forming the social compact, ought to be explicitly ascertained and fixed—a free and enlightened people, in forming this compact, will not resign all their rights to those who govern, and they will fix limits to their legislators and rulers, which will soon be plainly seen by those who are governed, as well as by those who govern; and the latter will know they cannot be passed unperceived by the former, and without giving a general alarm.
>
> —Federal Farmer,
> October 9, 1787[1]

> The principal [rights] ... are the rights of conscience, personal liberty by the clear and unequivocal establishment of the writ of habeas corpus, jury trial in criminal and civil cases, by an impartial jury of the vicinage or county, with the common-law proceedings, for the safety of the accused in criminal prosecutions, and the liberty of the press, the scourge of tyrants, and the grand bulwark of every other liberty and privilege.
>
> —The Pennsylvania Minority,
> December 18, 1787[2]

It is interesting and useful to look back and see what rights were considered the principal ones two hundred or more years ago. The discussion here, however, is meant to give readers a reference for (and a bit of an introduction to) the later complexities of Ashcroftian and Bushian logic.

The rights I will focus on mostly are due process, free speech and association, legal representation, and freedom from unreasonable searches and seizures (also sometimes identified as the right to privacy).

Individual constitutional rights are not absolute. One of the tensions in representative democratic governments is between "the good of the one" versus "the good of the many." Most often, the question of how to balance these interests arises, then, between the individual right and the government interest in preserving and promoting the peace and security of the people.

Balancing Tests

The Supreme Court has come up with a variety of "balancing tests" to help them determine whether an individual right outweighs a government interest. The balancing tests have now been used by the Court for over forty years and no one questions them anymore. It is obvious that some constitutional provisions require some manner of weighing one thing against another. How do you determine whether a search is reasonable or not, unless you weigh it against or compare it to something else? How do you determine which interest to promote when you have two conflicting constitutional claims such as free press and fair trial? How about other potentially competing interests, such as national security and the right to privacy? Thus, balancing tests are essential to weighing interests.

Balancing, though, is also a dangerous practice that has come to be abused by the government in claiming more and more power to override individual rights for "national security" reasons. In 1961, Justice Black wrote a dissenting opinion which it is worth quoting at length.

> I think it is important to point out the manner in which this case re-emphasizes the freedom-destroying nature of the 'balancing test' presently in use by the Court to justify its refusal to apply specific constitutional protections of the Bill of Rights. In some recent cases in which it has 'balanced' away the protections of the First Amendment, the Court has suggested that it was justified

in the application of this 'test' because no direct abridgment of First Amendment freedoms was involved, the abridgment in each of these cases being, in the Court's opinion, nothing more than 'an incident of the informed exercise of a valid governmental function.' A possible implication of the suggestion was that if the Court were confronted with what it would call a direct abridgment of speech, it would not apply the 'balancing test' but would enforce the protections of the First Amendment according to its own terms. This case causes me to doubt that such an implication is justified. *** [T]he Court [now] relies upon its prior decisions to the effect that the Government has power to abridge speech and assembly if its interest in doing so is sufficient to outweigh the interest in protecting these First Amendment freedoms.

This, I think, demonstrates the unlimited breadth and danger of the 'balancing test' as it is currently being applied by a majority of this Court. Under that 'test,' the question in every case in which a First Amendment right is asserted is not whether there has been an abridgment of that right, not whether the abridgment of that right was intentional on the part of the Government, and not whether there is any other way in which the Government could accomplish a lawful aim without an invasion of the constitutionally guaranteed rights of the people. It is, rather, simply whether the Government has an interest in abridging the right involved and, if so, whether that interest is of sufficient importance, in the opinion of a majority of this Court, to justify the Government's action in doing so. This doctrine, to say the very least, is capable of being used to justify almost any action Government may wish to take to suppress First Amendment freedoms. [3]

If Justice Black were alive now, he would see how right he was.

Jethro Lieberman observes in *A Practical Companion to the Constitution*: "A random listing of various types of cases indicates the extraordinary range of the balancing in which the

Court engages."[4] Particularly when the national security hot-button is pushed, courts tend to weigh so heavily in favor of the government that they "balance" individual liberties right out of existence. As Supreme Court Justice Ruth Bader Ginsburg said to a group of women's rights lawyers who asked her if people's rights were in danger: "On important issues, like the balance between liberty and security, if the public doesn't care, then the security side is going to overweigh the other."[5]

Justice Black's formula is worth emphasizing. He writes that the court should inquire (1) whether there has been an abridgment of a right, (2) whether the abridgment of that right was intentional on the part of the Government, and (3) whether there is any other way in which the Government could accomplish a lawful aim without an invasion of the constitutionally guaranteed rights of the people. Perhaps this is a test courts should consider restoring.

Due Process

> The requirement of 'due process' is not a fair-weather or timid assurance. It must be respected in periods of calm and in times of trouble; it protects aliens as well as citizens.
>
> —Justice Frankfurter[6]

"Due process" is whatever legal process courts have decided is due in particular sets of circumstances. This is also called "procedural due process."[7] Due process only applies where the government intends to deprive a person of "life, liberty, or property." The process due for someone who has his public assistance terminated is not as extensive as the process due for someone who is arrested for a crime.

Furthermore, it's important to remember that due process is an individual right, not one that businesses or organizations can claim, unless Congress creates the right legislatively. This is significant in the context of certain provisions of the PATRIOT

Act, where a due process right is statutorily created for a foreign terrorist organization to challenge its designation, but not for an individual to challenge the designation if the individual is brought up on criminal charges of providing certain kinds of support to that organization.[8]

Due process also only applies where there is "state action," meaning that the *government* has deprived the individual of life, liberty, or property, and must therefore provide legal procedure in which the person may challenge the deprivation.

First Amendment Freedoms (Freedom of Religion, Speech, Press, Assembly & Association)

> You think that life is nothing but not being stone dead!
>
> —Joan of Arc[9]

> ...I'm the enemy 'cause I like to think, I like to read, I'm into freedom of speech and freedom of choice.
>
> —"Edgar Friendly" in
> *The Demolition Man*

The First Amendment states:

> Congress shall make no law respecting an establishment of religion, or prohibiting the free exercise thereof; or abridging the freedom of speech, or of the press; or the right of the people to peaceably assemble, and to petition the Government for a redress of grievances.[10]

Freedom of speech, religion, and expression are so essential to a free society that most people have a fairly good basic understanding of them. Yet not only are these freedoms threatened by the PATRIOT Act and other recent measures, but Ashcroft has actively defended the incursions. Law professor Jethro Lieberman declares that the First Amendment makes the U.S. "unique among nations by withdrawing from the government the power to dictate what people must feel or believe, how they may worship, what they may say, to whom they may say it, with whom they may mingle, and what they may demand from their government. The power to dictate or control these things is the power to enslave a nation."[11] Whether freedom of speech, expression, and religion make us unique or not, and whether it is true that our government does not dictate to us, certainly democracy cannot exist without these freedoms.

The portions that are most threatened by the Bush administration are the freedoms of speech and press, and the right to assemble. Case law has arisen abundantly over the years in relation to every clause of the First Amendment. Additionally, the Supreme Court has construed a "right of association" in the First Amendment, which has come to be viewed as an essential right and is also now under attack.

The Court has found in the First Amendment an associational right to engage in disfavored activities, such as membership in disfavored organizations, absent a showing of criminal activity. For example, in the Communist Party cases of the 1950's, the Court held unconstitutional laws that prohibited mere membership in a political organization that advocated violence or lawlessness. In other words, although the Court took many years to arrive fully at this approach, mere membership cannot be a crime, since it is protected by the First Amendment, even if that membership is in an organization that advocates the overthrow of the U.S. government. Any law that prohibits mere membership, therefore, is unconstitutional. Yet, the material support and designation provisions of the PATRIOT Act do just this.[12]

"Subversive advocacy" is another area the First Amendment protects. Justice Oliver Wendell Holmes wrote: "If there is any principle of the Constitution that more imperatively calls for attachment [e.g., favor] than any other it is the principle of free thought—not free thought for those who agree with us but freedom for the thought that we hate."[13] The Court has held that a state may not forbid "advocacy of the use of force or of law violation [sic] *except* where such advocacy is directed to inciting or producing *imminent lawless action* and is likely to produce such action."[14] This is a later development of the "clear and present danger test," made famous by Tom Clancy's movie: "Clear and Present Danger." Interestingly, the movie makes no reference to the test, but the title plays on the extent to which the term can be stretched by the U.S. government in protecting "national security." If it is politically desirable to view a group as a clear and present danger to the national security interests of the U.S., we can justify crushing it, even at the expense of our own soldiers, and that is exactly what happens in the film.[15]

The phrase "clear and present danger" was originally articulated in a 1919 case by Justice Oliver Wendell Holmes, who said that the defendant, who had distributed a leaflet against the draft, might have been within his constitutional rights to say what he did when the country was not at war, but not in wartime, when the words helped further a conspiracy to interfere with the war effort. Holmes wrote for a unanimous Court that "[the] question in every case is whether the words are used in such circumstances and are of such a nature as to create a clear and present danger that they would bring about the substantive evils that Congress had a right to prevent."[16] Although the Holmes test still exists in modified form, Lieberman concludes that the test "has repeatedly been misunderstood," "is not helpful," and further "[a]s famous as are the words ... they speak to only a part of the struggle for free speech."[17]

Advocacy is a form of speech. Membership is a form of expression, parallel to speech. Publication in the press is also a form of speech, but it is broader than individual speech. It is sometimes referred to as "the right of the public to know," which moves into the area of the right of the press to have access to trials.[18] Association is a form of expression. "Guilt by association" is prohibited.

The right to peaceably assemble is "one of the core political rights or Americans."[19] Chief Justice Hughes wrote in a 1937 landmark freedom of assembly case:

> [P]eaceable assembly for lawful discussion cannot be made a crime. The holding of meetings for peaceable political action cannot be proscribed. Those who assist in the conduct of such meetings cannot be branded as criminals on that score.[20]

The right to assemble has arisen in recent times, during protests against the World Trade Organization (WTO)(November 1999), the Free Trade of the Americas Agreement (FTAA)(November 2003), and the war on Iraq (February 2003). In New York, an organization called United for Peace and Justice (UFPJ) sued the city to permit demonstrators to march near the United Nations prior to the U.S. invasion of Iraq. They lost the suit, but hundreds of thousands of demonstrators from separate groups nonetheless marched spontaneously from and to so many different locations that the march happened anyway. In Seattle, however, demonstrators' right to assemble was restricted and violated in numerous ways.[21] Most recently, in Miami, tens of thousands protesting against the FTAA, including droves of buses with senior citizens on them, steelworkers' union members, and AFL-CIO members, were prevented from reaching protest sites.[22] Since Bush was elected, he has put into effect "First Amendment Zones," where protesters are kept at a distance from his location. The American Civil Liberties Union is challenging these zones.[23] Americans have a right to free speech everywhere, not just in special zones.[24]

Fourth Amendment Rights

The Fourth Amendment states:

> The right of the people to be secure in their persons, houses, papers, and effects, against unreasonable searches

and seizures, shall not be violated, and no Warrants shall issue, but upon probable cause, supported by Oath or affirmation, and particularly describing the place to be searched, and the persons or things to be seized.[25]

The Fourth Amendment governs the conduct of government officials who want to search our homes, belongings, communications, or persons, ensuring that they cannot do so without probable cause of criminal activity (which we discuss further in Chapter 4, *The Constitutional Code*). While it protects us, the protection is not absolute. The Supreme Court fashioned a rule called "the expectation of privacy" rule that limits Fourth Amendment protection.[26] The Court declared:

> What a person knowingly exposes to the public, even in his own home or office, is not a subject of Fourth Amendment protection...[b]ut what he seeks to preserve as private, even in an area accessible to the public, may be constitutionally protected.[27]

The Amendment "protects individual privacy against certain types of governmental intrusion but its protections go further, and often have nothing to do with privacy at all," declared the Supreme Court in the famous case that determined that there was no such thing as a "constitutionally protected area," and that the Fourth Amendment "protects people—not simply 'areas.'"[28] In this case, *Katz v. U.S.*, the Court determined that a person has "an expectation of privacy" in the content of his calls from a phone booth.[29] (Twelve years later, however, the Court decided that a person dialing from his home phone had no expectation of privacy in the numbers he dialed.[30])

Forty years before *Katz*, Justice Brandeis wrote in a dissenting opinion:

> To protect [the right to be let alone], every unjustifiable intrusion by the Government upon the privacy of the individual, whatever the means employed, must be deemed a violation of the Fourth Amendment.[31]

We shall see in the course of this book that Fourth Amendment issues arise frequently under the PATRIOT Act, particularly where it permits the government to mix standards from different, incompatible areas of law—such as the laws relating to foreign intelligence gathering (that is, spying on foreign countries and persons, which is not prohibited or regulated by the Fourth Amendment) and the laws relating to criminal investigations (which *are* required to adhere to the Fourth Amendment), or laws relating to immigration (which do not generally fall under the Fourth Amendment if they relate to asylum or deportation). The PATRIOT Act mixes all three of these types of laws into a veritable witch's brew, a dangerous mix of ingredients poisonous to a democratic government or way of life.[32]

The Sixth Amendment Right to Counsel

The Sixth Amendment states:

> In all criminal prosecutions, the accused shall enjoy the right to a speedy and public trial, by an impartial jury ...and to be informed of the nature and cause of the accusation; to be confronted with the witnesses against him; to have compulsory process for obtaining witnesses in his favor, and to have the Assistance of Counsel for his defence. [sic][33]

The Sixth Amendment right to counsel provides that defendants shall "have the assistance of counsel" in all criminal prosecutions. This right is more complex than it seems on its face. The Supreme Court has interpreted the Constitution to mean that the right is not limited to assistance during trial, but extends to the right to consult with a lawyer prior to trial—for example, after charges are filed or during custodial interrogation. Further, the Court has decided that the right includes an implied right to *effective* assistance and to free assistance in a criminal case, if you can't pay for a lawyer.

Lawyers are also required under the local code of professional ethics (which varies from state to state, but are all similar) to provide competent and zealous representation to their clients. There are also two doctrines relating to attorney/client relationships that are important: the first is attorney/client confidentiality; the second is attorney/client privilege. These require lawyers to keep confidential all client information and prevent incursions into lawyer/client communications.

There are four contexts in which the right to counsel has been threatened by the Bush administration: (1) under the PATRIOT Act, immigrants can be indefinitely detained without criminal charges or being granted access to counsel or a court of law, (2) the designation and detention of "unlawful enemy combatants," (which can include U.S. citizens, and as of this writing has been used against two of them), which is effectively the same as the indefinite detentions of immigrants, (3) Justice Department regulations promulgated by Ashcroft that allow the FBI to monitor attorney/client communications in certain instances, and (4) the prosecution of criminal defense attorney Lynne Stewart for her zealous representation of an alleged terrorist client.

We will touch upon all these areas at different points later in the book.

In Conclusion

Individual rights are protected by the Constitution. We have not covered ALL our constitutionally-protected individual rights—just those most at issue in the current climate. The terrorist attacks of September 11 created a deep shifting of values in America and pushed us to accept sacrifices we should never make. Yes, we must do everything we can to fight terrorism and protect our values, but that does *not, cannot,* include compromising those values themselves. The Abu Ghraib prison abuse scandal makes this vividly clear.

When I wrote the six-part series on the PATRIOT Act for Truthout, I included a section on torture. Around that time, a CNN poll announced that almost half of all Americans believed in using torture. I wrote that the PATRIOT Act opened the door for torture and cited an Amnesty report documenting cruel treatment of detainees.[34]

The circle from the acceptance of torture after September 11 to the revelations the Abu Ghraib torture scandal is an example of a reversal cycle.[35] While we can say that such reversals are overreactions that often occur during times of crisis, that is not an adequate response. Fundamental rights do not change due to conditions. Torture is wrong whenever and wherever it is perpetrated and by whomever perpetrates it. This precept and other fundamental precepts are embodied in our domestic and international laws. There is no excuse for such lapses. If we are a country of laws, not of men, we need to uphold the rule of law and hold all those accountable who are responsible, all the way to the top—and most especially to the top, for our leaders are the ones we look up to and follow.

While we have seen that balancing tests must be used where there are competing interests, individual interests should not be viewed as merely secondary to government interests, whether those government interests be in building a highway or in protecting national security. The test should *not* be whether, as Justice Black wrote, "the Government has an interest in abridging the right involved and, if so, whether that interest is of sufficient importance, in the opinion of a majority of this Court, to justify the Government's action in doing so." This is an exact reversal of the principles in our Constitution, which was adopted to protect individuals from government overreach. The question does not begin with the government interest, but with the individual right. The test therefore should be "(1) whether there has been an abridgment of a right, (2) whether the abridgment of that right was intentional on the part of the Government, and (3) whether there is any other way in which the Government could accomplish a lawful aim without an invasion of the constitutionally guaranteed rights of the people."

CHAPTER FOUR

The Constitutional Code

The primary constitutional concepts of separation of powers, judicial review, and probable cause are, in a sense, code words to the Constitution.[1] They describe principles that invest the Constitution with meaning and are central to an understanding of what has gone wrong in our government.

1. Separation of powers

Our government is made up of three branches. Why did the framers do this? So that no one person or body of persons has all the power. Powers are divided. The legislative branch has the power to make laws. The executive branch has the power to execute the laws. The judicial branch has the power to interpret the laws.

The circumstance of having three separate branches of government, each with separate powers, is called the doctrine of separation of powers.

In 1926, Justice Brandeis declared:

> The doctrine of the separation of powers was adopted by the convention of 1787 not to promote efficiency but to preclude the exercise of arbitrary power. The purpose was not to avoid friction but by means of the inevitable friction incident to the distribution of the governmental powers among three departments, to save the people from autocracy.[2]

Lieberman says: "Separation of powers is one of the deepest political principles of the Constitution, the core protection against tyranny. Safety lies in power divided, ambition checking ambition."[3]

Of course, it is one thing to say that we should divide

power and quite another to define how, as Supreme Court cases show. "The doctrine of separate of powers is porous and difficult to define ... [and is] greatly in need of clarification."[4] However, one does not need to be a constitutional scholar or Supreme Court justice to remember the reason behind the doctrine: to prevent too much power from falling into one person or group.

According to Lieberman, separation of powers issues usually arise in one of two situations: (1) encroachment on one branch's power by another branch, or delegation of one type of power to another branch, or (2) an attempt by Congress to dictate the outcome of a case in court.

The reason for raising separation of powers here, even though it is far too complex a subject to do justice in a short overview, is that the Bush administration is expert in over-accumulating power into the executive, and in stripping power from the other two branches. For example, Congress gave Bush the power to hunt down Al Qaeda, which Bush used as his rationale for unlawfully detaining hundreds of people in Guantanamo and several U.S. citizens in military brigs, without access to courts or attorneys (and many people still believe that he invaded Iraq for the same reason).

Ashcroft has said that if Congress repeals portions of the PATRIOT Act, Bush will veto it. That's a powers issue (although presidential vetoes have been upheld).

This is not to mention that the PATRIOT Act, itself, vests too much power in the Executive and strips courts of review powers. When government argues that national security compels the courts to let the Executive do as it pleases, that is a powers issue. Indeed, almost all of the issues arising under the Bush Plan, because they involve government power run amok, are separation of powers issues.

Another type of powers issue: in a case where the law prohibited any judicial review of the Department of State's designation of foreign terrorist organizations, a court found this violated due process. It then attempted to tell the Secretary of

State how to remedy this violation. This violated the separation of powers doctrine, because courts are not supposed to tell the other departments how to carry out their jobs. Courts may only decide what the law is.[5]

There is a related doctrine called the "delegation doctrine," which is chiefly concerned with limiting the bestowal of legislative power on the executive branch. When Congress creates an agency to carry out government policy, it cannot avoid conferring power on it to act. Lieberman says that "the delegation doctrine is the major prop of the administrative government, permitting most of the detailed federal law, from the tax code to environmental cleanup policies, to be devised not by Congress but by federal agencies."[6] The Supreme Court almost always sustains such authorizations. Lieberman adds that the Court "has been extraordinarily lax in holding Congress to the task of prescribing intelligible principles to guide executive policy-makers."[7] For example, the Court has said that in the area of foreign affairs, in which the president has broad independent powers, Congress may hand over a blank check.

Neither separation of powers issues nor delegation issues are raised in court very often, but it is nonetheless important to know about the doctrines so we can be alert to when such issues are raised in political situations, so we can judge the extent of powers we feel is warranted, and so that we can rein in an executive that takes too much power.

2. Judicial review

> To what quarter will you look for protection from an infringement of the Constitution, if you will not give the power to the judiciary? There is no other body that can afford such a protection.
>
> —John Marshall, during the 1787 Constitutional Convention Debates[8]

According to Leiberman, judicial review is "the power of courts to declare laws and acts of government unconstitutional."[9] It is easy to see how important judicial review is. If we do not have judicial review, there is no remedy for bad laws.

Without judicial review, there is no democracy. Recent laws and regulations that have been passed or promulgated at the behest of the Bush Administration and Attorney General John Ashcroft have severely undermined judicial review.

Judicial supremacy, on the other hand, means that the United States Supreme Court has the final say on all constitutional questions. "The claim," according to Lieberman, "is not merely that the Court has the final word in a particular case, but that the other branches of government, and the states, must follow the spirit of the Court's decisions in matters to which they are not parties in court."[10]

Judicial review is essential to the healthy existence and maintenance of democracy. That lower federal courts are capable of acting as checks on the laws and acts of government is also without doubt. As Lieberman states, "on a practical level, judicial review is the solution: it is one of the principal checks and balances in a complex system of separated powers."[11]

With judicial review so important, what, then, are we to make of the current Bush Administration assertion that terrorists simply do not deserve to have their day in court? What, then, of the denial of due process to the hundreds of Guantanamo detainees and the two American citizens in military brigs—while specifically denying the right to be heard in court, that is, the right of courts to review the detention? What about the new laws that say that immigrants can be indefinitely detained for nothing more than a minor visa violation— without judicial review? What of the PATRIOT Act, which Bush says he needs, that strips courts of jurisdiction in some instances? What about the Abu Ghraib prison abuse, responsibility for which goes all the way to the top, and Bush's insistence that the U.S. be exempt from prosecution in the

International Criminal Court?

The Bush Administration has run roughshod over federal courts. Courts are the last resort against executive power grabbing.

3. Court Stripping[12]

The 1996 Anti-Terrorism Law (AEDPA),[13] and the PATRIOT Act restrict the ability of courts to review executive actions. This is known as court-stripping. In September 2000, Congressman Conyers stated: "The Illegal Immigration Reform and Immigrant Responsibility Act of 1996 eliminated court appeal rights relative to judicial review of asylum determinations, decisions on apprehension and detention of aliens, document fraud waivers, orders issued in absentia, and denial of requests for voluntary departure. The statute also broadened the range of proceedings where secret evidence can be used against an immigrant."[14] In other words, IIRIRA limited the ability of federal courts to review appeals by immigrants. IIRIRA is still in effect.[15] And later laws were worse for immigrants.

Heidi Boghosian, the Executive Director of the National Lawyers Guild, points out that a goal of the habeas corpus restrictions in AEDPA "was to expedite and simplify the death row appeals process." However, "the resultant effect was an increase in the complexity and length of litigating capital appeals." David Cole, a professor at Georgetown University School of Law, states that the habeas corpus restrictions were included in AEDPA at the behest of then Judiciary Committee chairman, Senator Orrin Hatch, who had for years "sought to limit the right of habeas corpus."[16] Most of the Senate debate during the hearings on this provision, according to Cole, "centered around death penalty cases, but most of the changes sought by habeas opponents would apply to noncapital cases as well."[17] Senator Hatch "wanted to make it more difficult for federal courts to order retrials of prisoners where state courts had violated the U.S. Constitution."[18] However, "Hatch's provisions gutting habeas corpus ... are among [the] worst features [of AEDPA], but have nothing to do with terrorism."[19]

Boghosian continues:

> [T]he 1996 anti-immigration provisions [in AEDPA] and the 1996 IIRIRA ... intended to focus on controlling foreigners' rights. The laws placed severe restrictions on immigrants' access to judicial review both by creating the process of "summary exclusion" and by enacting provisions to deport non-citizens who committed crimes. Yet these laws, stripping away hard-earned civil liberties, were hastily passed in reaction to the quickly disproven theory that immigrants committed the [Oklahoma City] bombing. The result of these laws is that the ability of capital defendants to challenge the constitutionality of their convictions as well as immigrants' ability to challenge decisions by the Immigration and Naturalization Service (INS) in federal court is severely limited.[20]

Boghosian notes that these laws "allowed for the deportation of long-time residents for the commission of minor infractions that occurred years ago, obstructed refugees from receiving asylum, and reduced judicial oversight of the INS, a department traditionally requiring some judicial check on its exercise of power." [21] She concludes that "[t]hese ill-conceived 'court stripping' laws serve only to retract years of progress made in the areas of racial justice and equality with no documentable success in deterring criminal or terrorist activities."[22]

We will see that the PATRIOT Act strips courts among the following ways: the Act provides that the Attorney General or Secretary of State's "designation of foreign terrorist organizations" (FTO's) may be reviewed in no other court but the D.C. Circuit Court; it prohibits defendants charged with material support of a designated FTO from challenging such designation in any court; it mandates indefinite detention of aliens on the

Attorney General's say-so, without court review, and; it mandates that courts rubber stamp certifications for obtaining records (and a subsequent expansion of the PATRIOT Act that authorizes the use of "national security letters" to obtain certain third-party records without any court review).

4. Probable Cause

The Fourth Amendment says that neither an arrest warrant nor a search warrant may be issued except on a showing of probable cause of criminal activity.[23] That means that police must have reason to believe that there is "more than bare suspicion" and "less than evidence which would justify ... conviction" that the suspect is engaged in criminal activity.[24] A mere conclusion in the absence of facts cannot amount to probable cause.[25]

Ralph B. Strickland, Jr., Agency Legal Specialist at the North Carolina Justice Academy states: "Not all search and seizures require warrants (e.g., automobile searches, arrest in a public place), but the Supreme Court has interpreted warrantless searches and seizures as unreasonable unless preceded by probable cause. This means that as a general rule, most searches and seizures require probable cause."[26]

He continues: "On the one hand, [the probable cause standard] protects from arbitrary intrusions into liberty and privacy, but on the other hand, it gives sufficient leeway to government officials by not being as strong of a standard as proof beyond a reasonable doubt."[27]

Strickland discusses the various definitions of probable cause used by courts. For an arrest:

> Probable cause is where known facts and circumstances, of a reasonably trustworthy nature, are sufficient to justify a man of reasonable caution or prudence in the belief that a crime has been or is being committed. (reasonable man definition; common textbook definition;

comes from Draper v. U.S. 1959).[28]

For a seizure:

> Probable cause is what would lead a person of rea-
> sonable caution to believe that something connected with
> a crime is on the premises of a person or on persons them-
> selves. ([This is] sometimes called the nexus definition;
> nexus is the connection between [probable cause], the per-
> son's participation, and elements of criminal activity;
> determining nexus is the job of a judicial official, and it's
> almost always required in cases of search warrants, not
> arrest warrants).[29]

Notice that the probable cause is always in connection with
criminal activity. While it is often not spelled out, the standard,
therefore, for obtaining an arrest or search warrant in a criminal
investigation is "probable cause of criminal activity." This fact
becomes important when we start looking at warrants used in
national security or terrorist investigations, which do not require
probable cause of criminal activity, but only probable cause that
the target is a foreign power or an agent of a foreign power.

Probable cause also invokes the notion of privacy, for a
search or arrest is an invasion of privacy.

In Conclusion

This chapter covered a few concepts that are important in
understanding how our Constitution is applied. These concepts
also help in assessing the actions of our government. When
Cheney says he does not have to reveal internal documents or
processes from his Energy Task Force meetings, which might
reveal how much his policy decisions were influenced by such
corporate giants as Enron, which dealt with speculations on
energy contracts, later collapsed, and was found to have
engaged in cooking its books and misinforming stockholders,
the question of government accountability arises. It also brings

judicial review into play. The case has ended up in the Supreme Court, where argument was heard in April 2004.

Where the government claims that national security trumps judicial review or trumps an individual right, the question of powers arises. How much power will we allow the executive branch to possess? And how much power can be taken away from the courts? What happens when courts are stripped of the authority to review certain questions? What then? Where does the issue go? Does it simply disappear? If not, how does it get handled?

In an article I wrote a few years ago, titled *The Silent World*, I talked about what happens when someone is silenced. I described "the invisible world" as the theoretical realm of silenced persons and wrote that that invisible world "cannot be eradicated by being silenced," adding that "[r]epression causes an increase in the repressed energies."[30] Where presidential vetoes are used to override congressional decisions (such as the veto Bush promised of any PATRIOT Act rescissions), or where government overrides that amorphous thing: the will of the people, or even overrides individual rights enough to wake that will, where it removes the power of judicial review, or where, in fact, it removes democratic processes and replaces them with oligarchic or fascist dictates, the people are not silenced:

> If the messages of the invisible world are ignored, they increase and increase until some catastrophic event occurs, some explosion, in which the buried information spews out untidily onto the hitherto clean and neat visible world, wreaking havoc.[31]

Similarly, basic human rights *cannot* be overridden without eventual backlash. The answer is always *constant dialogue*, and that is what the Constitution and its precepts are intended to preserve. These things are worth remembering as we move forward into our discussion of the types of legal systems and standards of review that exist in our country.

CHAPTER FIVE

Types of Courts and Standards of Review

There are a variety of different types of courts that are important in the Bush "war on terrorism," and the standards they contain are crucial to assessing what the Bush Administration is doing to democracy. One of the central features of this Administration's approach to government, and especially to legal strategy, is the mixing of standards from different laws and different courts.[1] Thus, it is important to look at what these different courts and standards of review are.

Among the types of courts are: (1) regular federal civil and criminal courts (called Article III courts because they were created under Article III of the Constitution),[2] (2) immigration courts,[3] (3) military courts & military tribunals, and (4) the Foreign Intelligence Surveillance Act (FISA) court (also called FISC, for Foreign Intelligence Surveillance Court). Each of these types of courts, or court systems, contains different procedures and, more importantly, different standards.

Let me spell it out briefly before discussing each in more depth:

(1) Civil courts are distinct from military courts and include both civil and criminal cases. These courts function as long as the government functions.

(2) Executive branch courts. These include immigration courts which decide asylum and deportation issues and military courts or tribunals. Technically, the military is under the Executive branch but since there has been a Department of Defense, it helps to separate military courts and tribunals from other executive courts.

(3)   Thus military courts and tribunals. Military courts are the regular courts for trying soldiers for crimes (e.g., courts martial). These courts function year round, separately from other courts. Military tribunals or commissions are specially established courts for trying spy or war cases. Normally, military tribunals are not created unless civil courts are nonfunctioning. Nonetheless, although civil courts continued to function fine after 9/11, the Bush administration created military commissions for trying terrorists.

(4)   The FISA court is for obtaining foreign intelligence surveillance warrants. The PATRIOT Act, however, amended FISA to allow for surveillance of American citizens where the intelligence is deemed "relevant to an ongoing foreign intelligence investigation."

There are different standards for each legal system and type of court, and the ramifications of these varying standards to civil liberties is huge. For example, a military tribunal to try enemy combatants seems to make sense, until you realize that three military officers, none of whom need be trained as judges, can put a suspect (who may be a U.S. citizen) to death based on hearsay and with no appeal.

Immigration courts make sense, too, until you find out that the already constitutionally-diluted standards of immigration law are being gradually transferred via the PATRIOT Act to certain criminal proceedings in federal courts.

And the FISA court? Well, who knew it even existed? It's fine as long as all it does is authorize warrants to places taps on foreign spies and terrorists, but what about under PATRIOT Act amendments, which allow such FISA warrants to issue without probable cause to get your library records, your educational, financial, or medical records, as long as an FBI agent can say that those records are "in connection with an ongoing foreign intelligence investigation"?

Clearly, these parallel legal systems are subject to abuse

and the Bush Administration, as we shall see in more detail in the latter half of this book, has abused them. Such abuse affects all of us.

Civil Courts

The civil court system is made up of courts that try both civil and criminal cases. In the federal system, civil courts are the district and circuit courts. These courts, as mentioned above, were formed under Article III of the Constitution, and the 1789 Judiciary Act. In the state court system, civil courts can be village or city courts, county or state courts (which may, in turn, be divided up into "circuits," which are not to be confused with the federal circuits). Federal civil courts are the ones referred to in the rest of this book, unless otherwise indicated. They are also the ones discussed in the judicial review section.

Criminal cases tried in federal courts must adhere to federal law and federal constitutional standards. Thus, to arrest someone for a crime and bring him before a federal court, there must have been probable cause of criminal activity. To convict someone of a crime, there must be proof beyond a reasonable doubt. The standards in civil federal cases are somewhat less demanding, requiring only a "preponderance of the evidence" to find fault. Guilt of a civil wrong, however, does not lead to incarceration; it generally leads to monetary damages. The distinction between the two standards is clearly illustrated in the O.J. Simpson case. Simpson was found not guilty of the criminal charges of murdering his wife, but was found guilty of the civil claim of "wrongful death" and was required to pay damages to his wife's family.

Civil courts are equipped to deal with all kinds of cases, including those involving national security, terrorism, and immigration. Even military officials may be tried in civil courts sometimes (but not for military infractions). In some instances, civil federal courts are the courts of first resort and in some cases they are the courts of last resort. For example, asylum and deportation claims must be tried first in immigration court, which is an executive branch court. Immigration court decisions may then be appealed to the Board of Immigration Appeals, and thereafter may sometimes be appealed in federal court. The anti-terrorism laws, including AEDPA and USAPA, however, have foreclosed appeals in many of these cases, as described in the previous chapter section on court stripping. National security cases may prompt the government to request the sealing of documents, as well any other necessary procedures (like closed hearings, admission of redacted documents, *in camera* judicial review of documents or examination of witnesses.), but they can still be prosecuted in federal court.[4] Terrorist cases can also be readily tried in federal civil courts. In fact, there is a high conviction rate in terrorist cases in these courts.[5]

The FISA Court (FISC)

The FISA court (or Foreign Intelligence Surveillance Act court), or FISC (Foreign Intelligence Surveillance Court) is a court that meets solely for the purpose of granting or denying foreign intelligence surveillance warrants. The FISC is made up of 11 district court judges, each eligible to hear and approve surveillance applications.

However, what's important to know about FISC are the standards it applies. A September 4, 2003 U.S. Navy memorandum on FISA and PATRIOT Act changes puts it succinctly: "FISA is the statute which authorizes federal agents to conduct electronic surveillance, as part of a foreign intelligence or counterintelligence investigation, without obtaining a traditional, probable-cause search warrant."[6] Later chapters discuss in more detail why this is bad. However, it is important to note here that while it may be appropriate to circumvent Fourth Amendment protection on searches of foreign targets who are not being brought to trial on criminal charges, but when these searches result in criminal prosecution, the use of FISA sets dangerous, constitutionally-damaging precedents.

Immigration Court

Immigration Court, also known as the Executive Office of Immigration Review (EOIR), is part of the Department of Justice (which in turn is part of the Executive Branch). According to the EOIR's web site, "EOIR's primary mission is to adjudicate immigration cases in a careful and timely manner, including cases involving detained aliens, criminal aliens, and aliens seeking asylum as a form of relief from removal, while ensuring the standards of due process and fair treatment for all parties involved."[7] More specifically, "EOIR administers and interprets Federal immigration laws and regulations through the conduct of immigration court proceedings, appellate reviews, and administrative hearings in individual cases."[8]

EOIR contains:

°   The Board of Immigration Appeals (BIA or Board), which hears appeals of decisions made in individual cases by Immigration Judges, Department of Homeland Security District Directors, or other immigration officials;

°   The Office of the Chief Immigration Judge (OCIJ), which oversees all the Immigration Courts and their proceedings throughout the United States; and

°   The Office of the Chief Administrative Hearing Officer (OCAHO), which adjudicates cases concerning employer sanctions, document fraud, and immigration-related employment discrimination.[9]

Again, according to the web site:

> The purpose of these proceedings is to provide a process through which individuals can defend themselves against Government charges, complaints, or denials of benefits; or through which they can seek relief from penal-

ties imposed against them. Every proceeding adheres to statutory and regulatory guidelines ensuring the uniform application of law and the fair and equitable treatment of all parties involved.[10]

Further:

> Immigration Judges are responsible for conducting judicial proceedings and act independently in their decision-making capacity; their decisions are administratively final, unless appealed or certified to the Board of Immigration Appeals. The Judges conduct hearings concerning the removal of illegal aliens throughout the United States. Through its Criminal Alien Institutional Hearing Program, OCIJ currently has programs coordinated and in place in all 50 states, including Puerto Rico, the District of Columbia, and selected municipalities and Bureau of Prison facilities to adjudicate the immigration status of alien inmates incarcerated by Federal, State, and municipal correctional authorities as a result of convictions for criminal offenses.[11]

It is important to know about immigration courts because some concerns about the PATRIOT Act involve the application in regular federal courts of immigration standards, and immigration law does not apply the same standards as civil or criminal law. Nor are the same constitutional standards applied to immigration proceedings as are applied in federal courts. For example, immigrants in a deportation or asylum proceeding do not have a Sixth Amendment right to counsel. They are allowed to obtain an attorney and are given full notice of proceedings against them, so that they can prepare to make their case. But if they cannot afford an attorney, the state will not supply one for them.

Immigrants also do not necessarily have a due process right to a hearing. If the immigrant is caught at the border, she may simply be turned back without a hearing. If she is caught within the borders, up until 2001, she was considered to have a due process right to a hearing to determine her status. The PATRIOT Act amended immigration law to allow for indefinite detentions of immigrants merely on the Attorney General's say-so.[12]

Additionally, when INS brings a deportation claim against an alien, under immigration law prior to the PATRIOT Act, the alien could only be detained if he was either a flight risk or a danger to the community. Under the PATRIOT Act, any alien may be indefinitely detained even if he has only violated his visa.

Finally, under both the pre-2001 anti-terrorism law, AEDPA, as well as under the PATRIOT Act (which removed some exclusions), in a especially odious mixing of immigration law and criminal law, a person can be sent to jail for the rest of his life for providing material support to a designated foreign terrorist organization (FTO), without the government having to prove that the person either *knew* the FTO was engaged in unlawful activities or ever *participated* in those unlawful activities. The material support provision is in the criminal code. The FTO provision is in the immigration statute. The Secretary of State is authorized to designate the FTO and no defendant charged under the provision may challenge the designation. Thus, the combination of these two statutes forms a "strict liability" crime. Neither knowledge of nor intent to participate in a crime matter. A person may be given a life sentence if he gave baby food for humanitarian purposes to a designated FTO.

Military Courts & Tribunals

Military courts are not under Article III of the Constitution and so are not part of the federal civil justice system. They are formed under Article I, which gives Congress the authority to "make rules for the government and regulation" of the armed forces. Since 1950, military courts have operated under the Uniform Code of Military Justice (UCMJ), which continues the tradition of trial by court-martial for all uniformed military members, whether in war or peacetime.

The UCMJ provides for several stages of review, including appeal to the Court of Military Justice, a court which consists of three civilian judges appointed by the president and subject to Senate confirmation, but court-martial verdicts may not be appealed directly to civilian courts. A form of habeas corpus (the right to be brought before a court to challenge one's detention) is allowed, but the only issues that may be raised are whether the military had jurisdiction over the defendant and the offense charged and acted within its powers.

The UCMJ provides for most of the rights contained in the Bill of Rights, including the right against double jeopardy, self-incrimination, Miranda-type warnings, and appointed or retained counsel. However, the Fifth Amendment specifically states that the indictment by grand jury is not applicable to "cases arising in the land and naval forces." This means that there are no grand jury indictments handed down in military cases. Indictments are brought by military prosecutors only. There is also no right to trial by jury in courts-martial. Trials are held before a panel of military personnel appointed by the commanding officer who convenes the court-martial, or before a military judge sitting alone.[13]

Lieberman says that although the UCMJ "provides for trial of many crimes that are not military in nature—for example, rape and other assaults of civilians and robberies committed off-base,"

> [m]any of the offenses for which members of the armed forces may be tried are peculiar to the military; there simply is no analogue to "absent without leave" in civilian life. Because the military is a largely closed society with traditions and necessities far different from those of society at large, the Court has been willing to relax many constitutional rules that would apply to prosecutions in civil courts.[14]

This difference is generally without significance outside of the military. However, with the increasing militarization of police,[15] use of military forces for peacekeeping purposes overseas, and the increasing mixing of the parallel legal systems and standards, the relaxation of constitutional rules under the UCMJ becomes troubling.

Another important distinction is between martial law and military justice. Military justice is what a soldier gets at a court-martial. Martial law is a military rule of law for all persons, with government run by the military. In 1866, after President Abraham Lincoln declared martial law and ordered the army to try spies, the Supreme Court declared that martial law was unconstitutional when the civil courts are open and functioning. Only when the civil courts are "actually closed and it is impossible to administer criminal justice according to the law" may military tribunals, and only in the war zone itself, try civilians according to its own rules and the law of war. Additionally, the Court determined that martial law may be declared only by Congress and only during wartime.[16]

The Bush Administration has nonetheless erected military tribunals here on domestic soil, by declaring a perpetual state of war. On September 18, 2001, Congress enacted a Joint Resolution authorizing the President "to use all necessary and appropriate force against those nations, organizations, or persons he determines planned, authorized, committed, or aided the terrorist attacks on September 11, 2001, or harbored such organizations or persons, in order to prevent any future acts of international terrorism against the United States by such nations, organizations or persons.[17] The American Bar Association (ABA) states: "It can reasonably be argued that Congress' authorization to use 'all necessary and appropriate force' includes authority for the President's order, at least with respect to offenses relating to the September 11 attacks," but adds that "[t]he scope of the President's power to act alone with respect to military commissions has not been developed in case law."[18]

However, subsequent to the Joint Resolution, "on November 13, 2001, the President announced that certain non-citizens would be subject to detention and trial by military authorities."[19]

According to the ABA:

> Military commissions have existed, albeit under different names, since before the beginning of the Republic. George Washington ordered the trial of John Andre for spying by a "Board of Officers," which was, in all but title, a military commission. The term "military commission" came into use during the Mexican War, and by the time of the Civil War was well embedded in usage. Military commissions have had the authority to try persons not otherwise subject to military law for violations of the law of war and for offenses committed in territory under military occupation.[20]

In 1952, the Court stated: "Since our nation's earliest days, such [military] commissions have been constitutionally recognized agencies for meeting many urgent governmental responsibilities relating to war. They have been called our common-law war courts."[21] However, the Supreme Court in 1942 reserved determination of the extent to which "the President as Commander in Chief has constitutional power to create military commissions without the support of Congressional legislation."[22]

Bush's military tribunals create a frightening precedent. More frightening, there has already been talk of declaring martial law if another terrorist attack occurs.[23] Most frightening of all, as we shall see in the upcoming chapters, the Bush Administration has already set the stage for a military dictatorship.

In Conclusion

One of the most common misconceptions held by people as they consider what should be done with terrorist suspects is how our legal systems work. In my own personal experience, many people to whom I have spoken believe that all our legal systems require "guilt beyond a reasonable doubt" to convict and "probable cause of criminal activity" to arrest or search. While these standards do exist in criminal prosecutions and investigations in general, they do not exist in all areas and the mixing of standards from other areas of law which is found in the PATRIOT Act, severely undermines criminal constitutional procedural standards.

Almost forty years ago, in the famous case *Katz v. U.S.*, in which the Supreme Court decided for the first time that a person talking on a pay phone in a phone booth had a right to privacy and the government could not perform a wiretap of his phone calls without a warrant, Justice White wrote a concurrence in which he noted that "there are circumstances in which it is reasonable to search without a warrant," namely "national security cases." He continued:

> Wiretapping to protect the security of the Nation has been authorized by successive Presidents... We should not require the warrant procedure and the magistrate's judgment if the President of the United States or his chief legal officer, the Attorney General, has considered the requirements of national security and authorized electronic surveillance as reasonable.[24]

This was, of course, eleven years before FISA was passed with the purpose of regulating exactly this process so it was *not* left without review by a court. Justice Douglas wrote a concurrence in the opinion of the court, but especially replying to Justice White's remarks, which Douglas viewed "as a wholly unwarranted green light for the Executive Branch to resort to electronic eavesdropping without a warrant in cases which the Executive Branch itself labels as 'national security' matters."[25] Douglas' further remarks are enlightening in light of government actions since September 11:

> Neither the President nor the Attorney General is a magistrate. In matters where they believe national security may be involved they are not detached, disinterested, and neutral as a court or magistrate must be. Under the separation of powers created by the Constitution, the Executive Branch is not supposed to be neutral and disinterested. Rather it should vigorously investigate and prevent breaches of national security and prosecute those who violate the pertinent federal laws. The President and Attorney General are properly interested parties, cast in the role of adversary, in national security cases. They may even be the intended victims of subversive action. Since spies and saboteurs are as entitled to the protection of the Fourth Amendment as suspected gamblers...I cannot agree that where spies and saboteurs are involved[,] adequate protection of Fourth Amendment rights is assured when the President and Attorney General assume both the position of adversary and prosecutor and disinterested neutral magistrate.[26]

We now move on to Book II, *The Bush Plan*, where we look first at the elements of fascism and then at Bush's own actions. As I explain more fully at the end of Part One of Chapter Six, I have not categorized Bush's actions, but have kept them separate so that readers could discern the threads running through them. Following this, Chapter Seven briefly discusses some of the threats to civil liberties under the PATRIOT Act, while for brave souls Chapter Eight delves more deeply into the PATRIOT Act morass. Chapter Nine, then, discusses the so-called "Cheney Plan for Global Dominance," and Chapter Ten questions Bush's views on the invasion of Iraq and the doctrine of "military necessity," and raises the question of war crimes.

BOOK II
The Bush Plan

The Demise of Democracy

The Elements of the Bush Plan for America[1]

> As a citizen, as a senior citizen now, I am troubled by a society that has become increasingly insecure and, there-fore, increasingly willing to reach for what, at least in my day, would be thought quite extravagant uses of the terri-ble power of government coercion, government detention and doing so under a cloak of secrecy.
>
> —Lyle Denniston[2]

PART ONE:
Britt's List: Is America Becoming Fascist?[3]

As I noted earlier, the Bush Plan may or may not be an intentional plan to subvert democracy and establish fascism. Whether it's purveyors intend this result or not, the result is the same. The mainframe of the Bush Plan can be discerned in the combination of numerous disparate components: the enact-ment of the PATRIOT Act and MATRIX, the 2000 election, the detentions at Guantanamo, the invasion of Iraq, the coup in Haiti, the withdrawal from the International Criminal Court, the Free Trade of Americas Agreement (FTAA), legal actions against Greenpeace and Lynne Stewart and other activists, the subversion of environmental protections and cor-porate invasion of the environment, and a broad policy of secre-cy.

Before taking a look at those components, however, let's review the fourteen "common threads" of fascism compiled by

Laurence W. Britt, posted in Chapter 1, *Down the Road to Fascism*.[4] Here's the list:

1.   Powerful and continuing expressions of nationalism.
2.   Disdain for the importance of human rights.
3.   Identification of enemies/scapegoats as a unifying cause.
4.   The supremacy of the military/avid militarism.
5.   Rampant sexism.
6.   A controlled mass media.
7.   Obsession with national security.
8.   Religion and ruling elite tied together.
9.   Power of corporations protected.
10. Power of labor suppressed or eliminated.
11. Disdain and suppression of intellectuals and the arts.
12. Obsession with crime and punishment.
13. Rampant cronyism and corruption.
14. Fraudulent elections.

Now let's just do a quick survey and see to what extent actions of the Bush Administration fit into Britt's list.[5]

1. Powerful and continuing expressions of nationalism.
Immediately after 9/11, expressions of nationalism appeared everywhere in America. Drivers attached flags to their cars, placed them on their windows, and attached "God Bless America" bumper stickers. The Department of "Homeland Security" was created.[6] Bush sent troops to Iraq in the name of American "democracy," and security, then went aboard an air-craft carrier a month later, declaring "Mission accomplished." Bush's campaign ads for his re-election ride on expressions of nationalism.

Expressions of support for our country are natural in the

wake of a cataclysm like 9/11. The difference here is that Bush has shamelessly co-opted and capitalized on these feelings and made them his campaign slogan, even going so far as to post images of Ground Zero in his campaign ads.

2. Disdain for the importance of human rights (and the rule of law).

The Bush Administration has become identified with disdain for human rights. From the withdrawal from the International Criminal Court (for fear of prosecutions of Americans for war crimes, including human rights violations and crimes against humanity), to the enactment of the PATRIOT Act (parts of which violate basic human rights), from: the illegal and indefinite detentions of Guantanamo Bay and in the U.S. of so-called "unlawful enemy combatants," onto the Abu Ghraib prison abuses and to mass, arbitrary arrests and prosecutions of protesters, activists, and even a defense attorney (Lynne Stewart), the so-called war on terrorism has caused more human rights abuses and less safety. Indeed, Amnesty International reported recently that the U.S. has set an example of disregard for human rights worldwide.[7]

3. Identification of enemies/scapegoats as a unifying cause.

The Administration has continued to label suspects as "enemies" and has used that label as a political tool, even where such identification was not relevant to hunting down terrorists. For example, the "Axis of Evil" and the Bush assertion that "If you're not with us; you're against us!" Another example: we went after Saddam, even though there was never any evidence that he was in any way tied to the 9/11 attacks or al Qaeda and the pretext for going to war (weapons of mass destruction) was a sham. Yet another example: while the PATRIOT Act specifically eschews discrimination against Muslims and Arabic persons, thousands of Arabic-speaking persons or followers of Islam were rounded up and detained after 9/11 without probable cause of criminal activity, but apparently solely on the basis of their ethnic origins or religious practices.

4. The supremacy of the military/avid militarism.

Under Bush, military spending and the mobilization and use of military force has increased radically. Even civil society has become increasingly militarized: the popularization of the idea of war (invasion of Iraq, the war on terrorism), the glorification of the military (ads for army on television and in movie theaters), and the increase in ROTC programs in high schools. While one would expect an increase in militarization after 9/11, the invasion of Iraq was not compelled or justified by that attack. The Cheney doctrine of global dominance, discussed later in this book, specifically promotes escalation and supremacy of the military.

5. Rampant sexism (and racism).

Both the sexism and the racism in the Bush Administration are covert. While Bush's National Security adviser is an African-American woman and his Secretary of State is an African-American man, any pro-women/pro-African-American agenda they may represent is so vapid as to be turned against itself by Bush's demands for absolute loyalty to him and his policies. In other words, it is not that Bush won't hire women and African-Americans. It's that they must endorse policies that are subtly anti-women and anti-African-American.

Bush's policies include his insistence that women abrogate their reproductive rights, his refusal to continue funding parental planning programs overseas that educate about contraception, and the partial-birth abortion ban in the U.S. (recently found unconstitutional by a federal court).

With respect to African Americans, Bush's 2000 election (which I discuss in Part Two of this chapter), riding as it did on a specious equal protection argument, was a complete slap in the face to African-Americans who were never able to get the Supreme Court to uphold equal protection on such grounds.

The outrageous disenfranchisement of thousands of voters, a great majority of whom were African-American, is another indicator, as is, perhaps, the unlawful removal of President Aristide of Haiti. As one Haitian said to me: "Do you think this would have happened if Haiti had been a white country?"[8]

6. A controlled mass media.

There are a number of obvious ways in which the Bush Administration has increased control over mass media. One is the practice of embedding reporters. Reporters were embedded with army units in the Iraq invasion. The reporters were brought to the places where the military wanted them to go and were told exactly what the military wanted them to hear. The Bush Administration gave the media misinformation prior to the invasion of Iraq in order to legitimize that invasion. They falsified information about the presence in Iraq of chemical and biological weapons, and fissionable material. They were openly claiming that Saddam was trying to acquire nuclear materials from Africa in order to build a nuclear bomb.

Not quite as well known is the fact that reporters were also embedded with the police in the November 2003 protests in Miami against the Free Trade of Americas Agreement (FTAA) ministerial meeting. Embedded mainstream reporters were given protection by police during the demonstrations but independent media who were working within the demonstrations were tear-gassed, shot at and arrested.

The FCC recent rulings against Howard Stern for obscenity and Bono for profanity, certainly encouraged at least in part by the climate set by Bush Administration views on women's reproductive rights, birth control, dissent, and religion, are, according to Robert Corn-Revere, a prominent First Amendment attorney, simply unconstitutional. "What constitutionality?" he remarks, "The FCC has done its best to prolong the longevity of this doctrine [the FCC's indecency/profanity standards] by keeping it out of court."[9]

A coalition of two dozen broadcasters, performers and First Amendment groups, according to Jeff Jarvis of *The Nation* magazine, just petitioned the FCC to reconsider its Bono ruling, arguing that "attacking profanity (*a k a* blasphemy) dances perilously near the line between church and state, that this 'is fundamentally incompatible with the First Amendment' and that it 'already is exerting a substantial chilling effect on constitutionally-protected speech.'"[10]

But the assault on free speech isn't coming just from the FCC. Jarvis points out that "legislation coming out of Congress goes even further and raises even more troubling constitutional issues" ("Senator Fritz Hollings would extend FCC authority to restrict violent programming"), the Federal Trade Commission "just stepped up monitoring of media violence," and Attorney General Ashcroft "has launched a multimillion-dollar war on pornography."[11]

Recently, the *New York Times* apologized to its readers for its past failures of reporting on Iraq. But even this *mea culpa* has now been clearly shown by Christopher Carson, a private-practicing attorney, to be as vapid as that which was apologized for.[12] According to Carson, the newspaper was indeed "remiss in its coverage," but not for the reasons it stated. Carson noted that, "in the wake of a steady accumulation of evidence of Iraqi WMD stocks and programs, and ties to al Qaeda, [the *New York Times*] was not apologizing for the near-uniform negativity of its assessments of the Bush administration's pre-war intelligence. The *Times* is sorry it wasn't negative *enough*."[13] Carson's article makes vividly clear that the *Times* was still leaving out significant facts.

Of course, American media nowadays is routinely recognized as controlled by corporations. NBC is owned by General Electric. CBS is owned by Viacom.

The Administration's penchant for secrecy is also another way of controlling media. What the media doesn't know, they can't air.

7. Obsession with national security.

Once Bush learned how useful the national security wild card was, he did not fail to use it as often as possible. Programs that were not counted as homeland security a few years ago have now suddenly been shifted into the homeland security category. The government is spending about $5 billion a year more just on airport baggage and passenger screening. They have expanded the size of the customs service and the immigration service. They have begun implementation of the US VISIT Program, a tracking program which requires millions of foreign visitors to submit biometric information consisting of digital finger scans and a digital photograph upon arrival in the United States. They have had a significant growth in law enforcement activities, from new computerized data-mining programs to face and license plate recognition traffic lights.

National security was used as an excuse to pass the PATRIOT Act and several expansions of it. It is used to justify invading privacy and indefinitely detaining suspects. It's used to prevent defendants from exercising their Sixth Amendment rights to confront the evidence against them, by justifying increasing use of secret evidence against them. The list goes on and on.

8. Religion and ruling elite tied together.

The Christian Right has been a major power in the Republican Party since Ronald Reagan and George W. Bush has used this power to promote his agenda. He professes to be a strong Christian who believes he is guided by God and has advanced these beliefs as the equivalent of patriotism and democracy. The Administration's faith-based initiatives, refusals to fund parental planning programs, attempts to amend the Constitution to pass laws to further limit the rights of women to choose, and to ban gay marriages, all mix religion or religious doctrines with government.

Bush even opened the door for the Billy Graham ministries to start doing evangelical work in Iraq despite the objections of many Islamic leaders.

While Bush may be the centerpiece of the religious, ruling elite, he's not the only one who mixes his religion with his office. Our Attorney General Ashcroft advances his moral/religious beliefs by covering the breasts of the statute of Justice and praying every morning with his staff, while making frequent appearances to defend legislation in which he is ethically supposed to have no vested, personal interest and announcing suspects' guilt before they have been tried.

9. Power of corporations protected.
The Bush Administration has touted corporate power through it's tax cuts for the wealthy, it's attempts to make Miami the permanent home of the FTAA Ministerial, it's favoritism of Enron and other big companies at the expense of the environment or the little person. It's aggressive undermining of environmental protections also favors big business. NAFTA and the FTAA favor corporations over labor, as does the World Trade Organization (WTO) and the World Bank, all which Bush supports.

The president had every opportunity to pursue fiscally responsible policies to help the struggling middle class, but for three consecutive years chose massive supply-side tax cuts for the most fortunate Americans.

10. Power of labor suppressed or eliminated.
In November 2003, police agreements with the AFL-CIO and Steelworkers Union for the Miami FTAA protests were disregarded, and peaceful union members were assaulted, some shot with rubber bullets, and some arrested.

Early in his term, President Bush repealed ergonomic safety standards, halted a potential strike by Northwest Airlines mechanics, and suspended Clinton-era rules that required the government to favor unions with federal contracts. Bush plans to expand the North American Free Trade Agreement to include all countries in the Western Hemisphere (except Cuba), and to privatize nearly 500,000 federal positions.

The money given to candidates by organized labor unions is usually just a fraction of the money that business gives. The United Auto Workers, for example, gave $3.3 million in 2001-2002, while the automotive industry contributed $14.9 million, more than four times as much. The bulk of labor's money is in the form of PAC contributions and soft money, with only a small amount coming from individuals. Thus the reason unions strongly opposed the 2002 campaign finance reform bill, and are hoping for a reversal in the Supreme Court this fall.

11. *Disdain and suppression of intellectuals and the arts.*
Perhaps the biggest area of suppression of intellectuals under Bush is his flagrant disregard for science, which can be seen in his dropping out of the Kyoto Accords, his increased allowances for polluters and insistence upon tearing up more wilderness areas for oil and gas in disregard of environmental science, as well as his disregard for the science behind global warming.

Bush is also not known for his promotion of the Arts. Funding for all arts-oriented school programs have also been cut back under Bush.

12. *Obsession with crime and punishment.*
Bush's own obsession with punishment is evident from his record as governor of Texas and his statements, some of which were noted in the Preface of this book, about the death penalty and punishment. Ashcroft mirrors Bush's penchant for punishment with his frivolous but dangerous prosecutions of activists. Bush has also focused on loading the courts with extremist judges who favor his draconian views.

13. *Rampant cronyism and corruption.*
As Richard Clarke writes in his book *Against All Enemies,* "Bush and his prep school roommate Clay Johnson [the White House Personnel Director] looked first to family loyalists and

political cronies to staff key positions. As one Republican columnist told me, 'These guys are more inbred, secretive, and vindictive than the Mafia.'"[14]

But we don't need to take Clarke's word for it. It's almost a given that Cheney allowed Enron to influence energy policies. And who gets to do the rebuilding in the unnecessary war on Iraq? Cheney's old company, Haliburton. And who goes duck hunting with Justice Scalia but Cheney, although Cheney's energy task force case was then pending in the Supreme Court.

14. Fraudulent elections.

One need not say anything more than "the 2000 election" to provide an example of a fraudulent election. See the section in Part Two of this chapter for more about the 2000 election. Disenfranchisement of thousands of legitimate voters whose names resembled those of convicted felons and preventing a paper ballot trail are two additional issues that came out of that election and still haunt us.

15. (Doublespeak).

I have added the category of doublespeak. Doublespeak is language deliberately constructed to disguise its actual meaning, such as euphemisms. Doublespeak is, in fact, a language of reversals. Doublespeak is not included in Britt's list, but it should be.

The word doublespeak was coined in the early 1950s. It is often incorrectly attributed to George Orwell and his dystopian novel *Nineteen Eighty-Four*. The word actually never appears in that novel (although he refers to several other types of "speak"). Whereas in the early days of the practice it was considered wrong to construct words to disguise meaning, this is now an accepted and established practice in government and business.

Mini-Summary

Using Britt's list, it is no stretch to call the Bush government fascist. Thus, despite the reservation of radical peace activist Stan Goff—who is certainly unafraid to criticize this Administration and to call a spade a spade—about whether this is yet a fascist government,[15] if Britt's list is believed, we're already there. But, let's take a look separately—without the benefit of Britt's list—at the elements of what I call "the Bush Plan"—those actions taken by the Bush Administration that, when viewed in terms of how they benefit those in power, add up to a pretty scary picture.

The reader will notice that these elements are disparate and I do not place them into categories. The reason I do not is that I want readers to engage in the difficult task of noticing the lines of the various threads and discerning the picture they weave, which is a wholly different task than reading in categories. To assist readers in this task, I have highlighted the "threads" in bold.

(For those who nonetheless still find this task too onerous, simply refer to my own summary at the end of the chapter and then go back and read through the separate elements at will. These elements, by the way, are in a loose order which it is not necessary to follow in reading. They may, in other words, be read or referred to in just about any order.)

PART TWO: THE BUSH PLAN

The PATRIOT Act

> With each USAPA Title building upon the other and linking together an entire federal investigative, surveillance, intelligence and law enforcement apparatus, a disturbing amount of unchecked power is now place in the Executive Branch. What is even more disturbing is that these ... provisions are permanent.
>
> —C. William Michaels,
> *No Greater Threat*[16]

The purpose of the PATRIOT Act can be construed by its result. While some provisions are not worrisome, others are troubling because they give tremendous powers to central authorities, undermine civil liberties, and enable suppression of opposition.

The PATRIOT Act is a mainstay of government oppressive power. The Act authorizes and codifies a near-absolute and permanent invasion of American's private lives, sets vast precedents in immigration law for nigh completely dissolving constitutional and/or international human rights, and finally erects a massive law enforcement apparatus that can be and has been used against immigrant and citizen alike, domestically and around the world.

The importance of the PATRIOT Act to the goals of this Administration was made clear by the Attorney General's speaking tour to defend it. It is also apparent in the DOJ's repeated efforts to obtain court decisions under the PATRIOT Act that eviscerate individual rights in order to take more executive power, often forcing prosecutors to make arguments that would in other contexts have gotten them laughed out of court. For example, a federal court wrote:

> When asked at oral argument how to distinguish being a member of an organization from being a quasi-employee, the Government initially responded 'You know it when you see it.' While such a standard was once an acceptable way for a Supreme Court Justice to identify obscenity, it is an insufficient guide by which a person can predict the legality of that person's conduct. Moreover, the Government continued to provide an evolving definition of 'personnel' to the Court following oral argument on this motion.[17]

Additionally, a remark made by General Frank in November 2003 that another major terrorist attack on Americans would likely cause "our population to question our own Constitution and to begin to militarize our country"[18] indicates a willingness in high levels of this Administration to consider, if not promote, martial law as a viable path. This conclusion is supported by the indefinite detentions of so-called "unlawful enemy combatants" at Guantanamo and the unprovoked invasion of Iraq. Such a public official willingness to overthrow the Constitution is unprecedented in American history.

Because of the unique importance of the PATRIOT Act to the Bush Plan and the Act's great complexity, I will discuss it in much greater depth in the next chapter.

Guantanamo, Enemy Combatants, & Abu Ghraib

The detentions in Guantanamo, Cuba (a.k.a. Gitmo), establish three important principles for the Bush Regime: **(1) the power to detain any foreign national without evidence, due process, habeas corpus, or counsel, and (2) the absence of accountability or judicial review.** These principles are also established by the indefinite detention provisions in the PATRIOT Act (affecting immigrants), the "unlawful enemy combatant" (UEC) designations of U.S. citizens (namely Padilla and Hamdi) on U.S. soil, and the ex-legal prison situations in Afghanistan and Iraq (most vividly, Abu Ghraib). The DOJ actively argues for both principles in its legal briefs and oral arguments.[19]

Gitmo, Abu Ghraib, and the UECs also establish **(3) the precedent of the American government's "right" to ignore the Geneva Conventions and other international instruments** such as the International Convention Against Torture. Geneva requires a status determination before a competent tribunal for every captured combatant. Claims of the use of torture at both Gitmo and, more prominently, Abu Ghraib have emerged.[20] The justification for the use of physical or psychological torture follows easily after the denial of legal process to an accused person.

Let's look at the first two concerns: the power to detain any foreign national without evidence, due process, or right to counsel, and the absence of accountability or judicial review. According to a paper written by Col. Daniel F. McCallum, a student of the National War College, Gitmo was chosen at least in part because it presented a minimal "litigation risk."[21] McCallum states baldly: "The litigation risk faced by DOJ was access to federal courts for the purpose of filing a writ of habeas corpus. Habeas corpus requires judicial review of the detention of a person to determine if the detention is lawful. An important factor in assessing this risk is that this only applies to citizens and foreign nationals if they are held within the United States." For Guantanamo, "since the property belonged to Cuba, DOJ assessed the litigation risk as minimal." Furthermore: "Considering the strained foreign relations we have with Cuba, DOS assessed the minimal negative impact acceptable."

Thus, it was the administration's intention in choosing Gitmo to deny due process and judicial review (including most alarmingly, habeas corpus review) to detainees. And in fact, that is exactly what the administration did with respect to Gitmo prisoners.

Furthermore, denying due process and judicial review to captured enemy combatants is a violation of the Geneva Conventions. The government therefore not only overtly sought to avoid the application of constitutional laws and processes, but had no fear in simply ignoring long-standing international law. This happens to be in violation of United States domestic law, too, since a grave breach of Geneva, such as denial of due process, is a violation of Title 18, Section 2441 of the United States Code, the war crimes statute (which is discussed at length in Chapter Ten, *Global Dominance in Action*).

The excuse given by the administration for these violations is that the United States is complying with the *spirit* of Geneva. However, Geneva does not allow anyone, signatories or not, to exempt themselves from the obligations of the Convention. Nor can signatories escape their positive obligations to abide by its rules. The Convention specifically requires that all signatories "respect and ensure respect" for the convention "in all circumstances," to adopt enabling laws to execute the Convention domestically, and to prosecute all serious violations of it.

The administration claims that an executive decision to declare a person an unlawful enemy combatant meets the standards of Geneva to provide a "status determination" by a "competent tribunal." This is not so, as we shall see in Chapter Ten.

However, in addition to the violations of Geneva occurring in the treatment of UECs and Gitmo detainees, the abuse of prisoners at Abu Ghraib in Baghdad is more egregious and illustrates even more vividly why international laws must always be strictly followed. Where carefully-developed, well-established international laws and customs are ignored by a government, no matter what the justification, there is a terrible human cost. More disturbingly, it is now clear that the use of torture was condoned and authorized by Secretary of Defense Rumsfeld himself. Although there is yet no evidence that Bush agreed, it is hard to imagine that he did not, as his policies having clearly endorsed these practices.

The classic lesson that we need checks and balances has rarely been more starkly revealed than by the episodes at Abu Ghraib. If anything, we must get over our disbelief, our disappointment and accept that the road to preventing abuses like this and like others described in this book lies not in weeding out rogue soldiers but in building solid law, resisting law that overreaches, and making sure that everyone accused has fair access to legal representation and review of the evidence in open court.

Iraq: Preemptive war and International law

The invasion of Iraq established the doctrine of preemptive war: the idea that the U.S. can unilaterally attack another sovereign nation to prevent or neutralize a perceived potential future threat. On September 20, 2002, six months before the U.S. invaded Iraq, the Bush administration unveiled its National Security Strategy. The Strategy, according to Senator Edward Kennedy, "claims that these new threats are so novel and so dangerous that we should 'not hesitate to act alone, if necessary, to exercise our right of self-defense by acting pre-emptively.'"[22] Kennedy pointed out in an address that was made on the floor of the Senate on October 7, 2002, that while the Administration "often uses the terms 'pre-emptive' and 'preventive' interchangeably[, i]n the realm of international relations, these two terms have long had very different meanings." Kennedy explains:

> Traditionally, "pre-emptive" action refers to times when states react to an imminent threat of attack. For example, when Egyptian and Syrian forces mobilized on Israel's borders in 1967, the threat was obvious and immediate, and Israel felt justified in pre-emptively attacking those forces. The global community is generally tolerant of such actions, since no nation should have to suffer a certain first strike before it has the legitimacy to respond.
>
> By contrast, "preventive" military action refers to strike that target country before it has developed a capability that could someday become threatening. Preventive attacks have generally been condemned. For example, the 1941 sneak attack on Pearl Harbor was regarded as a preventive strike by Japan, because the Japanese were seeking to block a planned military buildup by the United States in the Pacific.

Kennedy concludes that "[t]he coldly premeditated nature of preventive attacks and preventive wars makes them anathema to well-established international principles against aggression" and adds that "what the Administration is really calling for is preventive war, which flies in the face of international rules of acceptable behavior." Kennedy notes that "the Bush Strategy asserts that the United States should be exempt from the rules we expect other nations to obey." This Strategy "is not just an academic debate[; t]here are important real world consequences." It could "deprive America of the moral legitimacy necessary to promote our values abroad ... give other nations— from Russia to India to Pakistan—an excuse to violate fundamental principles of civilized international behavior ...[and] fuel anti-American sentiment throughout the Islamic world and beyond."

While Kennedy's discussion of the meanings of these two related terms shows that the Administration and media have been applying the term "preemptive" and "preventive" interchangeably and incorrectly, the former term (preemptive) seems to stick in the mind better. Thus, although it is technically incorrect, I use the term preemptive in quotes to mean "to strike a target country before it has developed a capability that could someday become threatening," e.g., to strike in order to preempt being attacked.

Bush's invasion of Iraq, the doctrine of "preemptive" war, and the detentions of enemy combatants are, taken together, yet one side of a broader series of avoidances or actual violations of international law which signal an end of the rule of law and avoid accountability on a global scale. As Lizzie Rushing, a student at the University of Colorado, Bachelor of Arts Program of International Affairs noted in a May 2003 essay, America's attempts to exempt itself from the International Criminal Court "could be interpreted as meaning that the Bush administration is not merely looking for protection for its nationals, but actual immunity with no apparent accountability."[23]

This view is supported by the breaking news about

Rumsfeld's memo to Bush on the Commander-in-Chief's "right" to violate international laws and torture terrorism suspects. Mainstays of international law are the Geneva and Hague Conventions, both of which the Bush administration is violating and which I will discuss further in Chapter Ten, *Global Dominance in Action*.

The Coup in Haiti[24]

"Regime change" seems to be the watchword of this Administration. The February 2004 military coup in Haiti was not only supported by the United States but was funded and organized by it. While the U.S. government announced that Aristide had resigned, and Cheney actually said that Aristide had "left of his own free will," it later became all too clear that he was given no choice. Had he not resigned, the U.S. was going to let the U.S.-funded and trained "rebels" kill him.

According to Marjorie Cohn, the Executive Vice President of the National Lawyers Guild and a law professor at Thomas Jefferson School of Law, Aristide's forcible removal by the United States violates the International Covenant on Civil and Political Rights, the U.N. Charter, the governing charters of the Organization of American States, and the Inter-American Democratic Charter.[25] The U.S. also violated the multilateral Prevention and Punishment of Crimes Against Internationally Protected Persons Treaty, of which both Haiti and the United States are signatories. Cohn makes it clear that the U.S. is violating even more laws than these and calls for an investigation by international human rights bodies.

But, by now, the reader knows that the U.S. has violated international laws left and right, totally apart from Haiti. So what is the significance of adding Haiti to the discussion? There is no "third world" country closer to the U.S. than Haiti. Haiti is also the first black republic in the world (and the only one in the Western Hemisphere) to have won its independence through armed revolution. This alone makes it a threat to U.S. power and hegemony.

Haiti is also a gateway to South America and a viable conduit for South American drugs. While stories have been coming out in the press insinuating that Aristide's government was corrupt and running drugs, the history of U.S. (and particularly the CIA) involvement in the Caribbean drug trade is long and prolific—and the same people involved in the Iran-Contra drug scandal are now back in office. The democratically elected President of Venezeula has claimed he put down several overthrow attempts backed by the U.S. **Haiti creates an additional stopover and source of recruits.**

The human rights situation in Haiti is appalling. As I write, news has just emerged that French troops and "Blue Helmets"—U.N. soldiers—raided the home of Jean-Charles Moises, the former democratically-elected mayor of a small northern town whom my team met with in April while he was in hiding. The troops took Jean-Charles' wife. There have been thousands of murders and buildings burnt. The Multinational Interim (Peacekeeping) Force of American marines, French and Canadian troops, have done little or nothing to stop these atrocities.

Withdrawal from the International Criminal Court[26]

Perhaps more revealing is America's refusal to endorse the International Criminal Court, the only potential tribunal in the world that would have the power to judge us and enforce the judgments. Indeed, Rushing wrote: "The fact that a court of which they are not a party could have jurisdiction for crimes alleged against any U.S. nationals seems to threaten their national security, as well as their interests as a military superpower in world politics."[27]

Simply put, **withdrawal from the International Criminal**

Court (ICC) frees the United States from international accountability for war crimes.

The ICC was created through an international agreement called the Rome Statute ("the Statute"), which was adopted on July 17, 1998 by an overwhelming majority of 120 participating countries. The Court sits in the Hague, and is a permanent court, empowered to try individuals accused of genocide, war crimes, crimes of aggression, and crimes against humanity that would otherwise escape prosecution. Only seven countries voted against the Statute, including China, the U.S., and Israel.

There are built-in safeguards in the Statute against frivolous or politically motivated prosecutions. An ICC investigation can be initiated by either the Security Council, a state party to the statute, or by the Independent Prosecutor (I/P). The I/P, however, must submit a "request for authority" to the Pre-Trial chamber before launching an investigation, which is granted only if the Pre-Trial Chamber determines both that there is a "reasonable basis to proceed" and that "the case appears to fall within the jurisdiction of the Court." The Statute also gives the UN Security Council the power to stop investigations or prosecutions for renewable one-year periods.

Another important stop-gap is the principle of complementarity, which is a mechanism within the Court that ensures that the ICC would complement rather than supersede national systems. When a state is investigating a case within its own legal system, the case is inadmissible before the ICC "unless the State is unwilling or unable genuinely to carry out the investigation or prosecution."[28]

Former President Clinton signed the Rome Statute but did not send it to the Senate for ratification before he left office.[29] However, in July 2002, the United States launched a full-scale multi-pronged campaign against the ICC, claiming that the ICC might initiate politically-motivated prosecutions against U.S. nationals. As part of its efforts, the Bush administration approached countries around the world seeking to conclude

Bilateral Immunity Agreements (BIAs), purportedly based on Article 98 of the Rome Statute, excluding its citizens and military personnel from the jurisdiction of the Court. These agreements prohibit the surrender to the ICC of a broad range of persons including current or former government officials, military personnel, and U.S. employees (including contractors) and nationals. These agreements, which in some cases are reciprocal, do not include an obligation by the US to subject those persons to investigation and/or prosecution at home.

Many governmental, legal and non-governmental experts have concluded that the bilateral agreements being sought by the U.S. government are contrary to international law and the Rome Statute.

Another facet of this crusade against the Court is the adoption of U.S. legislation known as the American Service Members' Protection Act (ASPA). This law, passed by Congress in August 2002, contains provisions restricting U.S. cooperation with the ICC, making U.S. support of peacekeeping missions largely contingent on achieving impunity for all U.S. personnel, and even granting the President permission to use "any means necessary" to free American citizens and allies from ICC custody (prompting the nickname "The Hague Invasion Act"). The legislation also contains waivers that make all of these provisions non-binding. However, the Bush administration has been using these waivers as bargaining chips to pressure countries around the world into concluding bilateral immunity agreements—or otherwise lose essential US military assistance.

The European Parliament stated that the bilateral agreements which the Bush administration was conducting were undermining the ICC as well as "jeopardizing its role as a complementary jurisdiction to the State jurisdictions and a building block in collective global security."[30]

Mini-Summary

If you combine the precedents set by the PATRIOT Act, Guantanamo, Iraq, Abu Ghraib, and the withdrawal from ICC, you need little more proof of a U.S. rolling coup-in-progress, not just in the United States, but beyond it. Although the Administration has declared this coup in the name of freedom, compassionate conservatism, national security and the war on terrorism, the main features of it are exactly the opposite: dissolution of the rule of law, arbitrary arrests and detentions, violations and abuses of human rights and dignity, disregard for the sovereignty of other nations and even for the most basic principles of widely accepted international norms.

These conclusions will not altogether surprise those who have closely followed the covert "interventions" of previous administrations or the history of covert American projects on its own citizens.[31] However, these disparate components of U.S. foreign and domestic policy are generally viewed piecemeal by media and average Americans; they are not generally added up. Yet, there are other clear indicators of the Bush Regime's goals.

"Free Trade" and corporate dominance

The Free Trade of Americas Agreement (FTAA) is the latest in so-called free trade agreements that, contrary to the suggestion that they benefit workers, establish the "right" of corporations to override local, state and federal laws, including worker's rights, individual constitutional rights, and environmental protections, in favor of FTAA-promulgated rules. Such rules, of course, have been decided between ministers and cabinet secretaries who are not elected officials.

The FTAA is modeled after the North American Trade Agreement (NAFTA). Like NAFTA, the FTAA purports to embrace the idea of free trade between nations. In fact, it promotes corporate plundering of communities and natural resources and undermine environmental and human rights protections. One investigator wrote that "[w]hat I found out was that free-trade agreements like the North American trade agreement that we have with Mexico and Canada are very bad for us in the U.S. and very, very bad for people to the south of us."[32] The FTAA, she said, "could cause Americans to lose even more jobs, settle for lower wages, settle for a weaker labor movement and erosion of workers' rights and environmental regulations."[33] Leonidas Iza, leader of the Confederation de Indigenous Nationalities of Ecuador, called it "a perverse U.S. plan that will bring more hunger and misery and widen the gap between rich and poor ... a social time bomb."[34]

Bill Moyers, speaking about a provision of NAFTA called "Chapter 11," says the provision is now being used by corporations "to challenge the power of governments to protect their citizens, to undermine environmental and health laws, even attack our system of justice." [35] Tamara Straus, senior editor of AlterNet.org, writes that Chapter 11 "hobbles the authority of government to act in the broader public interest. And, in fact, that was the idea in the first place."[36]

As bad as the FTAA may be, it is only a piece of a much broader problem. Amy Chua, a Yale Law School professor, writes:

> Contrary to what its proponents assume, free markets outside the West do not spread wealthy evenly and enrich entire developing societies. Instead, they tend to concentrate glaring wealth in the hands of an 'outsider' minority, generating ethnic envy and hatred among frustrated, impoverished majorities.[37]

Charles Kupchan, author of *The End of the American Era,* writes that "globalization might be bringing newfound wealth to many quarters, but it is also widening economic inequality both within countries and between them—a spillover effect that has contributed to anti-American sentiment and played a role in motivating extremist groups to direct violence against U.S. citizens and their territory."[38]

Marjorie Kelly, author of *The Divine Right of Capital*, writes that "treaties like the North American Free Trade Agreement," upon which the FTAA is based, "put[] financial concerns at the core and ... labor and environmental concerns into side accords."[39] Kelly attributes the philosophy behind such acts as arising from something akin to "the great chain of being" of the British aristocracy. Today, however, the aristocrats are the corporate barons who view the world through the lens of financial numbers, "where [they] see the numbers that belong to stockholders as the end point of the whole game."[40] "A primary bias," according to Kelly, "built into financial statements is the notion that stockholders are to be paid as much as possible, whereas employees are to be paid as little as possible."[41] Importantly, Kelly concludes that since "this is the only way corporations can see the world," they believe that their "worldview is rational, natural, inevitable."[42]

Jerry Mander, author of *In the Absence of the Sacred: The Failure of Technology & the Survival of the Indian Nations*, lists eleven "inherent rules of corporate behavior" that explain why the people within corporations follow "a system of logic that leads inexorably toward dominant behaviors" and destruction of social ties and the environment.

1.   The profit imperative

2.   The growth imperative

3.   Competition and aggression

4.   Amorality

5.   Hierarchy

6.   Quantification, linearity, and segmentation

7.   Dehumanization

8.   Exploitation

9.   Ephemerality (corporations are legal creations that exist

only on paper—as such, they have no physical nature or commitment to place)

10. Opposition to nature

11 Homogenization.

Mander explains:

> Corporations are inherently bold, aggressive, and competitive. Though they exist in a society that claims to operate by moral principles, they are structurally amoral. It is inevitable that they will dehumanize people who work for them, and dehumanize the overall society as well. They are disloyal to workers, including their own managers. If community goals conflict with corporate goals, then corporations are similarly disloyal to the communities they may have been part of for many years. It is inherent in corporate activity that they seek to drive all consciousness into one-dimensional channels. They must attempt to dominate alternative cultures and to effectively clone the world population into a form more to their liking. Corporations do not care about nations; they live beyond boundaries. They are intrinsically committed to destroying nature. And they have an inexorable, unabatable, voracious need to grow and to expand. In dominating other cultures, in digging up the earth, corporations blindly follow the codes that have been built into them as if they were genes.[43]

The NAFTA and FTAA are instances of corporate rule overtaking the rule of law. Police actions in Miami during the November 2003 demonstrations against the FTAA ministerial meeting there, decried even by the relatively conservative Miami Herald, illustrate the underlying goals of both the PATRIOT Act and the FTAA. Far from promoting local agriculture or business, appropriate local development and use of natural resources, or aiding local communities with funds or jobs, the FTAA Ministerial meeting in Miami resulted in the trampling of First and Fourth Amendment rights of thousands of demonstrators, media personnel, and legal observers. Miami Police Chief Timoney happily noted that his police actions set a precedent for homeland security. The federal involvement in police training, which began six months before the meetings and demonstrations, illustrate the extent to which the preemption of local law enforcement, hinted at by the PATRIOT Act, has already occurred.[44]

Prosecutions & Proceedings

The Bush administration has launched prosecutions of activists that could, if successful, establish a permanent framework for repression of free speech and dissent. The government is using several methods that build upon the PATRIOT Act: grand jury inquiries (which now allow sharing of secret grand jury information with the CIA and even with foreign powers); "national security letters" (which arise out of an expansion of the PATRIOT Act and demand information about clients from financial institutions); investigations by the FBI or other departments such as the Joint Terrorism Task Force (JTTF) and the army; and, of course, criminal indictments and prosecutions themselves.

The Prosecution of Greenpeace

In August 2003, the DOJ announced it was indicting Greenpeace under an obscure federal law that appears to have been used only twice since its 1872 enactment. The law criminalizes "sailor-mongering" or the luring of sailors with liquor and prostitutes from their ships—obviously not the sort of actions in which Greenpeace engages. The action was brought against Greenpeace because several of their members had boarded a ship that was carrying illegal mahogany and hung a banner off the ship demanding that Bush stop illegal mahogany trading. Normally, if any charges are brought for such an action, it is only misdemeanor trespass against the individual. This time, however, the Justice Department brought the sailor-mongering charge, which is a serious felony charge, against the entire organization.

If the Justice Department had been successful, Greenpeace would have been forced to "give a government employee access to its offices and membership and donor records" and to "regularly report its actions to the government."[45] A Miami federal judge threw the case out in May 2004.

Significantly, Greenpeace was the first group to demonstrate against Bush in Texas after his inauguration.

The prosecution of Greenpeace pulls together several elements in common with other items in the Bush agenda: **it targets environmental/activist groups, it goes after and into organizational records, and it represses First Amendment expressions that oppose the U.S. government or its corporate interests.**

The demand for unlimited access to records mirrors terrorist provisions in the PATRIOT Act. The targeting of activists also mirrors the uses of the PATRIOT Act. The targeting of environmentalists is similar to the dilution or eradication of environmental protections. The repression of First Amendment activities is found in the repression of FTAA demonstrations, as well as in some provisions of the PATRIOT Act.

Thus, it is difficult to view these components as random similarities. Rather, the prosecution of Greenpeace joins distinct ideas and tactics that the Bush Administration has used elsewhere in bits and pieces. Cleverly, the prosecution does *not* rely upon the PATRIOT Act or any anti-terrorism law. However, the tactics used are exactly those used under the PATRIOT Act. **This prosecution was meant to clear the way for the concept that "activists = terrorists." The joining of these tactics in this prosecution clarifies the Administration's underlying purpose in them separately: control, suppression, and eradication of opposition.**

The Demise of Democracy

The Prosecution of Lynne Stewart

The prosecution of New York attorney Lynne Stewart, on the other hand, is a carefully focused targeting of an activist criminal defense lawyer. While the case involves the use of electronic surveillance and invasion of Stewart's law practice, more importantly **the case targets the fundamental Sixth Amendment right to counsel, the sacrosanct attorney-client privilege, and attorney ethics that require attorneys to maintain attorney-client confidentiality and zealously represent the client.**

Stewart was originally charged with material support of a *designated foreign terrorist organization* and, when that failed, was subsequently re-indicted under a related provision: material support of *terrorists*.[46] (The difference is highly significant, as we shall see later when we discuss the PATRIOT Act in depth.) The DOJ charged Stewart with (1) having distracted prison guards while her translator passed messages to her convicted client, Shiek Abdul Rahman, and (2) having issued a press release for him. (Translators are paid to "pass messages" from attorney to client and back. And speaking publicly for one's client is part of the job of representing someone.)

Judge Koeltl, in her dismissal of the original material support charges against Stewart, summed up a major concern of the New York criminal defense bar when she stated that the government "fails to explain how a lawyer, acting as an agent of her client ... could avoid being subject to criminal prosecution."[47] The case puts attorneys in a double-bind situation by creating a conflict between the law (at least what the government claims is the law) and professional ethical obligations. Under professional ethics codes, attorneys are required to zealously and competently represent their clients. If they fail to do so, they can be sanctioned and possibly even disbarred. But Ashcroft is making it clear that criminal defense lawyers who do adhere to their ethical obligations may now be subject to criminal prosecution. This is a classic double-bind, a Catch-22, and it is a direct attack on the criminal defense bar.

The purpose of the Administration can be reasonably inferred in the same manner that courts determine intent: one is considered to intend the foreseeable results of one's actions. The DOJ clearly has no qualms about failing to distinguish between a lawyer, acting as a legitimate representative of her client, and a criminal. **Indeed, the government is creating a parallel between defense attorneys and terrorists. The result of such a prosecution is to scare criminal defense lawyers off of terrorist cases.**[48] Indeed, the prosecution threatens the very existence of the criminal defense bar. Without defense attorneys, innocent people unlawfully detained won't have much recourse. The Executive will retain absolute and final power. Defense lawyers are the last line of defense from government abuses of constitutional rights. Without the defense bar, democracy falls.

Grand Juries & Actions Against Activists

Activist groups are now being targeted by the DOJ with a very sneaky technique: grand jury subpoenas.[49] An activist is called in to testify to the grand jury about unspecified violations of federal law. Later on, the activist's testimony is used against him, usually to bring charges of perjury for some incorrect statement. Anyone who has read trial transcripts knows how prosecutors can weave a chain of innocent affirmative responses into an appearance of lies and/or guilt. Juries convict innocent people all the time. The Innocence Project, led by Barry Scheck, is an entire organization built on this fact.[50]

Shutting down animal rights activists has become a stated priority of the Administration, who justify investigations and prosecutions by labeling the activists as bio- or eco-terrorists. One activist wrote to me a fairly detailed compilation of incidents. He wrote that:

> ...feds were handing out grand jury subpoenas to animal rights activists like the subpoenas were candy (vegan

candy). This has been somewhat typical in the animal rights movement for awhile now. We have had grand juries pop up without our knowledge in some instances. There was one in Massachusetts in 2002 that we only found out about after they subpoenaed a new activist and arrested two other activists. One Seattle activist was subpoenaed to appear before a NJ state grand jury that was set to meet on Sept 12, 2001. He went, wasn't going to talk, and left and that was the last thing we heard about that grand jury.

Mostly now it has been [the] federal one in NJ and one in Arkansas. [One activist] from Texas … was subpoenaed to appear before that Arkansas grand jury. She eventually appeared twice and a third subpoena was quashed. Then in August, days apart, they raided her home in Dallas and the family home of a Huntington, New York activist. The above[-]mentioned Seattle activist had his home raided in April, the same day the feds executed a search warrant at the Stop Huntingdon Animal Cruelty office…So these grand jury problems have been fairly [constant] for animal rights activists.

There have been a few instances of arresting activists for not even showing up. [A California activist was] taken into custody and dragged across the country to testify.][51]

After asserting her Fifth Amendment privilege, she was allowed to leave.

Discussing proceedings against "Stop Huntingdon Animal Cruelty" (SHAC), an organization dedicated to stopping testing on animals by Huntingdon Life Sciences, a company that runs animal testing labs in both the United States and Great Britain, the activist wrote that SHAC:

> has fought more than a dozen civil suits, including a RICO suit that started when the campaign got going in this country (April 2001). That racketeering suit was for $1[2] million dollars and went nowhere. Toward the end,

they tried adding more defendants and started handing out email subpoenas left and right.[52]

Under the PATRIOT Act, investigations, surveillance, and prosecutions can be brought for activities that do not rise to the level of probable cause of criminal activity. This means that activists can be targeted for expressing their beliefs. In February 2004, Mara Verheyden-Hilliard, an attorney and co-founder of the Partnership for Civil Justice, a Washington, D.C.-based public interest law firm that litigates constitutional rights and civil rights cases, said about the tactics used against animal rights activists:

> We have to make a distinction between things exploding and people protesting outside...We have very serious concerns when we see the government and aligned business entities trying to use the power of law enforcement and the threat of law enforcement activity against political opponents, and they do that post Sept. 11 using the language of terror.[53]

More recently, the PATRIOT Act has been used to go after artists. Stephen Kurtz, a professor at the University of Buffalo, and two others were served subpoenas to appear before a federal grand jury. The grand jury will be considering whether or not to charge Kurtz, whose art involves the use of biology equipment, with "possession of biological agents." Apparently, Kurtz found his wife dead of a heart attack one morning in May and called 911. When paramedics arrived, according to the Christian Science Monitor, "one of them noticed that Kurtz had laboratory equipment, which he used in his art exhibits. The paramedics reported this to police and the FBI sealed off his house."[54]

One of those subpoenaed, Beatriz da Costa, who is an art professor at the University of California and a member of Critical Art Ensemble, an art collective that Kurtz founded, said:

I have no idea why they're continuing (to investigate). It was shocking that this investigation was ever launched. That it is continuing is positively frightening, and shows how vulnerable the PATRIOT Act has made freedom of speech in this country.[55]

Another recent tactic is "an apparent effort on the part of the United States Army to gather information about students engaged in a civilian academic conference."[56] The National Lawyers Guild (NLG) press release states:

On February 9, [2004,] two Army officers came to the University of Texas Law School seeking information about a conference that had been held on February 4. The agents requested a roster of attendees and sought to interview the organizer of the event. The conference was entitled, "Islam and the Law: The Question of Sexism?" and was co-sponsored by the U.T. student chapter of the National Lawyers Guild[, as well as numerous other student law, university, and local organizations.] The conference was apparently also attended by military personnel in plain clothes.[57]

NLG President Michael Avery said:

It appears that the government is stepping up surveillance of innocent activity at academic institutions. Two weeks ago a federal grand jury in Iowa attempted to subpoena information about [the conference.] An element of racial profiling is present in this case, given the Muslim-related content... Government spying on student conferences has no place in a free society.[58]

It is clear from the Greenpeace and Stewart prosecutions and the grand jury subpoenas of and actions against activists that the DOJ is specifically targeting activists. The Greenpeace prosecution also dovetails with the Bush administration's sabotage of environmental laws and makes clear that Bush is targeting environmental protections from every angle. When viewed in the larger context of the other elements mentioned in this chapter, the DOJ tactics lead to a frightening conclusion: **the DOJ, an arm of the Executive Branch, is ensuring that there will be no witnesses, no protesters, and no defenses.**

MATRIX[59]

> The progress of science in furnishing the Government with means of espionage is not likely to stop with wire-tapping. Ways may some day be developed by which the Government, without removing papers from secret drawers, can reproduce them in court, and by which it will be enabled to expose to a jury the most intimate occurrences of the home....Can it be that the Constitution affords no protection against such invasions of individual Security?
>
> —Justice Louis Brandeis[60]

MATRIX is a new "data mining" system being used by police and federal authorities in some states. MATRIX stands for *Multistate Anti-TeRrorism Information eXchange*. Data mining, according to an ACLU White Paper issued in May 2004, "is controversial because it involves not the attempt to learn more facts about known suspects, but mass scrutiny of the lives and activities of innocent people...to see whether each of them shows any signs of being a terrorist or other criminal."[61]

MATRIX was designed by Seisint Inc. in Boca Raton, Florida. Florida Governor Jeb Bush "has personally taken a lead role in selling the program," according to the ACLU, and Vice President Cheney "was given a personal briefing on and plea for support" for it in January 2003 by Governor Bush.[62] It is not only financed but managed by the Department of Homeland Security.

The MATRIX creates a "terrorism quotient" that measures the likelihood that individuals in the databases are terrorists. Seisint calls this measure a "High Terrorist Factor" or HTF score. According to a Seisint slide presentation obtained by the

ACLU, the company's aim is to "use the power of the super-computer to analyze massive amounts of data in order to identi-fy potential terrorists in the general population."[63] One slide declares "When enough insignificant data is gathered and ana-lyzed, <u>IT BECOMES SIGNIFICANT</u>."[64]

Seisint has already provided the INS, the FBI, the Secret Service, and the Florida Department of Law Enforcement with a list of 120,000 names with the highest HTF scores.

The ACLU believes that MATRIX is "an effort to recre-ate the discredited Total Information Awareness (TIA) data[-]mining program at the state level."[65] When information about TIA was leaked in 2002, people were so outraged that Congress shut it down. TIA disappeared, but neither the idea nor the practice of data-mining did. They have simply been moved to the state level.

The ACLU earlier said about MATRIX that it shows that "the federal authorities have been deeply involved in develop-ing the state-run effort to spy on citizens."[66] Barry Steinhardt, Director of the ACLU's Technology and Liberty Program, in his earlier report, stated that the capability of MATRIX "is com-pletely unprecedented in our history, and remains unrestrained by our legal system."[67] Steinhardt said: "This kind of data min-ing has the potential to change forever the relationship between private individuals and their government in the United States of America; it is not something that should be taking place in the shadows."[68]

The White Paper concludes that MATRIX "constitutes a massive invasion of privacy, and a violation of the core demo-cratic principles that the government not be permitted to vio-late a person's privacy unless it has reason to believe that he or she is involved in wrongdoing."[69]

If the PATRIOT Act places a disturbing amount of unchecked power in the hands of the Executive, MATRIX consolidates and solidifies that power. Again, this is

unchecked power, as Steinhardt point out. It completely overrides and subverts judicial checks.

Indeed, by erecting this system "in the shadows," as
Steinhardt notes, MATRIX avoids both congressional oversight and judicial review, the only checks on abuse of
Executive powers (other than voting an administration out of
office). It can therefore also be said to violate separation of
powers and our system of checks and balances, since it intrin-
sically arrogates to itself and only to itself any review or oversight. It is completely undemocratic and anti-civil libertarian.
Most worrisome is that once the power is in place, it cannot be
undone. Moreover, it is tremendous power that could be used
both against its own citizens and globally.

Environmental Laws

According to a recent article by Robert F. Kennedy, Jr.,
"Bush is sabotaging the laws that have protected America's
environment for more than thirty years."[70] Kennedy writes that
"the Bush administration has initiated more than 200 major
rollbacks of America's environmental laws, weakening the protection of our country's air, water, public lands and wildlife."

Kennedy connects Bush's environmental policies with a
wider, global picture. He writes that "the deadly addiction to
fossil fuels that White House policies encourage has squandered
our treasury, entangled us in foreign wars, diminished our international prestige, made us a target for terrorist attacks and
increased our reliance on petty Middle Eastern dictators who
despise democracy and are hated by their own people."
As with the Patriot Act, the purpose of Bush's energy policies
can be seen from the results. The invasion of Afghanistan
opened a corridor for construction of a gas pipeline between
Turkmenistan and Pakistan. The invasion of Iraq put business
opportunities into the hands of Cheney's Haliburton and other
big companies. **Rollbacks of domestic environmental laws give**

Bush's corporate constituents greater profits. Invasions of oil-rich countries (or, as with Afghanistan, poor corridor countries) do the same.

Whether one believes that Bush invaded Iraq or Afghanistan for their oil or for revenge or for purely humanitarian reasons, the fact remains that Bush has turned back controls on coal and oil polluters and enabled corporations to profit from these invasions.[71] He has also expanded oil drilling, making repeated attempts to invade the Artic Wilderness area, a protected wilderness, for the same pursuit, although drilling will untold and permanent damage to this last remaining tundra wilderness area.

Opposition to nature, you might recall, was one of Mander's eleven rules of corporations. Dehumanization is another. It is interesting to note that Unocal, the company that had most to gain from the invasion of Afghanistan, has been accused of human rights crimes in other areas of the world. In fact, there is even a verdict against Unocal in a law suit for human rights abuses, and it was that verdict the prompted Republicans to begin their crusade to have the Alien Tort Claims Act, under which the suit was brought, repealed.[72] This illustrates how far the government has gone down the road to becoming an arm of powerful corporations.

The 2000 election

It is natural for men, who wish to hasten the adoption of a measure, to tell us, now is the crisis—now is the critical moment which may be seized, or all will be lost: and [then] to shut the door against free enquiry whenever [they become] conscious [that] the thing presented has defects in it, which time and investigation will probably discover. This has been the custom of tyrants and their dependants in all ages.

—The Federal Farmer,
Oct. 8, 1787[73]

Bush v. Gore set several ominous precedents that are important to the Bush Plan: it showed an utter disregard for established law, which means it showed itself willing to utterly throw out law, and, more importantly, it created the "right" to attain to the presidency through a unilateral Supreme Court decision.

The 2000 election was the most shocking election—and perhaps one of the most shocking events—in America's history and, more than any other act of this administration (or any of its predecessors), can be said to have paved the way for American empire. There is much that could be said about that debacle, but I focus only on the two primary legal issues which decided the case: Bush's bogus (and truly ludicrous) equal protection claim and the legal notion called "standing." The first issue, equal protection, decided the case and shouldn't have. The second issue did in fact decide the case by not being handled at all, where it should have been—and the court should have considered standing *sua sponte* (of its own accord), but did not even mention it. Had they done so, they would have had to thrown the case out. And they knew this.

Vincent Bugliosi, one of the most successful prosecutors in this country, minces no words:

> From the beginning, Bush desperately sought, as it were, to prevent the opening of the door, the looking into the box—unmistakable signs that he feared the truth. In a nation that prides itself on openness, instead of the Supreme Court doing everything within its power to find a legal way; to open the door and box, they did the precise opposite in grasping, stretching and searching mightily for a way, any way at all, to aid their choice for president, Bush, in the suppression of the truth, finally settling, in their judicial coup d'état, on the untenable argument that there was a violation of the Fourteenth Amendment's equal protection clause—the Court asserting that because of the various standards of determining the voter's intent in the Florida counties, voters were treated unequally,

since a vote disqualified in one county … may have been counted in another county, and vice versa. Accordingly, the Court reversed the Florida Supreme Court's order that the undervotes be counted, effectively delivering the presidency to Bush.[74]

Equal protection cases are invariably brought by the aggrieved party. In the 2000 recount, however, Bush never claimed that *he* was the aggrieved party (although he certainly made it sound like he was). Rather, he was claiming, *sub silentio* (silently), that *his voters* were the aggrieved ones and that he had what is called "third-party standing" to assert their claim. Bugliosi notes that "no Florida voter I'm aware of brought any action under the equal protection clause claiming he was disenfranchised because of the different standards being employed."[75] Bugliosi quotes constitutional law professor and scholar, Erwin Chemerinksy:

> Among the Supreme Court's errors [in Bush v. Gore] was not raising the issue of whether George W. Bush had standing to raise the equal protection claim. The law is clear that a person has standing only to raise injuries that he or she personally suffers. Bush's claim was that Florida voters were treated unequally by the counting of votes without standards because identical ballots might be treated differently elsewhere in the state. But since [Bush] did not vote in Florida, he would not suffer this injury.[76]

The Supreme Court's decision rested on a purported violation of the equal protection clause of the Fourteenth Amendment. This clause states that "No State shall … deny to any person within its jurisdiction the equal protection of the laws." One commentator noted that, on the equal protection issue, "the five conservative justices performed what can only be described as an ideological somersault, embracing an equal-protection claim that was not only unpersuasive on its own terms but irreconcilable with the basic tenets of their judicial philosophy."[77] Justice Thomas had written in an earlier case before the Court, in line with a long history of equal protection analysis:

> The equal-protection clause shields only against *purposeful* discrimination: a disparate impact, even upon members of a racial minority,...does not violate equal protection.... [W]e have regularly required more of an equal-protection claimant than a showing that state action has a harsher effect on him or her than on others.[78]

According to Bugliosi, as recently as 1996, Chief Justice Rehnquist affirmed the rule "that mere discrimination against a person or group was insufficient" to violate the equal protection clause.[79] In fact, the Supreme Court ruled in *City of Mobile, Alabama v. Bolden*, an election case, that "only if there is *purposeful* discrimination can there be a violation of the equal protection clause of the Fourteenth Amendment."[80] According to University of Virginia law professor Dick Howard, the decision in *Bush v. Gore* was "a remarkable use of the equal protection clause. It is not consistent with anything [the Court] has done in the past 25 years. No one even claimed there was intentional discrimination here."[81]

So, if there was no finding of *intentional* discrimination against or unfairness to one class of people (and of course there wasn't any such finding), there could not have been an equal protection violation. Think about it a moment. If the votes for Bush in different counties were counted differently, so were those for Gore. It is true that Gore, not Bush, requested a recount, so he got to choose which counties would recount, which means he could choose largely democratic counties. But Bush was not prevented from doing the same. Furthermore, whatever the methods used in different counties, the same disparities necessarily existed all over the nation. Different ballots, different voting machines, and different people doing hand recounts. But varying standards alone do *not* rise to the level of an equal protection violation. Not only that but the standard for determining a valid vote in Florida was nearly identical to the one Bush, himself, had signed into law when he was governor of Texas.

A tiny indicator of some part of the psychological under-current of the *Bush v. Gore* decision can be seen in the oft-repeated post-election Republican phrase: "Get over it!" This phrase seems to have worked like auto-suggestion on Democrats. I've heard many repeat it, their eyes glazing, like a mantra: "I'm trying to get over it, I'm just trying to get over it...." But it seems obvious now that getting over it is the very thing we must *not* do. December 12th, 2000, the day of the U.S. Supreme Court decision in *Bush v. Gore*, should be remembered as a day of infamy.

Yet, the behavior of the Supreme Court in *Bush v. Gore* was not the only concern the 2000 election raised. While Republicans banged on city doors, screaming that the recount was unfair, thousands of legitimate voters were disenfranchised because their names resembled a ex-felon's, who are prohibited from voting in Florida. Because the disenfranchisement affect-ed more African Americans than whites, the "mistake" hints at the possibility of intentional electoral manipulation. Further, some of the these concerns are turning to alarm as newspapers report that the new electronic voting machines can be used to steal elections.[82]

It may be tempting to view the 2000 election as an anom-aly—after all it was razor thin, and possibly unlikely to repeat. But the way in which Bush stole the election—brazen force on the judiciary, disenfranchising African Americans, interfering with a recount—gives a clear signal: the Bush administration will use anything they can to stay in power. That, even more than the events taken singly themselves, is ominous.

Secrecy

Everything secret degenerates, even the administra-

tion of justice; nothing is safe that does not show how it
can bear discussion and publicity.

—Lord Acton (1834-1902)

The Bush Administration has fostered and promoted secrecy from the outset, with Cheney's refusal to turn over to courts
minutes of his Energy Task Force, in the sequestering of and lack
of information about the Guantanamo detainees and the unlawful enemy combatants, as well as the thousands of aliens
detained under the PATRIOT Act, the names gathered under
the MATRIX system, to their refusal to cooperate and turn over
White House records relating to 9/11. The Creppy Memo, issued
by Immigration Chief Creppy, closed "special interest" immigration cases to the public.[83] Under Section 215 of the PATRIOT
Act, libraries and bookstores are required to turn over customer
usage and purchase information to the FBI upon request and are
not allowed to tell anyone. The list goes on and on. Secrecy is
the watchword of the Bush Administration.[84]

As James Hall wrote about Cheney's Energy Task Force in
The American Partisan:

> ... hiding behind the veil of secrecy to develop leg-
> islation only serves to increase the public's distrust of the
> policy-making process in general. Our citizens have the
> right to expect the machinations of their government to
> be as transparent as possible.[85]

"Democracy dies behind closed doors," said Judge Keith of
the Third Circuit Court of Appeals. He continued: "The First
Amendment, through a free press, protects the people's right to
know that their government acts fairly, lawfully and accurately
... When government begins closing doors, it selectively controls information rightfully belonging to the people. Selective
information is misinformation."[86]

The picture, then, is not hard to piece together: disregard
for civil rights and liberties and domestic and international

laws, blatant power grabs (again, both domestically and globally), exploitation and destruction of natural resources and communities, and the wielding of an ever-increasing police and military machinery to suppress dissent.

These are not new ideas. However, the canvas of this coup is so large, so comprehensive that we ordinary folks get mired in the over-abundant bits and pieces or disoriented by its grandiosity. An American coup, an American military dictatorship, an American fascist empire may seem improbable, but then so was Abu Ghraib a few months ago, and at one point in history no one could have imagined that Germany could gas tens of thousands of Jews.

September 11, 2001

What is most significant about September 11 is that 3,000 people (mostly, but not all, Americans) were killed on American soil and the U.S. government has still, over three years later, provided no explanation of how it happened or what they knew. As Kyle Hence, an investigative journalist who has researched and written a great deal about 9/11, writes, we don't know "what [the administration] did with multiple warnings from overseas regarding the threat of attack from the air, and what they were doing on the morning of the 11th, the day on which NORAD [North American Aerospace Defense Command] was conducting one of its annual readiness exercises." He continues: "How could they not have halted the attacks or at least shot down flight 77 when they had war-gamed for such a threat from the air (contrary to Condi Rice's lie on May 16 2002) and had approximately 30 minutes to respond after there could be no doubt we were under attack with a multiple hijacking underway?"[87]

The Bush administration has continually blocked the independent investigation into September 11th.[88] Kyle Hence notes that September 11th has conveniently "been a trump card played at every turn to justify [the administration's] plan for

America and the globe."[89] He adds that "as they recklessly project American might around the world in service to corporate interests and in the interest of securing control over dwindling fossil fuel reserves, they undermine our liberties here at home all the while lying about what they knew and when and obstructing the investigation into the matter."[90]

Enron & The Cheney Energy Task Force

James Hall wrote about Cheney's Energy Task Force in *The American Partisan*:

> The energy policy recommended by the Vice President's Energy Policy Taskforce created energy legislation giving billions of dollars in tax breaks to major energy corporations and recommended substantial deregulation of the energy industry. If the administration is embarrassed by the role that energy corporations played in writing self-serving legislation, it's understandable.[91]

Vice President Dick Cheney's repeated attempts to block disclosure of activities from his 2001 Energy Task Force reached the Supreme Court on April 27 2004. Despite two federal court rulings against these efforts, the Administration continues to insist the American public has no business knowing about the involvement of corporate executives like Ken Lay of Enron in shaping the nation's energy policy.

Summary

If you believe the Laurence Britt was correct in his assessment of what are the common threads found in all fascist states, the Bush Administration should scare you. There is not a single category under which Bush does not fit and in some categories, he fills out the list even more completely. But you do not have to agree with Britt's list or with the descriptions provided at the outset of this chapter of how the Bush Administration fits into the list. Britt's list is useful in helping one to see the Big Picture, of placing all the minutiae in perspective, but if you scan the various components listed in Part Two of the chapter on the Bush Plan, you may get a scarier picture. If you set aside the details of each component and review what each establishes and how the Administration benefits from it, the picture becomes clearer and more ominous.

The picture is of a government run by a ruling elite of religious fanatics that have set up a legal system of tremendous unrestrained oppressive power, are violating just about every one of the first ten amendments of the Constitution, our Bill of Rights, suppressed speech, arrested and physically injured people for nothing more than their dissent against the government, grabbed people off the streets and thrown them in prison with no access to an impartial judge to review their charges—and even without any charges at all—ignoring and violating the rule of law and customs of civilized society, waged "preemptive" war on a false pretext, freed themselves from all responsibility or liability for their actions, lied about facts, hidden other facts, and paid themselves a lot of money, undermined and further impoverished working people, and gone after anyone who they didn't like with prosecutions and legal proceedings. They've set up a system of electronic watchers so intrusive that the movie *Minority Report* no longer seems futuristic or remote and 1984 seems outdated. They are an immensely destructive administration, destroying the working class and labor, destroying the environment, destroying civil liberties, the rule of law, and the friendship of foreign nations the world over. They have sullied the name and reputation of the United States Supreme Court by using that Court to illegitimately place themselves in power. Despite increasing spending for military, straining the military machine almost beyond its endurance, unnecessarily risking the lives of young American men and women soldiers, they have not succeeded in capturing the one person responsible for the September 11 attacks.

CHAPTER SEVEN

The PATRIOT Act
Mainstay of Oppressive Power

> Slight encroachments create new boundaries from which legions of power can seek new territory to capture. "It may be that it is the obnoxious thing in its mildest and least repulsive form; but illegitimate and unconstitutional practices get their first footing in that way, namely, by silent approaches and slight deviations from legal modes of procedure."
>
> —Justice Black, *Reid v. Covert*[1]

Perhaps the most vivid component of the Bush Plan is the USA PATRIOT Act. Much has been written about this Act, a good deal of it disapproving.[2] Because numerous excellent critiques of the Act have been published, both on the internet and in book form,[3] there is no need to replay those arguments here. Instead, I want to focus briefly on the Act's clear purpose and then, also briefly, discuss the three main threats to civil liberties the Act creates. In the next chapter, I will respond to Ashcroft's defenses of the Act.

The PATRIOT Act[4] creates a structure that allows too much power in the executive branch. The Act creates an enabling structure for fascism and oligarchy. It is a structure that could consume democracy. The mere existence of such a structure in our government should alarm us.

How is it that the PATRIOT Act, purportedly designed to protect us from terrorists, can be a democracy-consuming monster? It is really very simple. The "foreign intelligence" provisions allow the Executive to avoid having to adhere to the Constitution, the immigration provisions set dangerous precedents for arbitrary use of power against persons, and the criminal provisions mix in with the foreign intelligence and immigration provisions to create a legal morass. All these together create "an entire federal investigatory, surveillance, intelligence and law enforcement apparatus, a disturbing amount of unchecked power...in the Executive."[5]

Here we will only look at a few of the threats to civil liberties posed by the PATRIOT Act. In the next chapter, we will consider Ashcroft's claims about the Act and discuss those provisions in more depth.[6]

But, before moving on to the PATRIOT Act threats to civil liberties, it is worth pointing out, again, that although the Act was passed under the Bush Administration, the forces that put this law into place are not exclusive to this Administration. As we shall see later in Chapter Nine, *The Cheney Plan for Global Dominance*, it was not just Bush (nor even just Cheney) who was responsible for the idea of an American Empire. As David Cole and James Dempsey point out in *Terrorism & the Constitution*, the causes of the constitutional dilutions in the anti-terrorism laws can be found in a history that goes back at least to the 1980's.[7] The Bush Administration, however, is almost a perfect embodiment of the worst mistakes America could make in the arena of civil liberties and human rights and the PATRIOT Act presents a template for a good number of those mistakes. Hopefully democracy will survive and future administrations, whether under Republicans or Democrats, will learn from Bush's mistakes.

The Threats to Civil Liberties

The main civil liberties threats of the PATRIOT Act are (1) the threat to due process, (2) the threat to freedom of association, (3) the Fourth Amendment threat to the right to be free of unreasonable searches and seizures and a consequent threat to privacy.

1. The Threat to Due Process

Threats to due process in THE PATRIOT ACT are found in the indefinite detentions of immigrants, and the so-called designation provision. The provision for indefinite detentions allows the government to, well, indefinitely detain immigrants—for as little as a visa violation. One purpose of this provision is to prevent foreign terrorists from escaping before information can be obtained about their plans and to prevent them from carrying out their plans. One would suppose that if this plan was a good one, law enforcement would have made a lot of arrests that led to charges and maybe even successful prosecutions by now. However, according to constitutional law professor David Cole:

> As of May 2003, only three of the 1,200 "suspected terrorists" arrested in the first seven weeks [after the enactment of the PATRIOT Act], and none of the nearly 4,000 more foreign nationals arrested since under related antiterrorism initiatives, turned out to warrant even a charge of terrorist-related criminal activity.[8]

But despite this "astoundingly low hit rate," the Bush Administration continues to defend the indefinite detention provision and has apparently continued, even as of this writing, to throw people into the abyss of indefinite detention. According to Jason Burke of *The Guardian*: "The United States government, in conjunction with key allies, is running an 'invisible' network of prisons and detention centres [sic] into which thousands of suspects have disappeared without trace since the 'war on terror' began."[9]

The use of indefinite detentions are thus a threat to due process, not just to aliens but to citizens. And arbitrary detentions and detentions without due process are prohibited by international law as well as the Constitution.

Indefinite Detentions

The indefinite detention provision only applies to *aliens*. So, *citizens* couldn't complain that *their* rights were violated. Thinking that dilutions or violations of human rights towards others cannot and will not affect oneself or one's own people is a common and dangerous mistake. As David Cole, author of *Enemy Aliens*, writes: "[W]hat we do to foreign nationals today often paves the way for what will be done to American citizens tomorrow."[10]

As if to illustrate this principle, it became clear very quickly after 9/11 that Bush didn't feel the need for any codified authority to detain U.S. citizens, as he declared several American citizens "unlawful enemy combatants" and had them thrown in military brigs, outside the reach of civil courts, denying them any legal process, access to legal representation, or even the International Committee of the Red Cross.

The Guantanamo situation is but a extension or variation of the indefinite detention and unlawful enemy combatant rules. Recent revelations of Rumsfeld's instructions to hide certain prisoners at Abu Ghraib so they could not be found highlights further the danger of Bush's position.

Designation

The designation provision authorizes the Attorney General or Secretary of State to designate a foreign organization as a terrorist group. So, what's the trouble with designation? These are foreign groups that are funneling funds and resources to carry out terrorist attacks, aren't they?

The trouble is we can't verify whether such a designation is just because there is no ability to challenge or review it. The administrative record can be sealed, so that although the designated group is allowed to challenge its designation under the statute, that challenge cannot be effective. Nor can judicial review be impartial. For one thing, review is limited to the District of Columbia Circuit court. For another, one-sided review of potentially largely hearsay evidence cannot be impartial. One court noted:

> The information recited [in the administrative record] is certainly not evidence of the sort that would normally be received in court. It is instead material the Secretary of State compiled as a record, from sources named and unnamed, the accuracy of which we have no way of evaluating.[11]

The due process provided, therefore, is illusory.

One may ask: "But wait a minute: isn't it better to detain or deport an alien who is associated with a terrorist group than wait around for due process to figure it out, only to have the person commit a terrorist act? If I was a politician or government official charged with protecting the country, I'd rather be safe than blamed for not taking such action." There are several problems with this line of reasoning. Due process does not prevent the government from taking measures to protect against terrorism. Nor does due process conflict with the right to detain someone who is considered as a threat or danger to society. Such persons who are considered dangerous to the community have always routinely been detained.

Further, deportation will not stop a terrorist act.

Finally, what is most troubling about this provision is not only the power to designate foreign groups as terrorist without any judicial or congressional oversight, but the authority granted in another statute that is often used in conjunction with the designation provision: that which criminalizes the giving of "material support" to a designated foreign terrorist group. The problem is that those charged under the material support statute are <u>not</u> allowed to challenge the designation of the group they are accused of supporting.

This leads to an interesting but dangerous paradox. A foreign organization that is designated as "terrorist" *can* challenge its designation, but someone who supports it can*not*. This means that a foreign group may be granted more due process than a criminal defendant.[12]

Of course, the due process granted the designated organization is not much process, since the administrative record will likely be classified, and since the organization is not allowed to contribute to that record. Nonetheless, it is *some* process. On the other hand, a criminal defendant could spend the rest of his life in jail based on having assisted a designated organization, without any ability to challenge the designation of the organization he is accused of supporting. (He is, of course, allowed legal process to challenge the charges against him, but that is wholly inadequate in the face of a closed record—e.g. a record which the defendant cannot view and to which he is not allowed to respond or contribute. This also violates the Sixth Amendment right to confront evidence against oneself.)

2. The Threat to Freedom of Association

Designation is also a threat to freedom of association,. The provision allows for exclusion of an alien from the United States on the basis of association with an undesirable group. Granted the United States government has every right to exclude people from entering the country, but it has always had the power to do so. The PATRIOT Act does not enhance this power. What it does is make it more difficult to appeal exclusion or deportation. The review process in immigration courts is an important safeguard that ensures that those who are denied entry or are being deported have a right to present facts in their favor. Designation, however, is not reviewable in immigration court. Any alien who is associated with a designated organization is excludable and/or removable and they may not challenge the designation.

In fact, as a side note, any alien—she does not need to be associated with a designated terrorist organization—can be punished for her associations, since the detention provisions in the PATRIOT Act permit holding and deporting people for nothing more than visa violations. Thus, as noted earlier, thousands of Arabic or Muslim aliens were rounded up after 9/11 and detained for no reason other than that they were Arabic or Muslim. David Cole writes: "Ashcroft's dragnet approach has targeted tens of thousands of Arabs and Muslims for registration, interviews, mass arrests, deportation, and automatic detention."[13]

Secondly, where material support of a designated foreign terrorist organization is charged, there is no requirement that the person accused of providing the material support have any knowledge of unlawful activity of the foreign terrorist organization, or any intent to participate in or further those unlawful ends. As David Cole says in *Enemy Aliens*, the "'material support' criminal statute imposes guilt by association" and "punishes moral innocents for constitutionally protected activity."[14] The knowledge and intent requirements are essential components of First Amendment associational doctrine. Over fifty years of Supreme Court case law stands for the proposition that where association is at issue, the issue may not be viewed as a "strict liability"one. An individual may not, in other words, be held liable for merely associating with criminals, if he does not know of and participate in their crimes. The matter of whether one's support of an organization is criminal or not, then, is a problem of proof, to be decided on the evidence by a court of law, not pre-determined by official edict.[15]

3. The Fourth Amendment Threat: Surveillance & Privacy

> The worse the government fails, the less privacy citizens supposedly deserve.
> —James Bovard, *Terrorism & Tyranny*[16]

Most of the provisions that relate to privacy in the PATRIOT Act fall under the Foreign Intelligence Surveillance Act, or

FISA. Some of these provisions threaten our Fourth Amendment protections to be free of unreasonable searches and seizures.

Surveillance under FISA is about gathering *foreign intelligence information*: that is, information with respect to a foreign power or foreign territory that relates to the national defense, national security, or conduct of foreign affairs of the United States.[17] Because FISA warrants were originally intended to apply only to foreigners, Congress did not think the warrants needed to be held to the Fourth Amendment protections. After all, this was spying on foreign nations and persons for national security reasons.

Well, that should be okay, shouldn't it? After all, these warrants only apply to aliens, right? No. Not anymore. Not under the PATRIOT Act.

As long as the target has "relevance to an ongoing investigation" and a "significant foreign intelligence purpose," it can be carried out.[18] This means that if you speak to a friend or relative in the Middle East and that person gave money at some point to an organization that provides humanitarian aid to a group suspected of ties to terrorism (even if neither you nor your friend is aware of that), you are a legitimate target for wire, phone, or computer taps under FISA. Prior to the PATRIOT Act, you could only be targeted if the *primary* purpose of the investigation was the gathering of foreign intelligence.

The FISA provisions will be discussed in a bit more depth in Chapter Eight, *Ashcroft's Way*. For the moment, let me address briefly only one of the most well-known and rightfully condemned provisions of the PATRIOT Act: Section 215, which allows the FBI to obtain library and book store records, among many others, if they are clamed to be relevant to an ongoing investigation. The library or book store (or other record-holder) is prohibited from informing the target of the FBI request. This provision has raised enough opposition to have been addressed by the International Library Association and resulted in a bill, called the "Safe Act," to partially rescind it. (This bill is still pending as of this writing.)[19]

However, the library and bookstore records are not the ones that should concern us. The provision authorizes search and seizure of *any* third-party maintained records, including medical, educational, and financial. Not only that but an additional provision was passed recently in the intelligence finance bill that actually expanded the powers of the FBI to obtain financial records by broadening the definition of "financial institution" and permitting the FBI to obtain such records without even going to a court to get a warrant.[20]

All requests for foreign intelligence warrants to tap or search are presented to the FISA Court. This is essentially a secret court, the existence of which was generally unheard of before the PATRIOT Act.[21] The FISA Court determines primarily one thing: whether to grant a request by the FBI to wiretap or search a foreign intelligence target. The criteria for this is that the target must be a foreign power or an agent of a foreign power. Note that "foreign intelligence target" does not mean: "foreigner." The target can be a US citizen suspected of engaging in supplying intelligence to parties outside the U.S. No probable cause of criminal activity is required for the warrant to be granted and the surveillance to be carried out. Even if you are not a foreign power or agent thereof, your phone or computer could be tapped and your home searched if you are viewed as in any way connected to anyone who is a foreign power or agent thereof.[22] Additionally, a new bill presently before Congress would allow surveillance or searches of persons not strictly in relation to foreign powers or agents. H.R. 3179 permits surveillance of "lone wolf" persons, ie. "persons acting alone, without any connection to a foreign terrorist group or government."[23]

Thus, the PATRIOT Act raises many concerns about whether it preserves our Fourth Amendment privacy protections.

The Church Committee that investigated FBI abuses in the 1970's stated:

> Personal privacy is protected because it is essential to liberty and the pursuit of happiness. Our Constitution checks the power of Government for the purpose of protecting the rights of individuals, in order that all our citizens may live in a free and decent society. Unlike totalitarian states, we do not believe that any government has a monopoly on truth.
>
> When Government infringes those rights instead of nurturing and protecting them, the injury spreads far beyond the particular citizens targeted to untold numbers of other Americans who may be intimidated....Persons most intimidated may well not be those at the extremes of the political spectrum, but rather those nearer the middle. Yet voices of moderation are vital to balance public debate and avoid polarization in our society.[24]

In Conclusion

It's almost impossible to sum up everything the PATRIOT Act affects. It's a huge piece of legislation. This chapter addressed only a few of the concerns via topical headings on three areas of civil rights protections: First Amendment, Fourth Amendment, and due process. Even in those selected areas, the Act goes way beyond the bounds prescribed by the Constitution. The threats to due process involve the combination of immigration and criminal laws. The threats to freedom of association similarly involve the combination of those two areas. The threats to privacy involve the combination of foreign intelligence laws and criminal laws.

The biggest problem, therefore, in the Act is this mixing of standards from different legal systems or sets of laws. Foreign intelligence law was originally intended to *limit* what the President could do in relation to foreign surveillance; it was not intended to *expand* what the FBI or other law enforcement could do in criminal investigations, or U.S. Attorneys could use in criminal prosecutions. Immigration law was intended to provide fair process for the admission and exclusion of aliens; it was not intended to be applied in criminal prosecutions. These encroachments on criminal constitutional procedural protections must be rescinded and the protections restored to their full constitutional reach. The peace and freedom of our nation depend upon it.

CHAPTER EIGHT

Ashcroft's Way

A Closer Look at the PATRIOT Act[1]

Many Americans think of Ashcroft as a religious zealot who is doing his best to destroy the Bill of Rights. I share this view. However, what if Ashcroft is right? What if we need the PATRIOT Act? What if the PATRIOT Act is the right balance of security and liberty? Ashcroft was not the progenitor of the PATRIOT Act,[2] but he has thrown his weight fully behind it, put out statements defending it, and even gone on a nationwide tour to promote it. This is a man with a strong sense of mission. One has to admire that. And surely there must be some truth to his arguments. After all, his shock troops—federal prosecutors—have won many rounds in courts across the nation.

Ashcroft posted his defense of the PATRIOT Act on a Department of Justice web page titled www.lifeandliberty.gov.[3] There he makes four main assertions: the PATRIOT Act (1) allows investigators to use tools to investigate terrorists that were already available to investigate organized crime and drug trafficking, (2) facilitates information sharing and cooperation among government agencies so that they can better "connect the dots," (3) updates the law to reflect new technologies and new threats, and (4) increases the penalties for those who commit terrorist crimes. This chapter takes some pains to delve into, discuss, and counter the first two of these four assertions in this chapter.[4]

Stick with me; this discussion reveals the real snake in the bag. If you really want to know what Ashcroft is doing, entering into the tangled web of his pro-PATRIOT Act discourses is revealing.

"Preserving Life & Liberty"[5]

Ashcroft starts out his defense with the following missive:

> The Department of Justice's first priority is to pre-
> vent future terrorist attacks. Since its passage following
> the September 11, 2001 attacks, the Patriot Act has
> played a key part—and often the leading role—in a num-
> ber of successful operations to protect innocent
> Americans from the deadly plans of terrorists dedicated to
> destroying America and our way of life. While the results
> have been important, in passing the Patriot Act, Congress
> provided for only modest, incremental changes in the law.
> Congress simply took existing legal principles and retrofit-
> ted them to preserve the lives and liberty of the American
> people from the challenges posed by a global terrorist net-
> work.[6]

It's comforting, isn't it? However, we shall see that the
"modest incremental changes" and "retrofitted" laws contain
some quite serious constitutional violations which, far from preserving the lives and liberty of the American people, are a great
threat to democracy.

1. Ashcroft's First Main Point: TOOLS
**The PATRIOT Act allows investigators to use the tools
that were already available to investigate organized crime and
drug trafficking for investigating terrorists.**

Appears to be unarguable, doesn't it? Supporting this
point, the DOJ quotes Senator Biden as stating that the FBI
could get a wiretap to investigate the Mafia, but they could not
get one to investigate terrorists. Biden said: "To put it bluntly,
that was crazy! What's good for the mob should be good for terrorists."[7] Who can argue with this?

But the DOJ's assertion is seriously misleading ... and
unless Ashcroft is wholly ignorant of the law, the assertion is
clearly *intentionally* misleading. Why? Because, yes, the PATRI-
OT Act *does* provide *tools* for terrorist investigations that have

already existed in criminal investigations (although these tools could still always have been used against terrorists, as well, if a criminal investigation was pursued). But what Ashcroft does *not* say is that the there are crucial differences in the *standards* under which these tools are used in terrorist investigations, and those differences are exactly where constitutional violations exist.

But bear with me a moment. Before I explain, we need to let Ashcroft say more explicitly what he's talking about.

Expanding on his assertion, Ashcroft states four succinct points: the PATRIOT Act allows (a) law enforcement to use surveillance against more crimes of terror, (b) federal agents to follow sophisticated terrorists trained to evade detection, (c) law enforcement to conduct investigations without tipping off terrorists, and (d) federal agents to ask a court for an order to obtain business records to national security terrorism cases.

Let's look at these point by point.

1.   SURVEILLANCE FOR MORE CRIMES OF TERROR
      (Sec. 808)

DOJ CLAIM: the Act allows law enforcement to use surveillance against more crimes of terror. On this point, Ashcroft writes:

> Before the Patriot Act, courts could permit law enforcement to conduct electronic surveillance to investigate many ordinary, non-terrorism crimes, such as drug crimes, mail fraud, and passport fraud. Agents also could obtain wiretaps to investigate some, but not all, of the crimes that terrorists often commit. The Act enabled investigators to gather information when looking into the full range of terrorism-related crimes, including: chemical-weapons offenses, the use of weapons of mass destruction, killing Americans abroad, and terrorism financing.

RESPONSE:

Nothing prohibited the DOJ from using electronic surveillance in terrorism investigations, just as in other criminal investigations, before the PATRIOT Act. The difference under the PATRIOT Act is that the Act expanded the categories under which FISA warrants could apply and FISA warrants do not require probable cause of criminal activity.

There are really two things that Ashcroft is mixing together here. First, the PATRIOT Act does add some new crimes and incorporates others into so-called terrorism investigations and prosecutions. While these provisions are not objectionable in themselves, the DOJ could have as easily gotten convictions on such crimes under regular criminal law that they now argue they can only prosecute as terrorism cases. For example, someone who commits murder is as guilty of the crime of murder whether it is part of an act of terrorism or not, and no matter what weapons he uses or where he commits the crime. And he could always be prosecuted for such a crime, no matter whether he was labeled a terrorist or not. The only difference is that by adding these categories to the list of *terrorism* offenses, the government can apply FISA to them, which allows them to avoid the Fourth Amendment standard of probable cause.

Ashcroft obscures a very important distinction here (and, as we shall see, throughout his defense of the PATRIOT Act): the distinction between <u>criminal procedural law</u> (which is governed by the Fourth Amendment) and <u>foreign intelligence investigations</u> (which aren't, because they involve foreign powers). **What Ashcroft is really saying is he wants to have (and the PATRIOT Act gave him) the same tools to use in so-called terrorist investigations as in criminal investigations, but *without the constitutional protections*:** for example, the Fourth Amendment right to be free of unreasonable searches and seizures.

So, whenever Ashcroft or anyone defending the PATRIOT Act uses the words *terrorist investigation, national security case, or foreign intelligence investigation*, remember that he is talking about evading the Fourth Amendment.

The Center for Democracy & Technology writes:

> The Justice Department had the ability to use wiretaps, including roving taps [see next section below for description], in criminal investigations of terrorism, just as in other criminal investigations, long before the PATRIOT Act. Then what are they talking about? A special wiretap technique, the roving tap was available in criminal investigations of terrorists and drug dealers but was not available under the government's separate authority to investigate terrorism as a foreign counterintelligence matter under the Foreign Intelligence Surveillance Act (FISA). No civil liberties groups objected to adding roving tap authority to FISA. We did object to the fact that an important procedural safeguard [e.g. probable cause] applicable to roving taps in criminal cases was not applied to roving taps in intelligence cases.[8]

The problem, of course, with applying the probable cause standard to a FISA foreign intelligence investigation is that FISA NEVER requires probable cause of criminal activity in order to issue a warrant, because FISA is meant to apply only to foreign powers or agents thereof. The trouble is, though, that under the PATRIOT Act, any subject that is *relevant to an ongoing foreign intelligence investigation* can be included in the tap and as long as at least a *significant purpose* of the investigation is to collect foreign intelligence, law enforcement can conduct the investigation under FISA, including taps and searches, *without probable cause*.

2.   ROVING TAPS (sec. 206)

("Roving wiretaps" are phone taps that apply to the person rather than the place. In other words, the person may use different phones and the tap will apply to all of them.)

DOJ CLAIM: the Act allows federal agents to follow sophisticated terrorists trained to evade detection.

Ashcroft says:

> For years, law enforcement has been able to use "roving wiretaps" to investigate ordinary crimes, including drug offenses and racketeering. A roving wiretap can be authorized by a federal judge to apply to a particular suspect, rather than a particular phone or communications device. Because international terrorists are sophisticated and trained to thwart surveillance by rapidly changing locations and communication devices such as cell phones, the Act authorized agents to seek court permission to use the same techniques in national security investigations to track terrorists.

RESPONSE:

Again, notice the use of the phrase: "national security investigations." This is a very clever way of diverting Americans from knowing that these investigations (and thus, these roving wiretaps) evade the Constitution. The taps evade the Constitution because they do not require probable cause of criminal activity.

Note that _criminal investigations_ of terrorism are _not_ the same as "terrorist investigations." Criminal investigations are brought by law enforcement where there is probable cause of criminal activity. A suspected terrorist may be investigated in a criminal investigation. A "terrorist investigation," on the other hand, is a _foreign intelligence_ investigation that affects national security or interests, and therefore does not require probable cause.

Terrorist investigations, foreign intelligence investigations, and national security investigations, therefore, are essentially synonyms, used interchangeably, in Ashcroft jargon.[9] In other words, a terrorist investigation is the same as a national security investigation is the same as a foreign intelligence investigation. Such investigations were originally defined in FISA as "foreign intelligence" investigations.[10]

Civil libertarians did not object to the use of roving wiretaps in terrorist investigations *per se*. As noted above, law enforcement had authority to use roving wiretaps in *criminal* investigations of terrorism before the PATRIOT Act. Criminal investigations adhere to the Fourth Amendment because they require probable cause of criminal activity. Terrorist/national security/foreign intelligence investigations do not.

The dispute, therefore, is not whether roving wiretaps should be used against terrorists, but whether such taps should adhere to the Constitution or not. Under the PATRIOT Act, the FBI no longer has to adhere to the Fourth Amendment in obtaining a warrant for a tap, as long as they can call the investigation a terrorist/national security/foreign intelligence investigation. Nor do they have to ascertain that the target of the roving wiretap is using the phone being tapped. Indeed, according to the Center for Democracy and Technology, "the combined effect of the PATRIOT Act and the intelligence authorization bill that passed a few months later is that the FBI can now get a warrant to wiretap a phone or computer without specifying either the suspect under surveillance or the phones or computers to be tapped."[11] Previously, third parties, such as phone companies and landlords, had to be specified in the warrant. Now, a "blank" warrant can be extended to unnamed and unspecified third parties. (This provision is subject to sunset in 2005, unless renewed by Congress.)

Furthermore, in order to put a roving wiretap into effect, law enforcement must place a "pen register" or "trap and trace" device on some piece of electronic equipment which allows monitoring of the phone. Section 214 of the PATRIOT Act removes prior restrictions on installing such devices. Previously, they could only be installed on "facilities used by terrorists or those engaged in international terrorist clandestine intelligence activities."[12] Now they can be installed anywhere, as long as the

FBI certifies to the court that the devices are likely to reveal information *relevant to a foreign intelligence* investigation. Finally, section 216 allows for so-called "universal jurisdiction" warrants: a single court may grant a warrant for any and all jurisdictions anywhere in the United States and expands the authority from use with telephones to other uses, such as for cell phones and email and allows for installation of electronic software (rather than an actual physical device) onto service provider equipment.

Some of these changes make sense, don't they? It makes sense that electronic surveillance methods be updated to fit new technologies. However, remember that Ashcroft is claiming that roving wiretaps merely give law enforcement tools to use in terrorist investigations that they already had in fighting crime. You can see now that the scene is far more cluttered that Ashcroft made it out to be. And if you think about it, there are a lot of little loopholes in these complex, interplaying laws. Roving taps can be applied to *any* phone that might relate to a moving targeted suspect. So if a terrorist calls a hotel and accidentally gets you, your home phone might then be tapped. All without probable cause that you are involved in criminal activity and all without you knowing it.

So, who cares? You're innocent, right? What do you have to worry about? Well, what if you also happen to give to an organization that is trying to help a Kurdish group learn peaceful negotiation skills, and that group was designated a foreign terrorist organization, unbeknownst to you? You could be put jail the rest of your life for having provided material support to that organization.

Even if you never give money or assistance to any humanitarian group or peace effort, under the FBI "mosaic theory," or the MATRIX's "terrorism quotient," your insignificant data could "BECOME SIGNIFICANT."[13]

3.   SNEAK & PEEK (DELAYED NOTICE) (sec. 213)

Delayed notice warrants are warrants issued with permission of a court which permit not notifying the subject of the search until some later time. They are also called "sneak and peek" searches.

DOJ CLAIM: the Act allows law enforcement to conduct investigations without tipping off terrorists. Ashcroft states:

> In some cases if criminals are tipped off too early to an investigation, they might flee, destroy evidence, intimidate or kill witnesses, cut off contact with associates, or take other action to evade arrest. Therefore, federal courts in narrow circumstances long have allowed law enforcement to delay for a limited time when the subject is told that a judicially-approved search warrant has been executed. Notice is always provided, but the reasonable delay gives law enforcement time to identify the criminal's associates, eliminate immediate threats to our communities, and coordinate the arrests of multiple individuals without tipping them off beforehand. These delayed notification search warrants have been used for decades, have proven crucial in drug and organized crime cases, and have been upheld by courts as fully constitutional.

RESPONSE:

Again, Ashcroft uses the terrorism trump card. Notice that he says that these delays have long been allowed "in narrow circumstances." True, but the standards applied under those narrow circumstances are not carried into Section 213. He also says this type of warrant has "been used for decades" and "upheld ... as fully constitutional." Yes, but that was when they were applied in the narrow circumstances and with the very narrow requirements that are not extended in Section 213.

The circumstances under which sneak and peek searches were previously permitted were where law enforcement could show a judge that if the target of the search were given notice, one of five things would happen: (1) someone's physical safety would be endangered, (2) someone would flee prosecution, (3) evidence would be tampered with, (4) potential witnesses would be intimidated, or (5) an investigation would be jeopardized or a trial unduly delayed. These searches were only allowed for searches of some forms of electronic communications that were in the custody of a third party.

Now, under the PATRIOT Act, this provision has been expanded to include any kind of search, physical or electronic, in any kind of criminal case. The standard—that an investigation may be jeopardized—is a very low one. Any time law enforcement feels inconvenienced, they can request delayed notice. Although law enforcement must still ask a court for permission to delay notice of the search, even when or if the searched party finds out he was searched, he may not view the warrant to ensure that it applies to him or to verify what was searched. Thus, illegal searches may occur without any check on their validity or constitutionality.

Under Fourth Amendment law, warrants must specify what items will be searched and remember this is always based on probable cause of criminal activity. Thus, courts have thrown out searches that were fishing expeditions that went beyond what was specified in the warrant. Where a suspect cannot view the warrant, he cannot challenge it. As the ACLU notes: "In a covert search warrant, there are often no limitations on what can or will be searched. Any protections afforded by a warrant are meaningless when the searching officer has complete and unsupervised discretion as to what, when and where to search and the individual owner is not provided notice so cannot assert and protect her rights."[14]

The "knock and announce" principle has long been recognized as required by the Fourth Amendment. That's the principle embodied in Rule 41 of the Federal Rules of Criminal Procedure (FRCP). The FRCP, of course, must adhere to the

Fourth Amendment. Federal courts, however, are divided over whether delayed notice even under the prior narrow requirements violates the Fourth Amendment. Section 213 capitalizes on this uncertainty.

This provision does not sunset in 2005.

4.   THIRD-PARTY RECORDS (sec. 215)

This is the provision that many identify with libraries, although it pertains to all "third-party" records, such as medical, financial, educational, purchase, rental, and lending records.

DOJ CLAIM: the Act allows federal agents to ask a court for an order to obtain business records to national security terrorism cases. Ashcroft says:

> Examining business records often provides the key that investigators are looking for to solve a wide range of crimes. Investigators might seek select records from hardware stores or chemical plants, for example, to find out who bought materials to make a bomb, or bank records to see who's sending money to terrorists. Law enforcement authorities have always been able to obtain business records in criminal cases through grand jury subpoenas, and continue to do so in national security cases where appropriate. These records were sought in criminal cases such as the investigation of the Zodiac gunman, where police suspected the gunman was inspired by a Scottish occult poet, and wanted to learn who had checked the poet's books out of the library. In national security cases where use of the grand jury process was not appropriate, investigators previously had limited tools at their disposal to obtain certain business records. Under the Patriot Act, the government can now ask a federal court (the Foreign Intelligence Surveillance Court), if needed to aid an investigation, to order production of the same type of records available through grand jury subpoenas. This fed-

eral court, however, can issue these orders only after the government demonstrates the records concerned are sought for an authorized investigation to obtain foreign intelligence information not concerning a U.S. person or to protect against international terrorism or clandestine intelligence activities, provided that such investigation of a U.S. person is not conducted solely on the basis of activities protected by the First Amendment.

RESPONSE:

Section 215 has raised more complaints that any other, probably because it requires libraries to turn over patron information and prohibits them from telling the patron the information was requested. Librarians, who far from being stereotypical Maid Marions are among the fiercest advocates of the rights to privacy and free speech, rose up so quickly against this provision that many Americans don't even know that the provision covers more than library records.

In fact, however, it is even *more* worrisome that most people know. Why? First, as noted above, it applies to ALL "third-party" records, such as medical, financial, educational, purchase, rental, and lending records. Second, while this provision falls under FISA and therefore is supposed to relate to *foreign intelligence*, it nonetheless allows the FBI to obtain records that have no relation to a foreign power or an agent thereof. The only requirement is that the "any tangible object" is "sought for an authorized [foreign intelligence] investigation," or an investigation "to protect against international terrorism or clandestine intelligence activities." Thus, the object or record sought can be *anyone's* records or things. Finally, any FBI agents in charge of a field office may apply for the warrant and the court is required to rubber stamp all requests upon mere certification by the FBI that the object or record is sought as stipulated above.

Note again the watchword: "national security cases." Notice Ashcroft says "where use of the grand jury process was not appropriate." Why not? Because grand juries only are called to determine whether there is sufficient evidence to bring *criminal* charges against someone. National security cases—e.g. foreign intelligence cases—were never meant to lead to criminal prosecutions. Grand jury processes, while not perfect,[15] protect against politically-motivated and unlawful prosecutions.

Of course, as noted earlier, there is no reason why terrorist suspects cannot be brought before a grand jury or why a grand jury cannot subpoena their records or things for a criminal investigation. What Ashcroft wants, though, is to get around the grand jury process to obtain records with no oversight.

This provision is set to sunset at the end of 2005, but the Intelligence Authorization Act (IAA) of 2004 nonetheless enacted an expansion of this provision.[16] It permits "the FBI [to] acquire [financial] records through an administrative procedure whereby an FBI field agent simply drafts a so-called national security letter stating the information is relevant to a national security investigation."[17] The definition of "financial institution" includes such businesses as insurance companies, travel agencies, real estate agents, stockbrokers, the U.S. Postal Service and even jewelry stores, casinos and car dealerships. Like Section 215, subpoenaed businesses may not reveal they have been subpoenaed. Thus, where Section 215 diluted constitutional standards by permitting law enforcement to gain broad access to records of innocent persons and the court had to rubber stamp the request, Section 374 of the IAA permits such access to a broad array of financial information without even the protection of a court stamp.

Rep. Porter Goss (R-Florida), said "This bill will allow those tracking terrorists and spies to 'follow the money' more effectively and thereby protect the people of the United States more effectively."[18] This, of course, utterly ignores the constitutional concerns we raised above. Law enforcement was already able to track terrorists, both through pre-PATRIOT Act foreign intelligence investigations and through traditional criminal investigations. The only difference under the IAA is that now law enforcement doesn't have to answer to anyone to obtain financial records. They can do so on the basis of their say-so and no one can challenge it. Furthermore, those records do not even need to be exclusively those of terrorists. They can be anybody's.

2. Ashcroft's Second Main Point: INFORMATION SHARING

(secs. 203, 504, & 901)

DOJ CLAIM: The Patriot Act facilitated information sharing and cooperation among government agencies so that they can better "connect the dots."

Ashcroft argues:

> The Act removed the major legal barriers that prevented law enforcement, intelligence, and national defense communities from talking and coordinating their work to protect the American people and our national security. The government's prevention efforts should not be restricted by boxes on an organizational chart. Now police officers, FBI agents, federal prosecutors and intelligence officials can protect our communities by "connecting the dots" to uncover terrorist plots before they are completed. As Sen. John Edwards (D-N.C.) said about the Patriot Act, "we simply cannot prevail in the battle against terrorism if the right hand of our government has no idea what the left hand is doing." (Press release, 10/26/01)

He continues in a bullet point about sharing of grand jury information, which we will address after a more general discussion on information-sharing as a whole.

RESPONSE:

Ashcroft's First Point on Information Sharing

Ashcroft's first point relates to the separation that used to exist between "law enforcement, intelligence, and national defense communities." Ashcroft is telling half truths. The "government's prevention efforts" were never "restricted by boxes on an organizational chart." However, to be fair, there are two views of this.

According to Heather MacDonald, attorney and conservative commentator, the government prior to 9/11 was prevented from "connecting the dots" as a result of "senseless terror-fighting restrictions put into place by Attorney General Janet Reno in 1995."[19] These restrictions, known as "The Wall," "erected a mind-boggling and ultimately lethal set of impediments to cooperation among all relevant anti-terrorist personnel."[20] According to MacDonald:

> No sooner had the ink dried on the Wall guidelines than America's anti-terror operations suffered a nervous breakdown. Collaboration broke down almost completely. Says Mary Jo White, former New York U.S. attorney and the most seasoned al-Qaida prosecutor before 9/11: "The walls are the single greatest danger we have blocking our ability to obtain and act on [terrorist] information."[21]

Indeed, according to the Congressional Research Service: "Previous [to the PATRIOT Act], federal law enforcement officers who uncovered details of the activities of international terrorist organizations or of foreign agents in this country were often not free to pass the information on to federal intelligence officers."[22]

MacDonald declares outright that:

> According to Kenneth Bass, who helped draft FISA for the Carter administration, none of these Reno-man-

dated restrictions reflects the law's original intent. "The Wall is absolutely ludicrous," he says, "It is not in the national interest."[23]

However, FISA itself contains a so-called "minimization procedure" (designed to minimize the collection, retention, and dissemination of information about United States persons) that is known as an *"information-screening wall."* This "wall," according to the Electronic Privacy Information Center (EPIC), "require[s] an official not involved in the criminal investigation to review the raw materials gathered by FISA surveillance and only pass on information that might be relevant evidence."[24] The purpose of this practice is "to ensure that criminal investigators do not use FISA authority for criminal investigations."[25]

Nonetheless, although, according to law professor David Cole, "[v]irtually everyone agrees that better information sharing within the federal government, with other nations, and with state and local authorities, is essential...[b]y most accounts...the barriers to information sharing prior to September 11 were more bureaucratic than legal in nature." The "source of the reluctance" he says, "was principally Bureau culture, not law."[26] The FBI's problem internally, according to Cole, "was not so much that it was legally hamstrung by restrictions on its investigatory powers as that it was disorganized and decentralized, and did not sufficiently reward intelligence analysis as compared to more traditional law enforcement tasks."[27]

Cole's view is supported by Richard Clarke, former National Coordinator of Security[28] and author of *Against All Enemies: Inside America's War on Terror.* According to Clarke, the problem was "the secrecy of the FBI." "Institutionally, the fifty-six FBI offices talked only to the U.S. Attorneys around the country."[29] Clarke says Reno and National Security Advisor Anthony Lake came to an agreement in the mid-1990's about information sharing that became "the principle that we operated under and when I knew about people or events I was able to use the "Lake-Reno Agreement" to pry out information."[30] "Sometimes," Clarke wrote, "a few senior FBI personnel even volunteered information to us. Usually, however, the FBI acted like Lake-Reno was a resort in Nevada."[31]

Whether Janet Reno's "Wall" or the FISA "minimization procedures" were the cause of FBI secrecy, internally or externally, or not, the PATRIOT Act did change the rules—in two ways. First, it authorized the sharing of *criminal* investigative information with intelligence officials (sections 203 and 901) and, second, it amended the certification definition for a FISA surveillance order (section 218), making it easier to share information derived from it.[32]

It makes sense, doesn't it, for intelligence agencies to be sharing information that may stop a terrorist attack or result in bringing a terrorist to justice? Yes, it does—*as long as it doesn't compromise our civil liberties*. For, once those civil liberties are compromised, the terrorists have won. The ACLU says it well: we *can* be safe *and* free. The question is, then: how do we make sure our intelligence agencies can "connect the dots" while preserving civil liberties? And, does the PATRIOT Act achieve this balance?

The answer to the first question is certainly complex. David Cole goes a long way in answering the question in his book, *Enemy Aliens*. The solution, he believes, can be found, at least in part, in the way we treat aliens. He writes that "[a] different approach with substantially more hope for taming the time-tested proclivity to overreact would be to insist that, as much as possible, all persons share equally the costs and burdens that we have so often selectively imposed on foreign nationals."[33]

Whether this is indeed the answer, or at least part of it, the PATRIOT Act certainly does not achieve the proper balance and the information-sharing provisions, unfortunately, are not an exception to that failure. The ACLU identifies several problems with these provisions:

> It permits a vast array of information gathering on U.S. citizens from school records, financial transactions, Internet activity, telephone conversations, information gleaned from grand jury proceedings and criminal investigations to be shared with the CIA (and other non-law enforcement officials) even if it pertains to Americans. The information would be shared without a court order.[34]

The ACLU notes that FISA, enacted in 1978, "made it clear that the Department of Justice would have the leading role in gathering foreign intelligence in the United States." However, the PATRIOT Act "would tear down these safeguards and once again permit the CIA to create dossiers on constitutionally protected activities of Americans and eliminate judicial review of such practices." Finally, the ACLU says that the information-sharing provisions run "directly contrary to the statutory prohibition in the CIA's charter barring it from engaging in internal security functions."[35]

The PATRIOT Act information-sharing provisions (coincidentally, like the data-mining programs, Total Information Awareness (TIA) and MATRIX) rest on the idea that more information is better. But more information is not necessarily the answer. David Cole notes:

> As virtually all assessments of the government's failure to detect and prevent the September 11 attacks have concluded, the principal problem was not the government's lack of authority for gathering information, but its failure to analyze the massive troves of data it had...[If this is so,] sweeping initiatives that will inundate authorities with still more irrelevant information are not likely to provide a solution. The difficulty is that there are already too many extraneous dots. As a Markle Foundation Task Force comprised of national security and technology experts

founds, "Those who have called for endless mining of vast new government data warehouses are not offering the promise of real security. They instead evoke memories of the walls of clippings collected by the paranoid genius, John Nash, in A Beautiful Mind."[36]

Cole suggests that the best solution is the traditional "minimal requirement that the FBI's activities have some connection to federal crime." This requirement "serves to focus the agency on those who pose the greatest threat, and to forestall the expenditure of scarce resources on individuals and groups with neither an intention nor a capacity to commit a federal crime."[37] (Remember, too, that terrorism is also a federal crime.) In essence, therefore, the pre-PATRIOT Act separation between foreign intelligence and criminal information, as codified in the FISA "information-screening wall," is still the best and most appropriate safeguard to prevent intelligence agency and government abuse of constitutional rights.

So then, what about the second way the PATRIOT Act changed the information-sharing rules: section 218, the certification definition for FISA surveillance orders? Certification is (and has always been under FISA) a kind of preliminary hoop that all FISA warrants must jump through. The PATRIOT Act put this hoop substantially lower for law enforcement, changing it from an important safeguard into a mere mechanical exercise with no value. In the process, it diluted our Fourth Amendment rights just a tad more. Let me explain.

FISA warrants must pertain to foreign intelligence information, which is defined as "information that relates to U.S. ability to protect against possible hostile acts of a foreign power or an agent of a foreign power, sabotage or terrorism by a foreign power or agent, and clandestine intelligence activities by a foreign power or agent." Such information must relate to the national defense, national security, or conduct of foreign affairs of the United States.[38]

The Electronic Privacy Information Center (EPIC) notes that "[a]lthough FISA surveillances must have an intelligence purpose, courts allow FISA-obtained information to be used in criminal trials."[39] According to the Congressional Research Service (CRS), "[a]s originally enacted the application for a FISA surveillance order required certification of the fact that '*the* purpose for the surveillance is to obtain foreign intelligence information.'"[40] CRS explains:

> From the beginning, defendants have questioned whether authorities had used a FISA surveillance order against them in order to avoid the predicate crime threshold [ie., probable cause] for a [criminal warrant]. Out of these challenges arose the notion that perhaps 'the purpose' might not always mean the sole purpose.[41]

CRS notes that the Justice Department sought to obtain FISA surveillance and physical search authority (in the PATRIOT Act) on the basis of "*a*" foreign intelligence purpose. This would have meant that the DOJ could have freely mixed criminal investigative information with foreign intelligence information, with essentially no safeguards at all. But section 218 instead required certification that the foreign intelligence gathering is a "*significant* purpose" for the FISA surveillance or physical search order application.[42] This standard while not as bad as the "a purpose" standard, still significantly dilutes constitutional protections.

Section 218 also clearly "encourages coordination between intelligence and law enforcement officials."[43] So, isn't this a good thing? We do want coordination between these offices, don't we? The answer is the same as before: yes, *as long as it doesn't compromise our civil liberties*. According to EPIC, the PATRIOT Act amendment to FISA certification "is a serious alteration to the delicate constitutional balance reflected in the prior legal regime governing electronic surveillance."[44]

The pre-PATRIOT Act standard for certification maintained the delicate constitutional balance and safeguarded our liberties and it was not the cause of the FBI's intelligence failures. The PATRIOT Act amendment to this provision should be reversed or repealed. (Section 218, however, sunsets at the end of 2005.)

Ashcroft's Second Point on Information Sharing: Grand Juries

Ashcroft's second point is about sharing grand jury information. In full, he writes:

> Prosecutors can now share evidence obtained through grand juries with intelligence officials—and intelligence information can now be shared more easily with federal prosecutors. Such sharing of information leads to concrete results. For example, a federal grand jury recently indicted an individual in Florida, Sami al-Arian, for allegedly being the U.S. leader of the Palestinian Islamic Jihad, one of the world's most violent terrorist outfits. Palestinian Islamic Jihad is responsible for murdering more than 100 innocent people, including a young American named Alisa Flatow who was killed in a tragic bus bombing in Gaza. The Patriot Act assisted us in obtaining the indictment by enabling the full sharing of information and advice about the case among prosecutors and investigators. Alisa's father, Steven Flatow, has said, "When you know the resources of your government are committed to right the wrongs committed against your daughter, that instills you with a sense of awe. As a father you can't ask for anything more."

Flatow's statement raises an important point: that we don't want our government hampered by not being able to share information. However, as we discussed above, there are many problems with the information-sharing PATRIOT Act provisions. These apply also to grand jury information-sharing. But, with respect to sharing grand jury information itself, there are even more problems—some which should deeply concern us.

Before moving on to a discussion about these problems, however, it is worth pointing out that in posting these remarks to an official DOJ web site, Ashcroft shamelessly capitalized on a tragic death to point the finger at someone who has not yet been tried in a court of law—and to use that pre-determined guilt to promote a troubling law. Ashcroft is committing a highly unethical act here by talking about a pending case (Sami Al-Arian's). Nor should he be using his office to endorse particular laws.

In our system, people are supposed to be innocent until proven guilty. Ashcroft's behavior raises questions about the propriety of the prosecution. Where a United States official "preemptively" declares the guilt of an arrestee, he is not only acting as prosecutor, but judge and jury; and he also risks tainting the trial. Finally, Ashcroft's behavior also raises the question of his own fitness as an Attorney General.

However, despite Ashcroft's unethical behavior, it is important that we discuss his point about sharing of grand jury information, for, as we have seen from Ashcroft's legal tactics, discussed in Chapter Six, Part Two, grand juries can be (and *are* being) used to discourage and suppress activism and dissent, e.g. constitutionally protected First Amendment activity.

Grand juries were provided for in the Fifth Amendment, which states: "No person shall be held to answer for a capital, or otherwise infamous crime, unless on a presentment or indictment of a Grand Jury."[45] The grand jury is, according to James Dempsey and David Cole in *Terrorism & the Constitution*, "[o]ne of the most powerful tools of the criminal justice system."[46] The grand jury "serves not merely to indict but to gather information."[47] In other words, it was "an institution originally designed to protect against prosecutorial abuse but since turned into an investigative tool" for prosecutors.[48]

Because the purpose of grand juries is to gather information relating to a possible crime, not to convict someone, they are not required to consider a suspect's side of the story. Witnesses may be summoned without being told who or what is being investigated or who (including the person summoned) might be indicted as a result. Lawyers for witnesses may be excluded from the proceeding, the grand jury may use information obtained from an unlawful search or seizure, and a vote of twelve jurors is sufficient to issue an indictment, even where the grand jury may contain up to twenty-three jurors.[49]

While the Fifth Amendment right to silence may be invoked during a grand jury proceeding, Dempsey and Cole note that the grand jury "can compel anyone to testify before it under oath [and] [a]nyone who refuses to testify can be sent to jail."[50] On the other hand, a "witness who lies can be prosecuted for perjury."[51] Further, "the grand jury can compel anyone with any record or tangible thing to produce it, irrespective of probable cause, again with the threat of jail time for those who refuse."[52]

While "technically subject to the oversight of a judge," in practice, the grand jury "operates as an arm of the prosecutor who convenes it," and "the prosecutor issues subpoenas without the prior approval of the judge."[53]

Although it is not a constitutional requirement, Rule 6(e) of the Federal Rules of Criminal Procedure (FRCP) prohibits disclosure of grand jury matters.

The PATRIOT Act substantially changes the constitutional role of grand jury proceedings by permitting disclosure (ie. information sharing) to federal law enforcement officers of information acquired by the grand jury. This is troubling because of the lack of proper constitutional safeguards in these new information-sharing provisions, as discussed above.

However, more troubling is that now grand jury information can be shared with the Central Intelligence Agency. Why does this matter? Don't we want the CIA to have the information they need to pursue foreign terrorists?

Well, for one thing, when the CIA was created in 1947, "Congress explicitly said that the Agency was to have no subpoena or domestic police powers."[54] Dempsey & Cole explain:

> Congress did not want this secret intelligence agency engaged in domestic security activities. Instead, the CIA's operations were intended to be directed overseas, focused on foreign nationals, in the world of spy-versus-spy and relations between states, where the criminal law was largely inapplicable. The information the CIA secretly collected was intended to inform the President in carrying out foreign affairs and national defense, not to be used to arrest people or prosecute crimes. The secrecy with which the CIA operated—collection activities could go on for years, even decades, without being publicly revealed—was fundamentally incompatible with the criminal justice system, where investigations must have a clear criminal objective, and the information collected and the means by which it is acquired must in most cases ultimately be shared with the accused and tested in open court.[55]

Indeed, an accused person's right to confront the evidence and witnesses against him and have that evidence tested in open court is required by the Sixth Amendment of the Constitution: "In all criminal prosecutions, the accused shall enjoy the right to a speedy and public trial, by an impartial jury ...and to be informed of the nature and cause of the accusation; to be confronted with the witnesses against him; to have compulsory process for obtaining witnesses in his favor, and to have the Assistance of Counsel for his defense."

Dempsey and Cole note that "[s]ince the CIA was not supposed to engage in law enforcement and since its agents were not supposed to appear in court, the CIA was not granted law enforcement powers."[56]

Finally, Dempsey and Cole point out that "history suggests that when the CIA gets involved in domestic activity, abuses are likely to follow" because the agency "is simply not trained in adhering to domestic legal limits on its conduct, [since] its principal field of operation is espionage overseas, where domestic rules do not apply."[57] The PATRIOT Act changes, "give the CIA and other intelligence agencies a much greater domestic role, while leaving them shrouded in secrecy and largely immune to judicial or public oversight."[58]

Section 203(a) permits law enforcement agents to provide to the CIA, without a court order, foreign intelligence information that has been revealed to a grand jury. The sharing of grand jury information is also not limited to information about the person being investigated. Other subsections of 203 allow for sharing of electronic intercepts and foreign intelligence or counterintelligence information obtained as part of a criminal investigation. There is also no prohibition against the CIA or FBI or other federal agencies sharing personal information obtained under this provision with foreign governments.

In Conclusion

Ashcroft has been less than truthful in his assertions about the PATRIOT Act. He has touted what he views as the benefits of the Act not only without revealing its severe weaknesses but simultaneously obscuring the very real dangers it poses to civil liberties and democracy. It is impossible to view Ashcroft's choices as errors of ignorance or failure to understand. Upon careful review, it is clear that his choices were intentional. And deceptive.

But beyond the personal, more important are the principles. Congress needs to reconsider these provisions and take into consideration whether it is *ever* appropriate to mix such laws, whether it is *ever* appropriate to allow such dilutions of constitutional standards, whether it is *ever* wise to leave our liberty and our country in the unaccountable hands of those who by their positions must always be "cast in the role of adversary" against those whose liberties they seek to invade.

CHAPTER NINE

The Cheney Plan for Global Dominance

> We should not break faith with this nation's tradition of keeping military power subservient to civilian authority, a tradition which we believe is firmly embodied in the Constitution. The country has remained true to that faith for almost one hundred seventy years. Perhaps no group in the Nation has been truer than military men themselves.
>
> —Justice Bradley, *Boyd v. U.S.*
> (1886)[1]

If there remains any doubt about the fascist and imperial objectives of the Bush Administration, a review of the Cheney Plan for global dominance must quell it. The genesis and history of this Plan was painstakingly sketched by David Armstrong, an investigative reporter for the National Security News Service, in an October 2002 article published in Harper's Magazine. The article, titled, Dick Cheney's *Song of America: Drafting a Plan for Global Dominance*,[2] provides clear and convincing evidence of Bush's objectives. Armstrong says,

> The overt theme is unilateralism, but it is ultimately a story of domination. It calls for the United States to maintain its overwhelming military superiority and prevent new rivals from rising up to challenge it on the world stage. It calls for dominion over friends and enemies alike. It says not that the United States must be more powerful, or most powerful, but that it must be absolutely powerful.

Because of Cheney's "consistent...dedication to the ideas in the documents that bear his name...and [his] close association with the ideologues behind them," Armstrong dubs the plan: the Cheney Plan. The Plan, Armstrong says,

> ...is disturbing in many ways, and ultimately unworkable. Yet it is being sold now as an answer to the "new realities" of the post-September 11 world, even as it was sold previously as the answer to the new realities of the post-Cold War world. For Cheney, the Plan has always been the right answer, no matter how different the questions.

The Plan did not start with the administration of George W. Bush. Rather, the Plan was in the works for at least a decade before Bush II came into office. It started around 1990, when Congress declared that the Pentagon's threat assessment was "rooted in the past." Colin Powell, President Reagan's chairman of the Joint Chiefs of Staff and national security adviser, and Paul Wolfowitz, undersecretary of defense for policy, responded with a "new rationale for [a] Base Force approach." This approach, which Powell originally referred to as the need for a military "forward presence," with fewer troops but in more places, eventually evolved into the practice of erecting U.S. bases around the world.

With the Berlin Wall falling in November 1989 and the Soviet Union rapidly "becoming irrelevant," Powell argued that the U.S. "could no longer assess its military needs on the basis of known threats," but needed to shift to a "capability based" assessment: "the ability to address a wide variety of new and unknown challenges." Armstrong notes that this assessment became a key theme of the Plan.

Congress was pushing for reductions in military spending and threatened to withdraw funding if planners did not develop a new and cheaper strategy. When Wolfowitz recommended reducing U.S. forces to levels proposed by Powell but included a "crisis response/reconstitution" jump-out clause which would allow for increases when necessary, Cheney adopted the Plan as his own. Cheney had always been "deeply suspicious of the Soviets and strongly resisted all efforts to reduce military spending," but the Wolfowitz compromise did the trick for him, and he presented it to President Bush the Elder. By remarkable coincidence, Bush I first unveiled the Plan on the very day Saddam Hussein invaded Kuwait.

Then, in August 1991, the Soviet Union collapsed. According to Armstrong, the U.S. had a choice:

> It could capitalize on the euphoria of the moment by nurturing cooperative relations and developing multilateral structures to help guide the global realignment, or it could consolidate its own power and pursue a strategy of unilateralism and global dominance. It chose the latter course.

While the Plan thereafter went through numerous modifications, the primary theme remained always American world dominance. In order to ensure this, the Plan included the use of preemptive military force, the maintenance of a substantial nuclear arsenal, and of a global missile defense system (Star Wars). In short, the plan called for U.S. dominance through unilateral action and military superiority.

The updated Plan was leaked to the *New York Times* in March 1992 and according to Armstrong, "it met with bad reviews." Pat Buchanan said it would give a "blank check" to America's allies by suggesting the U.S. would go to war to defend their interests. Cheney "unconvincingly, tried to distance himself" from that early version of the Plan, but nonetheless continued in "unwavering adherence" to it over the years. Rumsfeld later added to Powell's "forward presence" doctrine, a "unilateralist, maximum-force approach."

The doctrine of preemptive military force included the concepts of "punishing" aggressors "through a variety of means," whenever the U.S. felt the need and a "U.S.-led system of collective security" that "implicitly precluded the need for rearmament of any kind by countries such as Germany and Japan." Delaware Senator Joseph Biden called the Plan "Pax Americana" (a nod to "Pax Romana," the "Roman Peace," which the Romans so kindly forced upon those they conquered), a plan in which "a global security system" would be erected "where threats to stability are suppressed or destroyed by U.S. military power."

The mindset of those who created the Plan is illustrated vividly in a passage in Richard Clarke's book, *Against All Enemies*, where he recounts a cabinet-level discussion on September 12, 2001. Even in the midst of the "Situation Room" emergency meetings, Rumsfeld and Wolfowitz were already talking about invading Iraq:

> At first I was incredulous that we were talking about something other than getting al Qaeda. Then I realized with almost a sharp physical pain that Rumsfeld and Wolfowitz were going to try to take advantage of this national tragedy to promote their agenda about Iraq. Since the beginning of the administration, indeed well before, they had been pressing for a war with Iraq.[3]

When Rumsfeld complained that "there were no decent targets for bombing in Afghanistan and that we should consider bombing Iraq," Clarke thought he was joking, but when President Bush, rather than rejecting the idea, "instead noted that what we needed to do with Iraq was to change the government, not just hit it with more cruise missiles," Clarke realized they were both serious.[4]

In May 2002, Rumsfeld began to add several complementary features to the Plan.

Preemptive strikes are now "unwarned attacks." "Forward presence" is now "forward deterrence." Overwhelming force is now "effect-based approach."

In a speech at West Point in June 2002, Bush the Younger publicly adopted the Cheney Plan.

The Cheney Plan, thus, is the Bush Plan. It is an exceedingly dangerous doctrine. As Armstrong points out:

> This country once rejected 'unwarned' attacks such as Pearl Harbor as barbarous and unworthy of a civilized nation. Today, many cheer the prospect of conducting sneak attacks—potentially with nuclear weapons—on piddling powers run by tin-pot despots. We also once denounced those who tried to rule the world. Our primary objection...to the Soviet Union was its quest for global domination...Having [rid ourselves and the world of the Evil Empire (the Soviet Union)], we now pursue the very thing for which we opposed it.[5]

In Conclusion

We, as individuals, as a people, and as a nation, must look into our own hearts and minds and determine who we are. Global dominance sure can sound tempting, especially when our nightmares are filled with the threat of terrorism. It's easy for America to be the bully and it is easy for Americans to accept this role. As singer/songwriter Jonatha Brooke sings:

> In the American day, you must give and I shall take,
> And I will tell you what is moral and what's just
> Because I want, because I will, because I can, so will I kill.[6]

But, as Stan Goff says, "The Army sent me to a kind of two-decade school, and in school I learned something. *The world is not fundamentally safe.*"[7] This is undeniably true. The world is not safe and it is a frightening thought to those Americans (such as Cheney, Bush, Rumsfeld, etc.) who have lived their lives in relative comfort.

But the un-safe-ness of the world does not compel us to become violators of international law and human rights, torturers, invaders, or murderers. It does not compel us to abandon democracy or the rule of law. It does not compel us to give up civil liberties, or to abdicate our right to "dissolve the political bands" which have connected us to an administration of which we do not approve.[8] Rather, it should compel us to think even more deeply about what principles we want to uphold so that maybe some part of what we do becomes some part of what others want to emulate.

CHAPTER TEN

Global Dominance in Action

Military Necessity or War Crimes?—Violating the Geneva & Hague Conventions[1]

> The accumulation of all powers, legislative, executive, and judiciary, in the same hands, whether of one, a few, or many, and whether hereditary, self-appointed, or elective, may justly be pronounced the very definition of tyranny.
>
> —James Madison,
> *The Federalist Papers*[2]

Back in the Spring of 2003, President Bush claimed that the invasion of Iraq was a military necessity, but we now know it was founded on forged documents.[3] The President claimed that the detention of persons at Guantanamo is "appropriate and consistent with military necessity, in a manner consistent with the principles of the Third Geneva Convention of 1949." He declared that the establishment of Military Tribunals in this country, even while the civil courts are open and fully functioning, is "necessary to meet the emergency."[4] And more recently, he has declared that he will not fire Defense Secretary Donald Rumsfeld despite Rumsfeld's criminal responsibility for the torture and killings at Abu Ghraib prison in Baghdad.

Is Bush violating international law and specifically the Geneva Conventions? If government officials, including Bush and Rumsfeld, are violating Geneva, are they thereby committing war crimes? Or does military necessity dictate—and justi-fy—their course? What do the Geneva Conventions require of the Administration? What is military necessity and what deter-mines it?

The United States Constitution expressly incorporates international treaties as "the supreme law of the land." Article VI of the United States Constitution states:

> The Constitution, and the Laws of the United States which shall be made in Pursuance thereof; and all Treaties made, or which shall be made, under the Authority of the United States, shall be the supreme Law of the Land; and the Judges in every State shall be bound thereby, any Thing in the Constitution or Laws of any State to the Contrary notwithstanding.[5]

All executive and judicial officers and members of Congress are bound by oath to support the Constitution, including Article VI. The term "treaties" includes those signed by the President and ratified by the Senate, as well as those not ratified or simply part of "customary international law"—mean-ing those principles which are recognized by most nations.[6]

The Geneva & Hague Conventions

The Geneva and Hague Conventions were signed and rat-ified by the United States in 1956. They have a long history. They were developed through many wars, starting in 1864. Their present versions arose out of the depredations of World War II. As the Geneva Convention requires, the United States codified their enforcement in the U.S. Code.[7]

Geneva forbids "the passing of sentences and the carrying out of executions without previous judgment pronounced by a regularly constituted court, affording all the judicial guarantees which are recognized as indispensable by civilized peoples." It is forbidden under the Hague Convention "to declare abolished, suspended, or inadmissible in a court of law the rights and actions of the nationals of the hostile party."[8]

Think about what Bush has done by detaining combatants at Guantanamo for over a year without trial ... or by taking persons out of civil courts and throwing them in military brigs for eventual trial before military tribunals ... tribunals that do not have judicial guarantees that meet basic Constitutional or international human rights standards. Think about the lack of judicial guarantees, the lack of access to a jury of peers, of basic rules of evidence (such as the rule that excludes hearsay evidence, for example), the right to confidential communications with and zealous representation by an attorney, and the right to appeal to an independent judicial body. The Bush Military Tribunals fail to guarantee any of these protections. Think about the photographs of the mistreatment of prisoners at Abu Ghraib.

In fact, the Geneva Convention not only requires due process by regularly constituted courts, but also requires that every captured person "whose status is in doubt" have his status determined by a "competent tribunal." The official Geneva Commentary states that "[t]his amendment was based on the view that decisions which might have the gravest consequences should not be left to a single person ... The matter should be taken to court." Because combatants might be subject to capital punishment, a further amendment was made, "stipulating that a decision regarding persons whose status was in doubt would be taken by a 'competent tribunal,' and specifically not a military tribunal."[9] A unilateral determination by the President that captives are "unlawful enemy combatants" does NOT meet the requirements of the Geneva Convention.

Some detainees have already been deported to other countries. (Some were deported to countries that use harsher interrogation methods than we do.) The 1945 Charter of the International Military Tribunal (IMT) forbids the deportation (not to mention the ill-treatment or murder) of "civilian population of or in occupied territory" for "any ... purpose."[10] Geneva forbids the "unlawful deportation or transfer or unlawful confinement of a protected person ... or willfully depriving a protected person of the rights of fair and regular trial."[11] Geneva defines protected persons as those "who, at a given moment and in any manner whatsoever, find themselves, in case of a conflict or occupation, in the hands of a Party to the conflict or Occupying Power of which they are not nationals."[12]

While Geneva makes rules for how combatants and civilians are to be treated, it also makes rules that apply to the nation who captures them—and to those that violate the treaty. The Geneva Conventions "were the first treaties to require States to prosecute violators, regardless of their nationality or the place where the offence is committed." Furthermore, under Geneva, "States must not only respect but 'ensure respect' for [international humanitarian] law."[13] The 1929 Geneva Convention abolished the provision that the Convention is binding only if all the belligerents are bound by it. In other words, Geneva is binding on all, no matter what.

Finally, Geneva is applicable in all circumstances. This means that "no Power bound by the Convention can offer any valid pretext, legal or other, for not respecting the Convention in all its parts." Whether the war is just or unjust, a war of aggression or of resistance to aggression, all parties are bound, not merely to take the necessary legislative action to prevent or repress violations, but to search for, and prosecute, guilty parties. No signatory can evade this responsibility.[14]

The Bush Administration is denying terrorist suspects hearings by a competent tribunal on their status, and is disobeying the intent of the conventions that combatants should be classified as POWs until such a hearing finds otherwise. The legal processes that will be used in the military tribunals violate both the Conventions and any rational concept of justice; they presume guilt, lack independent counsel, and lack appeal to independent competent authority. These are all deeply troubling flaws that cannot be ignored. Any one of those things by itself would be a war crime. Taken together, they are an outrage against humanity and the law of nations.

The War Crimes Act

The United States enacted section 2441 of Title 18 of the United States Code to enforce the Geneva Conventions. Section 2441 states that "[w]hoever, whether inside or outside the United States, commits a war crime ... shall be fined under this title or imprisoned for life or any term of years, or both, and if death results to the victim, shall also be subject to the penalty of death."[15] In its pertinent part, subsection (c) defines a war crime as:

(1)   a grave breach in any of the international conventions signed at Geneva 12 August 1949, or any protocol to such convention to which the United States is a party;

(2)   prohibited by Article 23, 25, 27, or 28 of the Annex to the Hague Convention IV, Respecting the Laws and Customs of War on Land, signed 18 October 1907;

(3)   which constitutes a violation of common Article 3 of the international conventions signed at Geneva, 12 August 1949, or any protocol to such convention to which the United States is a party ...[16]

Clearly, the Bush Administration is flagrantly violating Geneva, and in doing so, it is violating the United States Constitution, international humanitarian law, and domestic federal law. How can Bush get away with this? Military necessity.

The Doctrine of Military Necessity

The military necessity doctrine shifts the balance on most prohibitions. The Third Geneva Convention forbids:

> Willful killing, torture or inhuman treatment, including biological experiments, willfully causing great suffering or serious injury to body or health, unlawful deportation or transfer or unlawful confinement of a protected person, compelling a protected person to serve in the forces of a hostile Power, or willfully depriving a protected person of the rights of fair and regular trial prescribed in the present Convention, taking of hostages and extensive destruction and appropriation of property, **not justified by military necessity** and carried out unlawfully and wantonly.[17]

The Hague Convention prohibits destruction or seizure of "the enemy's property, unless such destruction or seizure be imperatively demanded by **the necessities of war.**"[18]

"Military necessity" is a term that has been thrown around quite a bit by this Administration. What is it? According to one scholar:

> Military necessity was first stated as a legal principle in General Orders No. 100, a codification of the law of war drafted by Francis Lieber and issued by President Lincoln in 1863. Controversial from the beginning, the principle was nevertheless intended as a new restraint on military discretion, as Lincoln's application of it during the Civil War demonstrates. Military necessity remains an important restraint on military operations in new situations for which specific rules have yet to be established.[19]

Francis Lieber, author of the famous *Code of War*, wrote that "Military necessity, as understood by modern civilized nations, consists in the necessity of those measures which are indispensable for securing the ends of the war, and which are lawful according to the modern law and usages of war."[20]

Lieber's language is reflected in the Commentary to the 1977 Protocol Additional to the Geneva Conventions, which states that military necessity "means the necessity for measures which are essential to attain the goals of war, and which are lawful in accordance with the laws and customs of war."[21]

The concept of military necessity comes from the idea of "just war," which is based on the idea of a human society with norms and morals that transcend national boundaries and apply to all humanity. According to the 16th century Dutch jurist, Hugo Grotius, war is just if

(1)   the danger faced by the nation is immediate,

(2)   the force used is necessary to adequately defend the nation's interests, and

(3)   the use of force is proportionate to the threatened danger.[22]

According to one commentator, there are three constraints on the free exercise of military necessity:

> First, any attack must be intended and tend toward the military defeat of the enemy; attacks not so intended cannot be justified by military necessity because they would have no military purpose. Second, even an attack aimed at the military weakening of the enemy must not cause harm to civilians or civilian objects that is excessive in relation to the concrete and direct military advantage anticipated. Third, military necessity cannot justify violation of the other rules of IHL [International Humanitarian law].[23]

> [T]he principle of necessity specifies that a military operation is forbidden if there is some alternative operation that causes less destruction but has the same probability of producing a successful military result.[24]

The Truth About Bush's Wars

The question must be asked, then: is the Bush Administration following Geneva, except to the extent that "military necessity" requires otherwise?

Clearly not. Military necessity cannot justify violation of rules of international humanitarian law, which include those provisions in the Geneva and Hague Conventions relating to status determination of captives, right to a fair hearing, legal representation, and full due process. Military necessity does not justify indefinite detention of suspects without charge. It does not justify torture. It does not justify violation of the United States Constitution. Nor can military necessity sanction the violation of federal criminal law.

And, where is the necessity in committing an act that is explicitly prohibited by law? (Remember 18 U.S.C. 2441 explicitly prohibits violation of Geneva and Hague and requires the United States to prosecute violators. This means that not only is every official who violates 2441 guilty of a war crime, but every federal prosecutor in this country who does not prosecute them is failing his or her duty.)

What about protecting our freedoms could possibly justify preventing our laws from being enforced? And since when does "necessity" entail doing anything that someone happens to think is a good idea without the least regard for any civilized standard of conduct?

A real necessity is obvious. When we launched the D-Day invasion we knew that there were French civilians living in the beachhead area who would very likely be injured or killed, but we also knew that warning them of the invasion would seriously jeopardize the chance of it's success. That is an example of a real military necessity: a specific instance where the specific circumstances require a specific method.

It is not necessity to simply do whatever you think might possibly give you some tactical advantage or leverage. If we were to capture some of Osama Bin Laden's children, we might be able to exert some pressure on him by roasting them one by one over an open fire, but there wouldn't be anything necessary about it—it would simply be another atrocity committed by an administration that has not the least understanding of necessity because they are lost in hysteria, greed, and the self-serving conviction of their own infallibility.

CHAPTER ELEVEN

Conclusion

Americans still have the chance to reverse the damage done by the Bush Administration. The comparison made at the outset of this book of the Bush Administration to Caesar's imperial rule is, in one way, accurate—Bush, like Casear, decided to make the world his empire—but in other ways it is not an apt comparison: Caesar had courage; Bush does not. Nor do Rumsfeld, Cheney, or the rest of the cabinet. Caesar went out and fought with is own hand. You will never see Bush or his ranks doing that. Bush sends others to die for him and hides, as he always has done, behind others as cowardly as he, others whose best defense is smoke and mirrors, and when those don't serve, outright lies. Caesar's laws provided important civil protections; Bush's do not. Bush's laws are some of the worst this country has ever known.

This book, though, is not just about Bush, as I've reminded readers numerous times throughout. His person has provided a concrete example of something we could juxtapose with the ideals of the Constitution and the rule of law. This is a task which sets Bush and those ideals in stark contrast and makes clearer to us the value and meaning, or lack thereof, in each.

It is no real comfort to me that I predicted Bush's ascension. It's no comfort that I was one of the first to articulate the faults of the PATRIOT Act. It is no comfort that I anticipated by two years the torture of Abu Ghraib, Gitmo, and other prisons. I do not feel glad about these insights on my part. I just feel sad about it all. It was never my intention to become a political commentator or activist and it is a mantle I wear uneasily and will shed as soon as I am able. The reason I wrote this book, though, is the same reason I speak to groups about the PATRIOT Act, which is the same reason I go out and organize events and protest. Why? Because it's important. Because it is necessary. And, as pedantic as it may sound, because I believe in democracy and the rule of law.

I agree with Stan Goff when he writes:

> Military operations have become the new linchpin of U.S. policy, and...are now among the disparate winds swirling toward some synergistic combination to form a perfect storm of generalized social and political disorder.[1]

Goff makes a strong case for the demise of U.S. global power. He sees revolution coming and he predicts it will not be pretty.

But Goff also suggests strategy. One of his suggestions is useful in providing me with some sort of graceful way to conclude this book, although of course he did not suggest it for the reason I now use it. Writing about "[m]averick military theorist John Boyd, who developed the warfighting theory that drove nearly all systems of development for U.S. fighter aircraft for the last two decades, studied chaos theory, entropy and dialectics, and dabbled significantly in epistemology,"[2] Goff writes:

> The centerpiece of Boyd's theory is that one's adversary is always human. The counterposition of two set-piece strategies, especially in modern warfare, is a recipe for a bloodbath of attrition. To defeat the leadership (a perceiving human) is the goal, according to Boyd, and that is accomplished by maintaining the initiative through audacious, often uncoordinated, rapid actions until the adversary is overwhelmed by the "mismatches" between perception and reality. These mismatches are not the result of your "plan." They are an outcome of your agility—your superior ability to accept chaos and adapt rapidly to changing patterns. Improvisation.[3]

I can't vouch for how Goff intended us to apply these interesting ideas. He discusses them in a chapter titled *Strategy, Chaos, and Agility*, towards the end of his book. At the close of the chapter immediately preceding it, Goff writes:

> My vision is that the American armed forces, when they are harshly taught as the current conjuncture will teach them, will unite with the people, and that sections of it will break away and become the defenders of their families, and thereby a liberatory force. As America's political class becomes ever more lawless, ever more compelled to scrap bourgeois democracy and slouch toward fascism, we shall need them and they shall need us.[4]

I don't know whether Goff's prediction will come to pass, but if it does, it means civil war. Revolution. It is not what I want, nor what I propose.

Still, Boyd's theory may be useful to peace and justice activists, despite, according to Goff, "the left's failure to grasp any but the most superficial aspects of military reality."[5] And, notwithstanding Goff's remarks that Boyd's theories "have been distorted both by the military itself...and the corporate sector, which is constantly hawking Sun Tzu, Boyd, and other war theory as an analogue to economic theory,"[6] I mean to apply this theory to pro-democratic activism.

Mismatches between perception and reality are beginning to occur for the Bush Administration. Bush will surely fight hard to retain his perceptions, no matter how far removed from reality these may be. But the further those perceptions are from reality, the more likely is the ultimate demise of the policies and practices based on those perceptions. And all we need do is to keep stirring up and revealing the mismatches. We must be able to rapidly adapt to the various changing patterns and we must, as Goff further points out, "stay inside the adversary's decision cycle."[7] This means to establish "a tempo in decision making and execution that outpaces the ability of the foe to react effectively in time."[8] We do not need to control events. We need only to keep exposing the mismatches and, within the Administration's reaction cycle, as each lie and deception unravels, we need only expose the next one.

As for being audacious and uncoordinated, the peace and justice movement has an advantage. We have no leaders telling us what to do or how to do it. We have no central organization and we are not temperamentally inclined to adhere to one. We are just a loose collection of ordinary people, or what Browning's unsympathetic man would have called "this rabble's-brabble of dolts and fools,"[9] We are like Hawkeye, in the Last of the Mohicans, who says "I do not call myself subject to much at all." We are like the "noisy crowd of electioneering Democrats" about whom Aaron Burr declared: *"They,"*—not the Founding Fathers—"are the expounders of the Constitution!"[10] We are The People.

Epilogue
Detainees and Torture

> The privilege of the Writ of Habeas Corpus shall not be suspended, unless when in Cases of Rebellion or Invasion the public safety may require it.
>
> —The U.S. Constitution[1]

> Why suspend [habeas corpus] in insurrections and rebellions? The parties who may be arrested may be charged instantly with a well defined crime. Of course the judge will remand them. If the public safety requires that the government should have a man imprisoned on less probable testimony in those than in other emergencies, let him be taken and retried while the necessity continues.
>
> —Thomas Jefferson[2]

A central goal of this book has been to substantiate the theme that "the Bush administration's legal policy has been nothing less than a broad assault against the fundamental principles of the rule of law that have existed for centuries."[3] This remark was made by an anonymous commentator on the recent Supreme Court detainee decisions, which many view as affirmations of civil liberties. Unfortunately, as I explain later, these decisions are not as good as they appear to be on their face. But, in discussing these decisions, I want to juxtapose them with a concept I wrote about two years ago: law that undermines or dilutes civil liberties invites officials to engage in human rights violations. I wrote a six-part series on the USA PATRIOT Act that included a section on torture, anticipating the revelations of abuse at Abu Ghraib.[4] Now it is possible to make the same inquiry with the recent decisions: e.g., to what degree do the legal processes or lack thereof, set forth by the Court permit and/or encourage torture? Another way to ask this is: what are the natural consequences of these decisions in their permeation through not just our courts but our society? I consider the answer clear and positive that the dilution of constitutional legal protections contained in these decisions not only open the door to bad lower court decisions, but set a bad example for members of society as a whole and open the door to human rights abuses, including torture, in our federal and state prison systems, as well as in our military detention systems.

The Supreme Court, ruling against the Bush Administration, decided in late June 2004 that both the Guantanamo detainees and so-called unlawful enemy combatants may challenge their detentions in U.S. courts. Justice Day O'Connor wrote for the plurality in the unlawful enemy combatant case: "A state of war is not a blank check for the president." In the Guantanamo detainee case, Justice Stevens wrote that non-citizens held in territory over which the U.S. exercises exclusive jurisdiction *may* challenge their detention in federal court.

In the Guantanamo detainee case, *Rasul v. Bush*,[5] the Department of Justice argued that the detainees, all foreign nationals held on Cuban territory, have no rights in U.S. courts. In the "unlawful enemy combatant" case, *Hamdi v. Rumsfeld*,[6] the DOJ argued that the executive may indefinitely detain without judicial review anyone (including U.S. citizens) it decides is an unlawful enemy combatant.[7]

As I pointed out recently,[8] the administration chose Guantanamo *in order* to avoid a legal challenge to the detentions. This was revealed in a 2002 essay by a student at the National War College who claimed he was privy to both classified and unclassified material. According to the student, Col. Daniel F. McCallum, Guantanamo was chosen, at least in part, because it presented a "minimal litigation risk." McCallum states baldly:

> The litigation risk faced by DOJ was access to federal courts for the purpose of filing a writ of habeas corpus. Habeas corpus requires judicial review of the detention of a person to determine if the detention is lawful. An impor-

tant factor in assessing this risk is that this only applies to citizens and foreign nationals if they are held within the United States.

For Guantanamo, "since the property belongs to Cuba, DOJ assessed the litigation risk as minimal," and "[c]onsidering the strained foreign relations we have with Cuba, [the Department of State] assessed the minimal negative impact acceptable" writes McCallum. Thus, it was the administration's intention in choosing Guantanamo to deny due process and judicial review to detainees.

The Administration's initiative in evading habeas corpus challenges points to a policy of subversion of the rule of law and civil liberties. This in turn indicates the possibility of human rights abuse. As Human Rights Watch observed in a recent report, the pattern of abuse at Abu Ghraib "resulted from decisions made by the Bush administration to bend, ignore, or cast rules aside" and that the administration "effectively sought to re-write the Geneva Conventions of 1949 to eviscerate many of their most important protections." The Pentagon and the Justice Department "developed the breathtaking legal argument that the president, as commander-in-chief of the armed forces, was not bound by U.S. or international laws prohibiting torture when acting to protect national security."[9]

A policy of subversion of civil liberties, therefore, is closely allied with a tendency to commit or promote the commission of human rights violations. Is it also true that erosions of civil liberties, without a *policy* of subversion, leads to human rights abuses? Incidental erosions of civil liberties may not *compel* human rights abuses, but those erosions certainly provide the *opportunity* for such abuses. But before we approach the question of whether the recent Supreme Court detainee decisions actively *erode* civil liberties, and potentially lead to human rights abuses, including torture, let us take a closer look at the underpinnings of torture.

Torture

Two years ago CNN polled Americans and found that nearly half endorsed torture. With the recent revelations of the abuse at Abu Ghraib prison in Iraq, the American public appears suddenly to view torture as an unexpected, unanticipated, and shocking event. But Abu Ghraib should not shock those who have witnessed the repeated violations of domestic and international law committed by and for the Bush Administration, many of which have been discussed in this book. It should not surprise those who noted the manner in which the Supreme Court put Bush into the presidency, or those who are aware of Bush's family connections or business dealings before 2000.[10] Nor should it shock those who followed the course from 9/11 to the unlawful invasion of Iraq.

A lawless administration cannot be expected to engender anything but lawless subordinates. As Human Rights Watch says:

> This pattern of abuse [at Abu Ghraib] did not result from the acts of individual soldiers who broke the rules. It resulted from decisions made by the Bush administration to bend, ignore, or cast rules aside.[11]

Abu Ghraib was not the beginning. The Administration recruited and elevated several previously indicted war criminals. As noted in the beginning of this book, Bush's frequent use of the death penalty and his indifference to human suffering while he was governor of Texas are well-established. John Negroponte, who was implicated in human rights abuses in El Salvador in the 1980's, recently was appointed ambassador to Iraq.[12] Bush attempted to appoint Henry Kissinger, who is under indictment for war crimes in numerous countries, to head the 9/11 commission.

But there have been those of us who spoke out against torture long before Abu Ghraib. I was one of those. When I wrote the PATRIOT Act series, I believed, and I continue to believe, that the Act foreshadowed and helped set the stage for government endorsement of torture.[13] In the article, I wrote that under the Act:

> ...evidence is already leaking out of cruel treatment toward detainees. A recent Amnesty International release states: "Reports of cruel treatment include prolonged solitary confinement; heavy shackling of detainees during visits ... and lack of adequate exercise."[14]

I quoted complaint papers in a case brought by the Center for National Security Studies (CNSS) to compel the Department of Justice to release information on detainees:

> There are...many reports about detainees being abused or treated improperly while in federal custody. Detainees have alleged that they have been beaten by guards. The Los Angeles Times reported that a Pakistani detainee was stripped and beaten in his cell by inmates while guards did nothing; that five Israelis were blindfolded during questioning, handcuffed in their cells and forced to take polygraph tests; and that a Saudi Arabian man "was deprived of a mattress, a blanket, a drinking cup and a clock to let him know when to recite his Muslim prayers."[15]

I noted that this was "the treatment afforded to detainees who are being held on routine visa violations, people who would not normally be detained at all," and that, according to CNSS and Amnesty International, "[l]ess than five of the [then] 718 immigration charges detailed by the government relate to terrorism" and that "[s]ome detainees have been held several months without being charged with any violation[, while o]thers report they continued to be held after bail had been granted and they were ready to meet it." I concluded that, according to Amnesty International (AI):

> These conditions are in direct contravention of international standards [and] AI has also called for a full inquiry into the conditions in the federal Metropolitan Detention Center in New York, to which AI was denied access, where some 40 detainees are reported to be confined in solitary cells for 23 hours or more a day.

The point here, of course, is that civil liberties and the rule of law are bulwarks which protect us from barbarian practices such as torture and that if we allow these rights and liberties to be sacrificed (as some suggested we should do) in supposed exchange for greater safety, we have, in effect, invited such practices and the consequent demise of those most sacred rights and liberties. There is really nothing new here. And the question must remain: why (and for what purpose?) would grown men and women throw out the considered wisdom of centuries of law-making by thoughtful persons on how to treat enemy combatants, whether "lawful" or not, or for that matter, how to treat persons, aliens or not, who are not yet even reasonably suspected of being enemies, let alone enemy combatants?

Did the Administration feel it was doing something new and novel? New procedures or new technology for "new" enemies? One can see the drive towards an army of new technology idea in its early form with the *Cheney Plan*, starting in the early 1990's, and with the intended use of preemptive military force, maintenance of a substantial nuclear arsenal, and of a global defense system. In his discussion on the 2003 invasion of Iraq in his book, *Full Spectrum Dominance*, Stan Goff frequently remarks on Rumsfeld's obsession with new technology.

But what is new about the idea of preemptive strikes? Or about treating others unfairly? What is new about deciding that because you have the power, you can be the prosecutor, the judge, jury, and executioner? What is new about tyranny? These ideas are as old as the Star Chamber, as old as Hammurabi, as old as Moses.[16]

Neither human wickedness nor human laws or justice are

new. What the Bush Administration did was to turn the clock back to barbarian times. With the invasion of Iraq, the indefinite and unlawful detentions, the disappearances,[17] and the torture at Abu Ghraib and elsewhere under American hands, we are but one step short of deciding to create a class of gladiators to quench the artificially-aroused public appetite for blood and violence.

The question, then, is raised: how did we get here? One way of looking at this is to trace ideas wrought by post-9/11 conservative analysts whose views mirror and expand upon those in the Administration. An interesting and valuable collection of such analyses is found in a special Spring 2002 issue of *Orbis: A Journal of World Affairs*, titled "The New Protracted Conflict."[18] Sam C. Sarkesian, Professor Emeritus of political science at Loyola University, Chicago, author of numerous publications on national security and a retired lieutenant colonel of the U.S. Army, wrote an article in this special issue in which he endorsed the use of a "culture" of special forces.[19] These forces, he noted, are indoctrinated in carrying out "unconventional warfare," which he defines as "following Sun Tzu's notions" of "sabotage, terror, and assassination." The special forces, according to Sarkesian, utilize "the notion that the center of gravity is the political-social milieu of the adversary." In other words, special forces carry out acts that - in language that the PATRIOT Act uses to define terrorism—"appear to be intended to intimidate or coerce a civilian population, to influence the policy of a government by intimidation or coercion, or to affect the conduct of a government by mass destruction, assassination, or kidnapping."[20] Terrorism by any other name is still terrorism.

Sarkesian claims that "[v]eterans of the early Special Forces era cherish their hard-won legacy and culture of the 'old' era, a culture many believe must endure if the Special Forces are to be successful in their primary mission of unconventional warfare." He continues with a description of these men, quoting from Charles Simpson's 1983 book, *Inside the Green Berets: The First Thirty Years*: "They are a grizzled, likeable, fantastically experienced bunch of tough old bastards who do not apologize to anyone for the wars they have fought and the things they have had to do."

Sarkesian also echoes the belief that the "strategic dimension of the U.S. effort beginning in September 2001 was termed a 'new kind of war,'" which he uses to justify the use of "unconventional warfare." Since World War II, Special Forces are "taught how to set up clandestine communications, avoid contact with regular enemy units, combine with the local civilian populace, and engage in night parachute operations."

Sarkesian sets forth five "critical characteristics of unconventional warfare." They are asymmetrical, ambiguous, unconventional, protracted, and involve "strategic cultures." Asymmetrical means that "the doctrine and tactics employed by those engaged in unconventional warfare avoids challenging conventional military systems conventionally." Ambiguous means that "the battle arena is not necessarily defined in conventional terms or with regard to a specific territory." Unconventional conflicts "require tactics that aim at disrupting the adversary in its weakest dimensions." This is where Sarkesian mentions "sabotage, terror, and assassination." He adds that the organizational structure and tactics "are fluid— flexible and adopted to local conditions in which operations occur." Protracted means, of course, over an extended period of time. As to "strategic culture," Sarkesian notes that it "differs sharply from the usual 'American way of war.'" Instead, "the strategic culture of those waging unconventional warfare must allow for moral ambiguity, shifting definitions of friend and foe ...and objectives that change constantly with the play of politics."[21]

Sarkesian's approach, the unconventional warfare approach, the Special Forces approach is, as he says, morally ambiguous. It is also morally troubling. His approach helps set the stage for human rights and international law violations. His article comes pretty close, without saying so, to being a blanket endorsement of torture. If sabotage, terror, and assassination are okay for us to do to our enemies, torture can hardly be questioned.

A better, less morally troubling approach is that of Bruce Berkowitz, a contributing editor of *Orbis* journal and a Research Fellow at the Hoover Institution, who also contibuted to the same issue of *Orbis* as did Sarkesian. Berkowitz writes:

> The executive branch needs a White House-level mechanism that decides whether the United States will take a law enforcement approach to a terrorist threat or an intelligence/law enforcement approach. Current policy assumes that the two approaches can be blended. They usually cannot (although both communities should be able to assist each other). Either the rule of law prevails in an environment, or it does not—in which case we need to turn to the rules of war...If it appears that other countries will not be cooperative—intentionally or not—the president should decide to shut down the law enforcement option and proceed with military action supported by intelligence.[22]

What is important about this view is that, although Berkowitz appears to be proposing almost the same thing as Sarkesian, e.g., a military solution, Berkowitz specifically recognizes "the rules of war." Sarkesian suggests that we should play by the rules of unconventional warfare, but makes no mention of the law of war, which is that body of international law (including the Geneva Conventions) that has been developed to ensure that even during hostilities between nations each party acts at or above a baseline level of conduct towards each other.

Berkowitz's distinction, however, is lost on another *Orbis* contributor, Michael Radu, who is a contributing editor, as well, a Senior Fellow at the Foreign Policy Research Institute, and

Director of its Center for the Study of Terrorism and Political Violence. Radu's view is that "Western Europeans believe that the Geneva Conventions regulating conflicts between states continue to govern even in the new age of global terrorism."[23] In other words, Radu believes that, despite what Europeans think, the Geneva Conventions do not govern, but rather should be chucked. Radu's approach, like Sarkesian's, resembles that of the Bush Administration. Human Rights Watch says that the Administration "seemingly determined that winning the war on terror required that the United States circumvent international law" and "effectively sought to re-write the Geneva Conventions of 1949 to eviscerate many of their most important protections."[24]

In 1945, it seems, the United States knew better. Provost Marshal General of the United States Army, Maj. Gen. Archer Lerch wrote: "The Geneva Convention, I might emphasize is law. Until that law is changed by competent authority, the War Department is bound to follow it."[25]

Radu's views reflect biases similar to those of Bush and his cabinet. Radu declares that the "terrorists exploit all the tolerant, human rights-oriented laws of Europe, and to a lesser extent the United States, to infiltrate, recruit, and raise funds in the West, whose culture they openly seek to destroy." He even goes so far as to state that "proliferation of human rights organizations seeking to make war between states impossible and to impose minimal standards on justice also aids and abets terrorism."[26] To Radu, the current definition of terrorism which has raised such a furor among civil libertarians "is obvious and simple," and that "[w]hile this is perhaps not sufficiently obscure for those academics (international law experts in particular) who thrive on complicating the simple, it is perfectly adequate."[27] However, as Deputy Director of the Americas Division of Human Rights Watch, Joanne Mariner, noted, "the decision to classify a given group as 'terrorist' is far from a mechanical one:

it involves political calculations as well as a factual assessment of a group's actions," and "the designation process is extremely vulnerable to political manipulation."[28]

Perhaps most biased and revealing of all Radu's remarks, however, is his view that:

> When not openly applauding the September 11 attacks, the European Left "explained" them by blaming the United States' policies and opposing any U.S. counterattack, in the name of peace, innocent Afghan civilians, or the need to seek the "root causes" of Osama bin Laden's Islamic fanaticism. In fact, all indications suggest that the "root causes" of terrorism are to be found in the dysfunctional middle classes of the West as well as of Muslim countries.[29]

Of course, Radu contradicts himself when he chastises the European Left for seeking the root causes of Bin Laden's fanaticism, but nonetheless opines that the causes are found in the (undefined) dysfunctional middle classes of the West, etc. But, the tone is dripping with a dehumanizing distain and indifference which closely resembles the tone conveyed by Mark Crispin Miller in his portrait of Bush, noted in the Preface to this book.

Dehumanizing others is exactly what torture does and it is exactly what is forbidden by international laws against torture. Common Article 3 to the Geneva Conventions prohibits "violence to life and person...cruel treatment and torture...outrages upon personal dignity, in particular humiliating and degrading treatment." Contrary to the Administration's assertions that Geneva does not apply to many of the prisoners, all persons are protected by the "fundamental guarantees" of article 75 of Protocol I of 1977 to the Geneva Conventions. Torture or inhumane treatment of prisoners-of-war or civilians are grave breaches of Geneva and are war crimes under federal U.S. law punishable for up to 20 years or the death penalty if torture resulted in the victim's death.

Even without the Geneva Conventions, the prohibition on torture is considered a fundamental principle of customary international law that is binding on all states and the widespread or systematic practice of torture constitutes a crime against humanity.[30]

Another *Orbis* analyst, University of Pennsylvania Professor of Law and a Senior Fellow of the Foreign Policy Research Institute, Jacques deLisle, in *The Roles of Law in the Fight Against Terrorism*,[31] compares the "law (criminal justice, or prosecutorial) paradigm" and the "war paradigm" of fighting terrorism. DeLisle's essay considers both sides of the issue for both paradigms, resulting in what appears to be an interesting, thoughtful, and fairly balanced analysis, but the odd effect is that every result seems as good or bad as every other and there is no moral imperative in anything.

DeLisle acknowledges "the corrosive effects on civil liberties" of "the blurring of legal and military frameworks," but adds that "much of the civil libertarian critique has been nearly blind to the fact of the war model's powerful grip and its implications in the context of a fight against terrorism," and concludes simply that "[w]ars exact sacrifices of many sorts, including some temporary surrenders of some civil liberties," as if there is no moral or practical difference between a society with full civil liberty protections and one without.

He notes that after 9/11, during which "the prospective means for meting out justice evolved," "[s]harp disputes arose over the legality, morality, and wisdom of U.S. forces seeking out identified individuals, trial by American military tribunals, prosecution before a special international court or criminal proceedings in the civilian judicial organs of the United States or other states with jurisdiction," adding that the "emergence of so many divergent means to a relatively clear end revealed a troubling ambivalence in grappling with the choice between a war paradigm and a criminal justice paradigm in responding to a terrorism threat."

The troubling ambivalence, however, seems to arise more from a lack of moral grounding than a rational difficulty in choosing. This is not a "Sophie's Choice," where one must choose a course of action where neither course is morally acceptable, or a "Catch-22," where you have to take a course of action to get where you want to get, but you cannot take that course of action until you are already there. On the contrary, when deLisle presents readers with the choice between the law paradigm and the war paradigm, he is presenting us with a false dilemma. There is, in fact, no dilemma between going to war and bringing criminal charges. There is no genuine dilemma between civil liberties concerns and deciding whether to bring charges or go to war. While deLisle acknowledges that the "war paradigm" and the "law paradigm" are not mutually exclusive, he does not recognize (and perhaps is not aware of) the fact that there are international *laws* that apply in situations of international, *armed conflict* (ie. war). DeLisle, rather, implies that the value and meaning of the resolution of this "troubling ambivalence" is no different either way one chooses, that what is important is simply that one *does* choose.

This reasoning is fundamentally flawed and ignores the rock solid moral bases of international laws. The outcome of deLisle's reasoning is the erosion and ultimate evisceration of morality. In the extreme situations in which military intelligence, special forces, front-line military engagements, or "front line" prison guards encounter, the laws of war, embodied in the Geneva Conventions, the International Covenant on Civil and Political Rights, the Convention against Torture, the United Nations Charter, and other international instruments provide for minimum morally acceptable conduct. DeLisle's approach, as balanced and civilized as it appears, would remove those imperatives.

Which brings us back to how our military came to torture prisoners at Abu Ghraib. The dilution of moral imperatives and guidelines is, as a practical matter, an invitation to human rights abuses. Psychologically speaking, of course, the issue is deeper. DeLisle notes that "the current enemy made diabolically effective use of the instruments of the United States' open, liberal, and liberty-protecting order." But this is what lawyers like to call a red herring. To the extent that our society is an open, liberty-protecting one, it neither justifies nor compels human rights abuses in response to a terrorist attack. It is no doubt true, as deLisle says, that "the exceptional sense of vulnerability at home and a shadowy enemy...magnify... the national taste [for war] and the force of consequentialist moral arguments for shifts in law and political practice that produce a stronger government in general and a stronger executive in particular," but, again, neither a sense of vulnerability nor a desire for a stronger executive justifies or compels torture. Indeed, many families who lost members on 9/11 exhorted Bush not to go to war, not to bomb, but rather to adhere to the rule of law.

In October 2003, Mark Bowden, a national correspondent for *The Atlantic Monthly*, wrote an in-depth look at *The Dark Art of Interrogation*.[32] Bowden endorses what Radu calls "the old Leninist 'dual-track' approach to the conquest of power: simultaneous use of legal organizations under the pretext of freedom of speech or religion and illegal, underground, and violent structures engaged in terrorism."[33] Bowden writes:

> The Bush Administration has adopted exactly the right posture on the matter. Candor and consistency are not always public virtues. Torture is a crime against humanity, but coercion is an issue that is rightly handled with a wink, or even a touch of hypocrisy; it should be banned but also quietly practiced. Those who protest coercive methods will exaggerate their horrors, which is good: it generates a useful climate of fear. It is wise of the President to reiterate U.S. support for international agreements banning torture, and it is wise for American interrogators to employ whatever coercive methods work. It is

also smart not to discuss the matter with anyone.[34]

This appears to be exactly what the Bush Administration did. "We now know that at the highest levels of the Pentagon there was a shocking interest in using torture and a misguided attempt to evade the criminal consequences of doing so," said Human Rights Watch executive director Kenneth Roth. Roth added, "[i]f [the Pentagon's] legal advice were accepted, dictators worldwide would be handed a ready-made excuse to ignore one of the most basic prohibitions of international human rights law."[35]

U.S. officials will answer that they are not encouraging dictators, they are fighting a "just war" against terrorism, fighting for democracy. Army General John Abizaid, chief of the U.S. Central Command that oversees Iraq, is quoted in *Time* as saying "Our openness about [the prison abuse] is a lesson about the rule of law" and Bush, who a few years back joked about how much easier it would be if he were a dictator, told Arab interviewers: "A dictator wouldn't be answering questions about this."[36] I guess we should be relieved.

The Detainee Decisions

The holdings of the Supreme Court detainee decisions are perhaps of greater importance to the future of this country than many realize. The question I consider here, however, looks beyond the legal holdings of these cases to the cultural consequences. Earlier I suggested that there is a correlation between the undermining of civil liberties and violations or abuses of human rights. The first part of the inquiry here, then, is whether these cases undermine civil liberties. The second part is whether the precedents established in these cases might contribute to or promote human rights violations, specifically abuses against detainees.

The three detainee decisions and their dissents and concurrences dovetail and interweave in complex ways. Each contributes to the other so that the final overview is like a mosaic, full of contrasts and patterns.[37] On the one hand, the Court upheld the right to due process for ALL detainees, whether in Guantanamo or on American soil, whether aliens or citizens. On the other, the Court determined that an "appropriately authorized and properly constituted military tribunal" with truncated procedures might suffice to consider challenges to detention.[38] The Court cited the Geneva Conventions but only as the basis for its assertion that "detention may last no longer than active hostilities" and as support for its suggestion that a military tribunal will suffice.[39] It made no reference, in the plurality opinion, to the fact that for two years the United States has been violating Geneva and that such violation is a war crime.

The Court in *Hamdi* utilized the balancing test from *Mathews v. Eldridge*, a civil case which involved the deprivation of welfare benefits. The original use of the Writ of Habeas Corpus—that of requiring the custodian of a person detained without charges to produce the person before a judge for a determination of the legitimacy of his detention—while ostensibly upheld by the Court, was at the same time subtly undermined by the application of the *Mathews* test in a clearly non-civil context.

This leads to another point: the Court points out that the lower court "apparently believed that the appropriate process would approach the process that accompanies a criminal trial."[40] The plurality rejects this approach, stating that Justice Scalia, who dissented, "can point to no case or other authority for the proposition that those captured on a foreign battlefield ...cannot be detained outside the criminal process."[41] Yet, considering that the "Great Writ" of habeas corpus arose out of unlawful detentions without probable cause,[42] it is hard to see why the plurality refuses to apply criminal procedural protections to challenges to the detention of persons who have claimed innocence, where innocent until proven guilty is supposed to be our standard.

Separate opinions by Justices Souter, Scalia, and Thomas in the *Hamdi* case cloud the picture further. Thomas, in his dissent, focuses on the powers of the President during insurrections, rebellions, and war. Conservative Justice Scalia oddly is the one who argues most extensively and effectively for civil liberties. While Justice Souter argues that the Government "has failed to demonstrate that the Force Resolution authorizes the detention complained of here even on the facts the Government claims,"[43] the plurality decided that the Authorization for Use of Military Force ("the AUMF") "is explicit congressional authorization for the detention of individuals in the narrow category we describe." [44]

These are just a sampling of the deceptive results and divergent opinions from only *one* of the three cases, *Hamdi*. There are equally divergent results in the *Rasul* case, which rules that United States courts have jurisdiction to consider challenges to the legality of the detention of foreign nationals captured abroad in connection with hostilities and incarcerated at Guantanamo Bay. The decision seems strong on civil liberties but it rests on a weak cobbling together of odd legal precedents. The stronger (or at least more intuitively correct) case was the one penned by Justice Kennedy, who argued that *Johnson v. Eisentrager*,[46] the case the Government argued was controlling, could be factually distinguished from the *Rasul* case and that because of these factual differences, the rule of *Eisentrager* made clear that habeas corpus *did* apply to *Rasul*.

The Great Writ of Liberty

Let's return for a moment to the Great Writ of Liberty, habeas corpus. Justice Scalia discusses the history of habeas corpus at length in his *Hamdi* dissent. He writes: "The very core of liberty secured by our Anglo-Saxon system of separated powers has been freedom from indefinite imprisonment at the will of the Executive."[46] Scalia quotes from the famed *Commentaries* of the British jurist and legal scholar, Sir William Blackstone:

> [C]onfinement of the person, by secretly hurrying him to jail, where his sufferings are unknown or forgotten, is a less public, a less striking, and therefore a more dangerous engine of arbitrary government.[47]

Scalia also quotes from the *Commentaries* of Joseph Story, a U.S. Supreme Court Justice and legal scholar:

> The Due Process Clause "in effect affirms the right of trial according to the process and proceedings of the common law."[48]

He quotes from Alexander Hamilton:

> The writ of habeas corpus protects against "the practice of arbitrary imprisonments...in all ages, [one of] the favorite and most formidable instruments of tyranny."[49]

And Scalia adds that "[i]t is unthinkable that the Executive could render otherwise criminal grounds for detention noncriminal merely by disclaiming an intent to prosecute, or by asserting that it was incapacitating dangerous offenders rather than punishing wrongdoing."[50] Scalia even quotes from a 1997 Supreme Court opinion, that, "[a] finding of dangerousness, standing alone, is ordinarily not a sufficient ground upon which to justify indefinite involuntary commitment."[51]

Scalia then notes that, of course, the allegations against Hamdi "are no ordinary accusations of criminal activity," but continues that "[c]itizens aiding the enemy have [traditionally] been treated as traitors subject to the criminal process."[52] He quotes from a 1762 treatise on treason that stated:

> The joining with Rebels in an Act of Rebellion, or with Enemies in Acts of hostility, will make a Man a

Traitor: in the one Case within the Clause of Levying War, in the other within that of Adhering to the King's enemies.[53]

Although Scalia does not point it out, this language is reflected in our Constitution, which states that "[t]reason against the United States, shall consist only in levying War against them, or in adhering to their Enemies, giving them Aid and Comfort." The provision continues that "[n]o Person shall be convicted of Treason unless on the Testimony of two Witnesses to the same overt Act, or on Confession in open Court."[54]

Finally, Justice Scalia points to our treason statute and other provisions that criminalize various acts of war-making and adherence to the enemy,[55] and notes that historically remedies for detention were "*not* a bobtailed judicial inquiry into whether there were reasonable grounds to believe the prisoner had taken up arms against the King[, but r]ather, if the prisoner was not indicted and tried within the prescribed time," he was discharged.[56]

This is, in fact, exactly what the Court's remedy is—a bobtailed inquiry—but what is even more odious is that the Court pretends to uphold the very thing it undermines: the Great Writ of Liberty. Instead of Congress having the courage to suspend the writ, as it and only it is authorized to do, or the Justice Department having the courage to bring criminal charges against Hamdi, or the Defense Department providing him with a real Geneva status determination, or the Court insisting that the *real* basis of habeas corpus be upheld by mandating criminal process be followed, we have gotten, instead, the *Mathews v. Eldridge* standard, meant for determinations of deprivations of welfare benefits.

That standard goes like this: the process due "in any given instance" is determined by weighing "the private interest that will be affected by the official action" against the Government's

asserted interest, "including the function involved" and the burdens the Government would face in providing greater process,
then an analysis of "the risk of an erroneous deprivation" of the
private interest if the process were reduced and the "probable
value, if any, of additional or substitute safeguards."[57]

What happened to probable cause of criminal activity?
What happened to the Fourth, Fifth, and Sixth Amendment
protections? What happened to innocent until proven guilty?

Given that Hamdi may now be heard by a military tribunal with procedures that allow for acceptance of hearsay evidence (not usually admissible in regular federal courts), a presumption in favor of the Government's evidence, and the burden on the detainee to prove the Government wrong, the result
will be what one conservative commentator recently wrote:
"[A]s long as Hamdi is given a meaningful opportunity to con-
vince his captors that he should be released, their denial of his
claim will probably be accepted by the Court."[58]

And, in the meantime, the standard that is established is
that the Executive can do whatever it wants to whomever it
wants, leading right on down the road to...Abu Ghraib. It is not
so unlikely as you might think. In fact, while we watch civil liberties whither away, prison abuse in this country has reached
staggering dimensions. Anne-Marie Cusac, a contributor at *The
Progressive*, asks in reference to unbridled domestic prison abuse:

> How could such things happen in the United States?
> For one thing, since the early 1990s, American prisons
> have acquired a distinctly military cast. This influence is
> evident in boot-camp-style punishment, in prison tech-
> nology, and also in prison and law enforcement confer-
> ences like the one I attended in 1996. That conference
> included long discussions on the ways military knowledge
> could help police and corrections to control crime. The
> sponsor of the conference, the American Defense
> Preparedness Association, was at the time sponsoring
> other conferences with such names as "Enhancing the

Individual Warrior," "Undersea Warfare," and "Bomb and Warhead."[59]

Cusac adds that "[t]he revelations at Abu Ghraib shock us because our soldiers abroad seem to have acted out behaviors that we condone, yet don't face up to, at home" and concludes:

> When we tolerate abuse in U.S. prisons and jails, it should not surprise us to find U.S. soldiers using similar methods in Iraq. George Bush said he was exporting democracy to Iraq, but he seems to have exported a much uglier aspect of American public policy—some of the most sadistic practices employed in the U.S. prison system.[60]

I would remark, however, that it is not just sadistic prison practices that we are now condoning at home and exporting; it is an entire culture that encourages lying, backstabbing, exploitation of others, indifference and unkindness to fellow human beings, and worse. A Supreme Court decision that lies about one of the most fundamental precepts of democracy—the right to be free of arbitrary detentions— as shocking as it should be to us, is just a symptom of a cultural disorder. If that disorder leads to craven behavior, there is nothing remarkable about it.

National Security Courts & Torture Warrants

Andrew C. McCarthy, a contributor to the *National Review* and a former chief assistant U.S. attorney who led the prosecution of Sheik Omar Abdel Rahman in connection with the first World Trade Center bombing,[61] writes intelligently and in great depth about torture, the laws of war, the laws prohibiting torture, the POW status, and finally torture warrants.[62] In a separate, but related article on *Abu Ghraib & Enemy Combatants*, McCarthy proposes a new court system which he calls a "national security court."[63] I admire the intelligence and clarity of McCarthy's analyses (and can overlook his occasional pot-shots at leftists and "pie-in-the-sky libertarians"), and he nearly convinces me, but in the end I find flaws and disagree with his conclusions. Let's look at them.

McCarthy admits that "the whole crossroad of terrorism and law enforcement is complex," but argues that terrorists "must be fought as military enemies rather than criminal elements" for three reasons: (1) "the justice system...is incapable on its own of neutralizing more than a tiny fraction of the hordes that oppose us," (2) "judicial proceedings that target a relative handful of committed (and some suicidal) jihadists do not dissuade them; they have the opposite effect," and (3) terrorist cases require us to "cut corners" constitutionally, which is not good for "our system's majesty" because if we say "we treat terrorists just like we treat everyone else...everyone else is [in fact] being treated worse, and that is not the system we aspire to."[64] McCarthy concludes that "[b]y stretching precariously to assimilate [terrorists] while accommodating national security, the system succeeds only in warping itself."

It's a compelling argument. McCarthy adds that "it's not fair that the barbarity of a few should be of such profound consequence, but anyone who thinks that 'trust us' carries the same assurances today as it did [before the revelations of Abu Ghraib] is hallucinating." With powerful concessions to the principles often relied on by civil libertarians (ie., that "the sanctity and dignity of human life is a bedrock premise of civilized society, expressed at the Founding in the Declaration of Independence itself"), McCarthy nearly has his cake and eats it too. And his consequent suggestion becomes nearly irrefutable: that in order to prevent the dilution of our constitutional system of protections, we need to create a new parallel legal system just for terrorists, which he calls a "national security court."

In McCarthy's vision, this court would be constituted much like the FISA court. It would "be drawn from the talented pool of experienced federal judges, would develop an expertise in issues peculiar to this realm: classified information, the

Geneva Conventions, the laws and customs of war, etc., and would have jurisdiction over matters related to the detentions and any resulting trials of alleged unlawful combatants." A special unit would be formed in the Justice Department that "could then report to the Court the fact that an alleged unlawful combatant had been captured and was being detained, and certify both that hostilities were ongoing and that it was in the national-security interest of the United States that the combatant be held." Again, it is compelling and McCarthy very nearly had me convinced.

However, there are two things wrong with this approach: first, it creates another parallel legal system, and, second, it forgets a primary condition of battle, visible combat. McCarthy's argument is based on an unexamined false premise: that terrorism is unlike any other "kind of war." Now, in some respects, he's right. Terrorism *is* different. Terrorists, as McCarthy notes, "are significantly different both in make-up and goals from run-of-the-mill citizens and immigrants accused of crimes." However, within his own definition of how different terrorists are, he includes an analogy to those they resemble:

> They are not in it for the money; they desire neither to beat nor cheat the system, but rather to subvert and overthrow it; and they are not about getting an edge in the here and now—their aspirations, however grandiose they may seem to us, are universalist and eternal, such that their pursuit is, for the terrorist, more vital than living to see them attained. They are a formidable foe...they have to be completely defeated, just like the Nazis, the Communists, and all tyrannically inclined, would-be hegemons.

Of course, if terrorists are like Nazis, Communists, or other "tyrannically inclined, would-be hegemons," the existing international systems are adequate, either the criminal laws or the laws of war may be used, and neither cancels out the possibility of the other.

However, in McCarthy's vision, we've created yet another parallel legal system. Earlier in this book, we considered the existence of three parallel legal systems in this country: the criminal/civil (federal) system, the immigration court system, and the FISA system. As noted earlier, each of these has genuine, legitimate, important uses. The problem arises when the three begin to be used in tandem, with standards from one of the "secondary" systems (immigration or FISA) being mixed with those from the primary, federal system. Why is this a problem? Because what necessarily happens when these standards mix is that the protections in the federal system, i.e., *constitutional* protections, are diluted and gradually eviscerated.

So then, what effect would the creation of an additional, fourth parallel legal system meant to handle the most difficult cases and kept outside of the Constitution have on democracy and the rule of law? I fear it would severely damage an already beleaguered society. And the question must be asked, too, if the laws of war and of treason, and the fundamental precepts contained in the Great Writ are extant and applicable (and, as Scalia shows, why should they *not* be?), why must we chuck them and create yet another, new, untried, untested, and inherently risky system? McCarthy makes a national security court system seem so *right*, so *compelled*, but that is only because we have bought the lie that everything *is* different now. We have bought the line that the world after 9/11 is somehow vastly different than the world before, when all that has changed is that violence has finally arrived at our own doorstep. But Europeans can tell you what it's like, Middle Easterners can tell you, Africans can tell you, anyone else in the world can tell you what violence in your homeland to your own people does to you. Yet, it was in Europe that the Hague and Geneva Conventions were promulgated. It was there that the Nuremburg trials were carried out under the rule of international laws and the Nuremburg Charter was set forth which allowed for *no* excuses or exceptions to these laws. And these precepts have been accepted and adopted worldwide and are now finally embodied, for the first time in world history, in an International Criminal Court, which the United States refuses to sign onto, while we say we need to make better protections by creating a new court system in our own country that ostensibly ignores those international laws and norms.

The second thing McCarthy fails to recognize, which arises in his other article on torture, is that laws of combat and war require visible combat. Where you have combat operations against populations that are visibly carried out, it's combat, whether the warring group is a sovereign nation or a disfavored group of insurgents, and if a person is found in active combat, the rules of war apply. This does not mean automatic POW status. The Geneva system of determining the status of a prisoner is fully adequate to the task of deciding this and where a person is not a legitimate POW, he is not accorded the protections of POW's, and, in any case, where the laws of war are violated, he may be tried as a war criminal, either in a military tribunal or in a federal court. But where a person is not captured in active combat, he should be tried as a criminal.

In his article on torture, McCarthy engages in another fascinating and useful discussion and analysis, which leads him to the conclusion that torture warrants should be considered in conjunction with his proposed national security court system.[65] McCarthy is surely correct that "many people—probably most people—who claim to be opposed to torture are not against it in all cases or in every form." His idea, following on the model proposed by Alan Dershowitz in his book, Why Terrorism Works, to "regulate how and under what circumstances [torture] could permissibly be done"…the idea that we should regulate what we don't want to look at it, because we let someone else do it secretly in the dark anyway, the idea to bring this consideration out into the open is well-intentioned, but wrong. Why? Because regulating rather than forbidding a wrong act makes it seem right.

I think the reason we should not do this is that in this situation once you bring it out into the open, you make it seem okay. Israel learned this lesson the hard way. They legalized torture for awhile. According to Mark Bowden in his article on interrogation, a 1987 commission led by the retired Israel Supreme Court justice Moshe Landau made a series of recommendations which permitted interrogators to use "moderate physical pressure" and 'nonviolent psychological pressure" in interrogating prisoners who had information that could prevent impending terror attacks.[66] Such methods were allowed only in "ticking bomb scenarios." However, "[t]welve years later the Israel Supreme Court effectively revoked this permission, banning the use of any and all forms of torture."[67] The use of coercive methods had apparently become increasingly widespread. "It was estimated that more than two thirds of Palestinians taken into custody were subjected to them."[68]

This should make obvious what is so deeply and fundamentally flawed with legalizing torture: if you are torturing two-thirds of all Palestinians, surely many of those people were not terrorists, but you have now just taught them how to hate and how to terrorize.

Unsurprisingly, according to Bowden, "[e]very effort to regulate coercion [in Israel] failed," because:

> [i]n the abstract it was easy to imagine a ticking-bomb situation, and a suspect who clearly warranted rough treatment [, b]ut in real life where was the line to be drawn? Should coercive methods be applied only to someone who knows of an immediately pending attack? What about one who might know of attacks planned for months or years in the future?[69]

Thus, dilution of international human rights norms *cannot* be successful in fighting terrorism. As the president of the Israeli Supreme Court, Ahron Barak, ("a judge much respected around the world," according to former *New York Times* columnist

Anthony Lewis) wrote in 2002:

> Terrorism does not justify the neglect of accepted legal norms. This is how we distinguish ourselves from the terrorists themselves. They act against the law, by violating and trampling it, while in its war against terrorism, a democratic state acts within the framework of the law and according to the law. It is, therefore, not merely a war of the state against its enemies; it is also a war of the Law against its enemies.[70]

A system of justice that is kept separate from the core federal constitutional system—that is, outside the protections of the Constitution and international laws—is dangerous to democracy. Already our Supreme Court lies to us about how it is undermining the Constitution. What would another parallel court, a secret court, do to our justice system? Instead of considering torture warrants and national security courts, which would lead to abuse of law and loss of human rights protections for *all* of us, increasing our enemies and making the world more unsafe, we need to learn about the lessons of our own sometimes violent history and recall and reclaim the fundamental, lost ideals that we have forgotten.

Appendix
THE BILL OF RIGHTS
Amendments 1-10 of the Constitution

The Conventions of a number of the States having, at the time of adopting the Constitution, expressed a desire, in order to prevent misconstruction or abuse of its powers, that further declaratory and restrictive clauses should be added, and as extending the ground of public confidence in the Government will best insure the beneficent ends of its institution;

Resolved, by the Senate and House of Representatives of the United States of America, in Congress assembled, two-thirds of both Houses concurring, that the following articles be proposed to the Legislatures of the several States, as amendments to the Constitution of the United States; all or any of which articles, when ratified by three-fourths of the said Legislatures, to be valid to all intents and purposes as part of the said Constitution, namely:

Amendment I

Congress shall make no law respecting an establishment of religion, or prohibiting the free exercise thereof; or abridging the freedom of speech, or of the press; or the right of the people peaceably to assemble, and to petition the government for a redress of grievances.

Amendment II

A well regulated militia, being necessary to the security of a free state, the right of the people to keep and bear arms, shall not be infringed.

Amendment III

No soldier shall, in time of peace be quartered in any house, without the consent of the owner, nor in time of war, but in a manner to be prescribed by law.

Amendment IV

The right of the people to be secure in their persons, houses, papers, and effects, against unreasonable searches and seizures, shall not be violated, and no warrants shall issue, but upon probable cause, supported by oath or affirmation, and particularly describing the place to be searched, and the persons or things to be seized.

Amendment V

No person shall be held to answer for a capital, or otherwise infamous crime, unless on a presentment or indictment of a grand jury, except in cases arising in the land or naval forces, or in the militia, when in actual service in time of war or public danger; nor shall any person be subject for the same offense to be twice put in jeopardy of life or limb; nor shall be compelled in any criminal case to be a witness against himself, nor be deprived of life, liberty, or property, without due process of law; nor shall private property be taken for public use, without just compensation.

Amendment VI

In all criminal prosecutions, the accused shall enjoy the right to a speedy and public trial, by an impartial jury of the state and district wherein the crime shall have been committed, which district shall have been previously ascertained by law, and to be informed of the nature and cause of the accusation; to be confronted with the witnesses against him; to have compulsory process for obtaining witnesses in his favor, and to have the assistance of counsel for his defense.

Amendment VII

In suits at common law, where the value in controversy shall exceed twenty dollars, the right of trial by jury shall be preserved, and no fact tried by a jury, shall be otherwise reexamined in any court of the United States, than according to the rules of the common law.

Amendment VIII

Excessive bail shall not be required, nor excessive fines imposed, nor cruel and unusual punishments inflicted.

Amendment IX

The enumeration in the Constitution, of certain rights, shall not be construed to deny or disparage others retained by the people.

Amendment X

The powers not delegated to the United States by the Constitution, nor prohibited by it to the states, are reserved to the states respectively, or to the people.

Notes

Title page

1   R. Carter Pittman, *Our Bill of Rights: How it Came to Be,* (essay, ca. 1950-60), http://rcarterpittman.org/essays/Bill_of_Rights/Our_Bill_of_Rights.html.

Preface

1   Comment by Charles W. Hodell (January 27, 1911), posted in an introduction to *The Ring and the Book*, at http://www.underthesun.cc/Classics/Browning/TheRingBook/TheRingBook1.html.

2   *Id.*

3   Mark Crispin Miller, *The Bush Dyslexicon: Observations on a National Disorder* (Norton, 2001). Bush's humor about the death penalty: George W. Bush, Presidential Debate, October 11, 2000, page 244; his parody of Tucker, page 121.

4   Renata Brooks, *A Nation of Victims*, http://www.thenation.com/doc.mhtml?i=20030630&s=brooks.

5   Anthony Lewis *One Liberty at a Time,From the cages at Guantanamo to a jail cell in Brooklyn, the administration isn't just threatening the rights of a few detainees—it's undermining the very foundation of democracy*(June 2004) http://www.motherjones.com/news/feature/2004/05/04_403.html.

6   *See* Chapter 1, *Down the Road to Fascism:* "The Bush Plan is nothing more nor less than what I see the Bush Administration doing."

Introduction

1   Charles A. Kupchan, *The End of the American Era: U.S. Foreign Policy and the Geopolitics of the Twenty-first Century* (Vintage, 2002), ("Kupchan, American Era")

2   In 1876, a presidential electoral tie between Rutherford Hayes and Samuel Tilden was resolved not by the Supreme Court alone, but by a special 15-member electoral commission, comprising 10 commissioners, with five selected by the House (controlled by Democrats) and five by the Senate (controlled by Republicans), and five Supreme Court justices. When the commission tied, one of the five justices broke the tie. This tie-break cannot be viewed in the same light as what the Justices did in the 2000 contest. The only other presidential electoral tie was in 1800-01 between Thomas Jefferson and Aaron Burr. That tie was resolved by Congress. See Jennifer Van Bergen, *Aaron Burr and the Electoral Tie of 1801: Strict Constitutional Construction*, 1 Cardozo Public Law Policy & Ethics Journal 91 (Spring 2003), available at

http://www.worth1000.com/cplpej/new/CAP102.pdf or http://www.puzzle-element.org/Burrarticle.pdf.

3   *See* Richard A. Clarke, *Against All Enemies: Inside America's War on Terror* (Free Press, 2004) 261, 286.

4   *See* Anthony Lewis, *One Liberty at a Time: From the cages at Guantanamo to a jail cell in Brooklyn, the administration isn't just threatening the rights of a few detainees—it's undermining the very foundation of democracy* (June 2004), http://www.motherjones.com/news/feature/2004/05/04_403.html.

5   Kupchan, *American Era*, ix-x. *See also* Clyde Prestowitz, *Losing Friends & Alienating People: U.S. diplomats and policy experts of all political stripes agree: Bush's unilateralist polices have been disastrous to our own interests* (June 2004),
http://www.motherjones.com/news/feature/2004/05/04_406.html, and David Rieff, *The End of Empire: The war in Iraq was supposed to launch bold new American foreign policy. But has the neoconservatives' grandiose dream ended before it began?* (June 2004), http://www.motherjones.com/news/feature/2004/05/04_405.html.

6   [Anonymous], *Julius Caesar Crosses the Rubicon, 49 B.C.*," Eye Witness to History," www.eyewitnesstohistory.com/caesar.htm (2002).

7   Alexander Hamilton, *The Federalist No. 1*. There is certainly a question whether the American Republic *ever* was an establishment of good government, particularly as it related to the equal rights of all peoples. The genocide of Native Americans and the abduction and enslavement of Africans are certainly not consistent with any notion of equality or good government.

8   Neither do its constitution-undermining legal strategies. *See* Jennifer Van Bergen, *Bush Uses Law to Undercut Bill of Rights* (L.A. Daily Journal, 16 March 2004), archived at http://www.puzzle-element.org/BushUsesLaw.doc.

9   Ambassadors Ed Djerejian (Syria, Israel) and Margaret Tutwiler (Morocco, presently under-secretary of State for public diplomacy), quoted in Prestowitz, *Losing Friends*, footnote 5.

10   Kupchan, *American Era*, at v.

Chapter One

1   *See* Jennifer Van Bergen, *The Bush Plan for America: The Rise of an American National Security State* (Dec. 14, 2003), http://www.ftaaimc.org/en/2003/12/3232.shtml.

2   Some call this shadow government "the octopus." *See* Kenn Thomas & Jim Keith, *The Octopus: Secret Government and the Death of Danny Casolaro* (Feral House, 1996).

3   For a recount of Goff's military career, see my July 16, 2003 interview with him: http://truthout.org/docs_03/073103A.shtml. For more on Stan Goff's views, *see* his new book *Full Spectrum Disorder: The Military in the*

New American Century (Soft Skull Press, 2004).

4   [Jennifer Van Bergen, interviewer], *Stan Goff on Iraq, FTAA, & Fascism* (December 18, 2003), http://www.ftaaimc.org/es/2003/12/3289.shtml

5   Laurence W. Britt, *Fascism Anyone?* (Free Inquiry Magazine, Vol. 23, No. 2 (Spring 2003)), http://secularhumanism.org/library/fi/britt_23_2.htm. (I am indebted to Mike Caetano for bringing this article to my attention, and for the many excellent ideas he raised in email conversations.)

6   John Armstrong, *Dick Cheney's Song of America: drafting a plan for global dominance* (Harper's Magazine, Oct. 2002), http://www.findarticles.com/cf_dls/m1111/1829_305/92589441/p1/article.j html.

7   Dante, *Inferno*, Canto XXIV:76-8.

8   Marcel Proust wrote in Chapter One of *The Guermantes Way*, that a name offers us "an image of the unknowable."

9   I borrow the phrase, "national security state" from C. William Michaels, *No Greater Threat: America After September 11 and the Rise of the National Security State* (Algora Publishing, 2002).

10   The mosaic theory began with the idea that "terrorists might use seemingly innocuous, disparate pieces of information to build a picture of what the United States is doing to combat terrorism and thereby expose governmental weaknesses and possibly render detention facilities vulnerable to attack." Kendall W. Harrison, *The Evolving Judicial Response to the War on Terrorism* (December 2002), http://www.wisbar.org/wislaw-mag/2002/12/Harrison.html. *See also, Center for National Security Studies v. United States Dep't of Justice*, 215 F. Supp. 2d 94 (D.D.C. 2002), http://laws.findlaw.com/dc/025254a.html, *and* Stephen Lee, *Cases: Taliban, al-Qaeda* (last updated April 13, 2002), http://www.newsaic.com/casetaliban.html. The theory was quickly adopted by the U.S. government as a rationale for why they had a right to invade privacy or indefinitely detain. According to David Cole: "This 'mosaic' argument essentially claims that immigration judges should presume danger even where the government offers only 'innocuous' information about an individual ... because it is always possible that at the end of the investigation, the innocuous may turn out to be inculpating—the precise inverse of the presumption of innocence that lies at the heart of the American justice system. When coupled with the claim that Al Qaeda 'sleepers' live quiet, law-abiding lives until they receive the call to strike, the 'mosaic' theory could justify the detention of virtually anyone." David Cole, *Their Liberty, Our Security* (Oct 27 2003), www.tompaine.com/feature2.cfm/ID/9242

11   For example, the provision authorizing the Secretary of State to designate foreign terrorist organizations (FTO's) is in the immigration statute, but it is used in conjunction with the provision criminalizing material support of FTO's. *See* Jennifer Van Bergen, *In the Absence of Democracy: The Designation and Material Support Provisions of the Anti-Terrorism Laws*, 2

Cardozo Public Law, Policy & Ethics Journal [ ] (Spring 2004).

12 Foreign intelligence information is "information that relates to, and if concerning a United States person is necessary to, the ability of the United States to protect against - (A) actual or potential attack or other grave hostile acts of a foreign power or an agent of a foreign power;(B) sabotage or international terrorism by a foreign power or an agent of a foreign power; or (C) clandestine intelligence activities by an intelligence service or network of a foreign power or by an agent of a foreign power. 50 U.S.C. § 1801(e)(1). A second definition of "foreign intelligence information," in 50 U.S.C. § 1801(e)(2), includes information relevant or necessary to "the national defense of the United States" or "the conduct of the foreign affairs of the United States." According to the Justice Department: "This definition, which generally involves information referred to as "affirmative" or "positive" foreign intelligence rather than "protective" foreign intelligence or "counterintelligence" information, is … rarely the object of surveillance in which purpose issues arise, because the affirmative intelligence information is usually not evidence of a crime. See Senate Intelligence Report at 11 & n.4." DOJ "In re: Sealed Case No. 02-001" Appeal to FISA Review Court (Decided November 18, 2002), http://www.fas.org/irp/agency/doj/fisa/fiscr111802.html.

13 Justice Ahron Barak, quoted in Anthony Lewis, *One Liberty at a Time: From the cages at Guantanamo to a jail cell in Brooklyn, the administration isn't just threatening the rights of a few detainees—it's undermining the very foundation of democracy* (June 2004), http://www.motherjones.com/news/feature/2004/05/04_406.html.

14 One conservative commentator, Chuck Baldwin, wrote that the passage of the "Constitution Restoration Act of 2004," which would prohibit federal courts from "interfering with any expression of religious faith by any elected … official," including displaying the Ten Commandments in the courtroom, "should be regarded as the most important item on the conservative agenda this year!" Chuck Baldwin, *The Constitution Restoration Act of 2004: The Most Important Legislation in the Last Fifty Years* (February 17, 2004),.chuckbaldwinlive.com/chuckwagon.html. In other words, Baldwin suggests that expressions of religious faith belong in the courtroom. Baldwin adds that he thinks "our Founding Fathers understood" the possibility of America being "controlled by a tyrannical oligarchy of federal judges," and "prescribed a way for Congress to deal with this matter." He means "court stripping," divesting courts of jurisdiction, which is discussed in Chapter 4.

15 Baldwin also notes that the Act would prohibit courts from "relying on foreign or international law in their decisions." *Id*. Under Article 6 of the Constitution, international law is incorporated into domestic law as "the law of the land," as I discuss later in Chapters 6 and 9. Thus, a statute that forbids judges from relying on international law would be unconstitutional.

16 Bernard Lewis, *I'm Right, You're Wrong, Go to Hell: Religions and the meet-

ing of civilizations (May 2003),
http://www.theatlantic.com/issues/2003/05/lewis.htm.

17   *Id.*

18   America, of course, is not strictly a democracy and never has been. It is a republic, a democratic republic, sometimes called a representative democracy. I use the term democracy loosely in this book to indicate a form of government wherein people have a say in their government and individual rights and liberties are protected. *See* Bernard Crick, *Democracy: A Very Short Introduction* (Oxford University Press, 2002). *Also see,* Jerry Mander, *In the Absence of the Sacred: The Failure of Technology & the Survival of the Indian Nations* (Sierra Club Books, 1991), Chapter 13, "The Gift of Democracy," which provides evidence that the U.S. Constitution was modeled after the Great Binding Law of the Iroquois Confederacy.

19   [Samuel Bryan], "The Address and Reasons of Dissent of the Minority of the Convention of Pennsylvania to their Constituents" (Dec. 18, 1787), in Ralph Ketcham, ed., *The Anti-Federalist Papers and the Constitutional Convention Debates: The Clashes and the Compromises that Gave Birth to Our Form of Government* (Signet Classic, 2003) 251. (*"Anti-Federalist Papers"*)

20   Mrs. Carrington to her sister, Nancy (March 1809) *in* Albert J. Beveridge, *The Life of John Marshall* (Houghton Mifflin, 1919) 1:145, n.3 (spelling modernized). ("Beveridge, *John Marshall*")

21   *See Anti-Federalist Papers, passim..*

22   Christopher Collier & James Lincoln Collier, *Decision in Philadelphia: The Constitutional Convention of 1787* (Ballantine Books, 1987) 348.

Chapter Two

1   Thomas Paine, *Common Sense* (Isaac Kramnick, ed.) (Penguin, 1982) 98.

2   *See* [Newsday] *Transition of Power: President-Elect Bush Meets With Congressional Leaders on Capitol Hill* (December 18, 2000), http://www.cnn.com/TRANSCRIPTS/0012/18/nd.01.html. [News clip with transcript of video clip of Bush speaking.]

3   *See Appendix.*

4   Sol Bloom, *The Story of the Constitution* (1986) (Washington, DC : National Archives and Record Administration, 1986, (c1937)), excerpt: "Questions and Answers Pertaining to the Constitution," http://www.archives.gov/national_archives_experience/constitution_q_and _a.html.

5   *Id.*

6   *Mathew v. Eldridge,* 424 U.S. 319 (1976). Notice that due process requires government or state action. This is about what process the government owes its citizens when it is going to deprive them of "life, liberty, or property."

7   *Camara v. Municipal Court,* 387 U.S. 523 (1967). Lieberman has an excel-

lent list of examples of balancing tests developed by the Supreme Court. *See*, Jethro K. Lieberman, *A Practical Companion to the Constitution: How the Supreme Court Has Ruled on Issues from Abortion to Zoning* (University of California Press, 1999) 63-64, *and* discussion in Chapter Three, *Our Individual Rights*.

8   The USA PATRIOT Act is an acronym. It stands for "Uniting and Strengthening America by Providing Appropriate Tools Required to Intercept and Obstruct Terrorism Act of 2001," Pub. L. 107-56, 115 Stat. 349. Hereafter I refer to it either as the PATRIOT Act.

9   Department of Justice, *National Security; Prevention of Acts of Violence and Terrorism; Final Rule*, 28 CFR Parts 500 and 501 (October 31, 2001) (66 Federal Register 55063), http://news.findlaw.com/cnn/docs/doj/dojbop66fr55062.pdf. *See also*, David A. Moran, *Ashcroft's monitoring order violates attorney-client rights* (November 28, 2001), http://www.detnews.com/2001/editorial/0111/28/a13-353317.htm.

10   Center for National Security Studies (CNSS), *Comments of the Center for National Security Studies on the Attorney General's Order Regarding the Monitoring of Lawyer-Client Communications*, 66 FED. REG. 55062 (Oct. 31, 2001), http://www.cnss.org/attorneyclientcomments.htm.

11   67 Federal Register 54878 (August 26, 2002).

12   *See Detroit Free Press v. Ashcroft*, 303 F.3d 681 (6th Cir.2002) *and North Jersey Media Group v. Ashcroft*, 308 F.3d 198 (3d Cir.2002).

13   Only an injured party may challenge a law or regulation. Citizens cannot challenge laws just because they think they are unconstitutional. This gives officials a great deal of wiggle room. The only remedy then is at the polls.

14   U.S. Constitution, Art. VI, para. 2 (ratified 12/15/1791)

15   Jethro K. Lieberman, *A Practical Companion to the Constitution* (University of California Press, 1999) 252 (*citing Le Paquette Habana*, 175 U.S. 677 (1900)).

16   *Id*.

17   *See Hamdi v. Rumsfeld*, 316 F.3d 450 (4th Cir. 2003) The Guantanamo and unlawful enemy combatant cases are presently, as of this writing, before the U.S. Supreme Court.

Chapter Three

1   "The Federal Farmer," (October 9, 1787) *in* Ralph Ketcham, ed., *The Anti-Federalist Papers and the Constitutional Convention Debates: The Clashes and the Compromises that Gave Birth to Our Form of Government* (Signet Classic, 2003) at 266. (*"Anti-Federalist Papers"*).

2   "The Pennsylvania Minority," (December 18, 1787) *in id.* at 247. The two quoted remarks here from the Federal Farmer and the Pennsylvania Minority were published in local newspapers during the period of the con-

stitutional ratification debates, before the Bill of Rights were added as the first Ten Amendments. These writers argued *for* the inclusion of the Bill of Rights.

3   *Scales v. U.S.*, 367 U.S. 203, 261 (1961) Justice Black (dissent).

4   Jethro K Lieberman, *A Practical Companion to the Constitution* (University of California Press, 1999) 63.

5   Gina Holland, *Justice Warns Against Civil Rights Apathy* (January 29, 2004), http://news.yahoo.com/news?tmpl=story2&u=/ap/20040130/ap_on_go_su_co/scotus_ginsburg_2.

6   *Joint Anti-Fascist Refugee Comm. v. McGrath*, 341 U.S. 123 (1951).

7   There is another type of due process called substantive due process which is simply the concept that all legislation be in furtherance of a legitimate governmental objective. This idea resulted in the Court formulating the balancing tests. Most rights issues are determined on the basis of whether the law is rationally related to a legitimate government goal. Some, however, which are considered "fundamental rights," require "strict scrutiny," in which the Court requires that the law furthers a compelling government interest to trump an individual right. Rights given strict scrutiny include First Amendment, voting, and sexual privacy.

8   Generally speaking the accused still, of course, has his criminal procedural rights, such as a right to a jury trial, right to counsel, and right not to be compelled to testify against himself in a court of law, although the Bush administration has attacked even these rights in its handling of the Guantanamo detainees and the so-called unlawful enemy combatants, Padilla and Hamdi, who have been detained in military brigs for nigh two years without access to courts or legal representation.

9   Bernard Shaw, *Saint Joan* (Penguin Books, 1966) 137.

10 U.S. Constitution, Amendment I (ratified 12/15/1791).

11 Lieberman, *Practical Companion to the Constitution*, at 189.

12 *See* Chapter 7, *The PATRIOT Act*, section on designation, and the discussion of the Lynne Stewart case in Part Two of Chapter 6, *Demise of Democracy*. *For an in-depth discussion on these provisions, see* Jennifer Van Bergen, *The Absence of Democracy: The Designation and Material Support Provisions of the Anti-Terrorism Laws*, 2 Cardozo Public law, Policy & Ethics Journal [ ] (Spring 2004).

13 *U.S. v. Schwimmer*, 279 U.S. 644 (1928) (J. Holmes, dissent).

14 *Brandenburg v. Ohio*, 395 U.S. 444 (1969).

15 In the movie, the U.S. sends half a dozen specially-trained soldiers on an undercover operation against insurgents in Colombia. For political reasons, the plug is pulled on the operation and most of the soldiers are killed.

16 *Schenck v. U.S.*, 249 U.S. 47 (1919). My description of the case is taken directly from Lieberman, *Practical Companion to the Constitution*, at 490. *See also* Lieberman, *id.* at 96, for a fuller description of the case. Holmes

later articulated the test as "clear and imminent danger." Id. at 97. (The Court did not return to anything resembling Holmes' test until 1969.)

17   Lieberman, *Practical Companion to the Constitution*, at 98.

18   The so-called "Creppy Memo," written by the Chief of the Immigration and Naturalization Service (INS), authorizing the closing of certain sensitive immigration hearings, was challenged by the press in several states and subsequently in two federal circuits on the basis of the right of the public to know. *See Detroit Free Press v. Ashcroft*, 303 F.3d 681 (6th Cir. 2002); *North Jersey Media Group v. Ashcroft*, 308 F.3d 198 (3d Cir. 2002).

19   Lieberman, *Practical Companion to the Constituion*, at 196.

20   *DeJonge v. Oregon*, 299 U.S. 353 (1937).

21   The protestors recently won a multi-million dollar settlement against the city. *See* Kirsten Anderberg, *Police at WTO 1999 Cost Seattle $250,000* (January 17, 2004), *http://sandiego.indymedia.org/en/2004/01/102642.shtml*.

22   There was also rampant police brutality and violations of other rights. *See* Mary (Beka) Economopoulos, *A Crisis in Democracy*, http://www.ftaaimc.org/en/2004/01/3563.shtm (November 26 2003).

23   *See* Editorial, *'First Amendment Zones' Restrict Free Speech* (January 25, 2004), http://www.commondreams.org/views04/0125-02.htm.

24   Time, manner, and place restrictions have been found constitutional, as long as they apply without discrimination to any class of persons, but the First Amendment Zones violate this criteria, since Bush supporters are allowed close access to him and protesters are not.

25   U.S. Constitution, Amendment IV (ratified 12/15/1791).

26   *See* Whitfield Diffie & Susan Landau, *Privacy on the Line: The Politics of Wiretapping and Encryption* (MIT Press, 1998) 135. This book contains an excellent overview of the history and law of privacy, particularly in the context of electronic communications.

27   *Katz v. U.S.*, 389 U.S. 347, 351 (1967)

28   *Id.*

29   *Id.*

30   *Smith v. Maryland*, 99 S. Ct. 2577 (1979).

31   *Olmstead v. U.S.*, 277 U.S. 438, 478 (1928)(J. Brandeis, dissenting)

32   *See* particularly discussion in Chapters 6 and 7.

33   U.S. Constitution, Amendment VI (ratified 12/15/1791).

34   *See* Jennifer Van Bergen, *Repeal the USA Patriot Act*, Part III, *Civil Rights Violations and Torture* (April 3, 2002), http://www.truthout.org/docs_02/04.04E.JVB.Patriot.htm. *Also archived at* http://www.puzzle-element.org/repealtheusapatriotactprt3.doc

35   *See* Jennifer Van Bergen, *The Madness of America* (October 9, 2002), http://www.truthout.org/docs_02/10.10Bb.jvb.madness.htm, for examples of reversals. *Also archived at* http://www.puzzle-element.org/themadnesso-famerica.doc.

Chapter Four

1   The list is a short one. There are other questions of equal importance,
    such as executive power and privilege, political questions, and foreign pol-
    icy questions that cannot be covered here. I recommend Jethro
    Lieberman, A Practical Companion to the Constitution, for further reading.

2   Myers v. United States, 272 U.S. 52 (1926).

3   Jethro K. Lieberman, A Practical Companion to the Constitution (University
    of California Press, 1999) 457.

4   Id. at 458.

5   See U.S. v. Rahmani, 209 F.Supp.2d 1045, 1057 (C.D.CA. 2002) (citing
    National Council of Resistance of Iran v. Dept. of State, 251 F.3d 192 (D.C.
    Cir. 2001) (noting this decision, the court stated that mandating proce-
    dure to the DOS violated separation of powers, that if the court found the
    provision was unconstitutional, it could strike it down, but it could not
    mandate procedure to an arm of another branch of the government).

6   Lieberman, Practical Companion to the Constitution, at 140.

7   Id.

8   Albert J. Beveridge, The Life of John Marshall (Houghton Mifflin, 1919),
    1:452.

9   Lieberman, Practical Companion to the Constitution, at 265.

10 Id. at 266.

11 Id.

12 This section relies heavily on Heidi Boghosian, Taint Teams And Firewalls:
    The Armor for Attorney-Client Privilege (Section II: "Court Stripping in the
    Name of National Security), 1 CPLPEJ 15, 17-19 ((May 2003).
    ("Boghosian, Taint Teams") All quotes in this section are from Boghosian,
    unless otherwise indicated. See also ACLU, "Court Stripping" -- Congress
    Undermines the Power of the Judiciary (Special Report, June 1996),
    http://www.aclu.org/library/ctstrip.html.

13 The Anti-Terrorism and Effective Death Penalty Act (AEDPA), Pub. L.
    No. 104-132, 110 Stat. 1214. AEDPA was the precursor to the PATRIOT
    Act. See James Dempsey & David Cole, Terrorism & the Constitution:
    Sacrificing Civil Liberties in the Name of National Security (The New Press,
    2002) 117.

14 John Conyers, Press Release (September 26, 2000),
    http://www.house.gov/judiciary_democrats/hr2121secreteviden-
    cepr92600.htm. Conyers was proposing the Secret Evidence Repeal Act
    (SERA) (H.R. 2121). The bill had received the full approval of the House
    Judiciary Committee and was widely supported before Bush was elected,
    after which nothing more was heard of it. SERA proposed using the same
    procedures as the Classified Information Procedures Act (CIPA), which
    provides procedures for the use of classified information in criminal prose-
    cutions, such that a defendant may challenge the information without
    classified information being compromised.

(Pub. L. 96-456, Oct. 15, 1980, 94 Stat. 2025, as amended by Pub. L. 100-690, title VII, § 7020(g), Nov. 18, 1988, 102 Stat. 4396; Pub. L. 106-567, title VI, § 607, Dec. 27, 2000, 114 Stat. 2855)
http://www.access.gpo.gov/uscode/title18a/18a_3_.html.

15   Illegal Immigration Reform and Immigrant Responsibility Act (IIRIRA), Pub. L. No. 104-208, 110 Stat. 3009-546 (1996). See Pulice v. INS, No. 98-4497 (6th Cir. 2000), http://laws.findlaw.com/6th/00a0198p.html, and U.S. v. Baldo-Figueroa, No. 01-50376 (9th Cir. 2004), http://216.239.51.104/search?q=cache:Tqv7RnQAmTcJ:www.ca9.uscourts.gov/ca9/newopinions.nsf/42DC0F0C2983D40488256E6F005B6C9A/%24f ile/0150376.pdf%3Fopenelement+IIRIRA+findlaw=en=3, for descriptions of how IIRIRA affects certain deportation cases.

16   Dempsey & Cole, *Terrorism & the Constitution*, at 114. *See also, id.* at 41-44, 93-95, and 121, for more on court stripping decisions and laws in recent years.

17   *Id.*

18   *Id.*

19   *Id.*

20   Boghosian, *Taint Teams*, at 18 (*citing* Ronald Weich, *Upsetting Checks and Balances: Congressional Hostility Toward the Courts in Times of Crisis* (ACLU, 2001) at 50).

21   *Id.* (Citations omitted.)

22   *Id.*

23   The Fourth Amendment states, in full: "The right of the people to be secure in their persons, houses, papers, and effects, against unreasonable searches and seizures, shall not be violated, and no Warrants shall issue, but upon probable cause, supported by Oath or affirmation, and particularly describing the place to be searched, and the persons or things to be seized." U.S. Constitution, Amendment IV (ratified 12/15/1791).

24   *Brinegar v. U.S.*, 338 U.S. 160 (1949).

25   *Aguilar v. Texas*, 378 U.S. 108 (1964).

26   (Untitled), http://faculty.ncwc.edu/toconnor/315/315lect06.htm. This appears to be from a faculty member, possibly Ralph B. Strickland, Jr., Agency Legal Specialist, of the North Carolina Justice Academy. (Internal links in the document lead to other documents with his name on them.) The document contains a useful list of the types of activities that might elicit probable cause to search or arrest.

27   *Id.*

28   *Id.* (Emphasis in original.)

29   *Id.* (Emphasis in original.)

30   Jennifer Van Bergen, *The Silent World* (November 10, 2002), http://www.truthout.org/docs_02/11.11B.jvb.silent.htm. *Also available at* http://www.puzzle-element.org/thesilentworld.doc.

31   *Id.*

Chapter Five

1   *See* Jennifer Van Bergen, *Bush Uses Law to Undercut Bill of Rights* (L.A. Daily Journal, 16 March 2004), *archived at* http://www.puzzle-element.org/BushUsesLaw.doc.

2   U.S. Constitution, Art. III, sec. I states: "The judicial Power of the United States, shall be vested in one supreme Court, and in such inferior Courts as the Congress may from time to time ordain and establish." The Judiciary Act of 1789 established the federal court system. 1 Stat. 73, (September 24, 1789), *see* http://air.fjc.gov/history/landmark/02a_bdy.htm.

3   As noted earlier, immigration courts were created within the Executive branch.

4   These cases often rely on the Classified Information Procedures Act (CIPA), which allows the government to substitute a summary of the information for classified documents, or to substitute a statement admitting relevant facts that the classified information would tend to prove. PL 96-456, 102 STAT. 4396 (1980), 18 U.S.C. App., Sec. 4, http://www.fas.org/irp/offdocs/laws/pl096456.htm. The Secret Evidence Repeal Act (SERA) that came close to passage in 2000 before Bush's election would have applied CIPA standards to immigration proceedings.

5   *See* chart of the relative numbers of terrorist case investigations, arrests and convictions and of terrorist acts prevented in the years leading up to 2000, *at* DOJ, *Annual Report* (Fall 1999), http://www.usdoj.gov/ag/annual-reports/ar99/chapter1.htm. *See also*, Michael Riley, *Feds Hype Conviction Rate in Terror Fight, Critics Say* (December 8, 2003), http://www.common-dreams.org/headlines03/1208-10.htm *and* John J. Goldman, *U.S. Atty. White's Modesty Belies Her Tenacity* (February 20, 2001), *http://www.twist-edbadge.com/solidarity/maryjowhite.htm*.

6   Deputy Assistant Judge Advocate General (National Security Litigation and Intelligence Law) to Judge Advocates, *Overview of FISA & Changes Implemented by USA PATRIOT Act*, (September 4, 2003), http://www.fas.org/irp/agency/doj/fisa/navy0903.pdf.

7   Department of Justice (DOJ), Executive Office of Immigration Review (EOIR), *Organizational Information* (no date), http://www.usdoj.gov/eoir/orginfo.htm.

8   DOJ, EOIR, *EOIR Responsibilities* (no date), http://www.usdoj.gov/eoir/responsibilities.htm.

9   *Id.*

10   *Id.*

11   Department of Justice (DOJ), Office of the Chief Immigration Judge (OCIJ) , *Fact Sheet* (revised April 2003), http://www.usdoj.gov/eoir/fs/oci-jbio.htm.

12   Section 412 of the PATRIOT Act also restricts judicial review of a detention to "review only under writs of habeas corpus issued out of any federal district court but appealable only to the United States Court of Appeals

for the District [of] Colombia." Charles Doyle (Congressional Research Service), *Terrorism: Section by Section Analysis of the USA PATRIOT Act* (December 10,2001) 35. ("CRS Report") http://fpc.state.gov/documents/organization/7952.pdf.

13   This description is taken from Jethro K. Lieberman, *A Practical Companion to the Constitution* (University of California Press, 1999) 304.

14   *Id.*

15   For example, the $8.7 billion diverted from the Iraq military budget to paramilitary training for police in preparation for the demonstrations in Miami against the Free Trade of Americas ministerial meetings in November 2003.

16   Lieberman, *Practical Companion to the Constitution,* at 300 (*citing Ex Parte Milligan,* 71 U.S. (4 Wall.) 2 (1866)).

17   Joint Resolution, Public Law 107-40, 115 Stat. 224.

18   American Bar Association Task Force on Terrorism and the Law, *Report and Recommendations of Military Commissions* (January 4, 2002) at 1, http://www.abanet.org/leadership/military.pdf. ("ABA, *Report*").

19   ABA, *Report,* at 6.

20   *Id.* at 3 (citations omitted).

21   *Madsen v. Kinsella,* 343 U.S. 341, 346-7(1952).

22   *Ex Parte Quirin,* 317 U.S. 1 (1942).

23   *See* Scott Loughrey, *Nightline Sells Martial Law,* http://infowars.com/print/ps/nightline_martiallaw.htm, *and* Wayne Madsen & John Stanton, *When the War Hits Home: U.S. Plans for Martial Law, Tele-Governance, and the Suspension of Elections* (May 14, 2004), http://www.counterpunch.org/madsen0514.html.

24   *U.S. v. Katz.* 389 U.S. 347, 360 (1967), *available at* http://caselaw.lp.find-law.com/scripts/getcase.pl?court=US&vol=389&invol=347.

25   *Id.* at 359-60.

26   *Id.*

Chapter Six

1   Many thanks to Bruce Glaser (Broward ACLU Vice Chair & State Legislative Liaison) for his excellent research and assistance in writing this chapter. Further thanks to anti-war activist and videographer, Raymond Del Papa for suggestions, additions, and rewrites.

2   Lyle Denniston, *Supreme Secrecy,* "On the Media" (NPR, January 9, 2004), http://www.wnyc.org/onthemedia/transcripts/transcripts_011604_supreme.html. (Denniston has been reporting for the Boston Globe on the Supreme Court for more than forty years.)

3   I am indebted to peace activist and former weapons designer Keith Kessler for his thoughtful insights and input on this section.

4   Laurence W. Britt, *Fascism Anyone?* (Spring 2003), http://secularhuman-

ism.org/library/fi/britt_23_2.htm.

5   In this section, I make little effort to document or provide sources, as the
        section is a simple survey, most of the information is either common
        knowledge or can easily be verified, and the rest of the book provides
        abundant citations to sources.

6   See Nazi Germany's War on Terrorism,,
        http://c0balt.com/resources/terror/terror.shtml ("Most Americans remem-
        ber his Office of Fatherland Security, known as the
        Reichssicherheitshauptamt and Schutzstaffel, simply by its most famous
        agency's initials: the SS.") and Al Martin, Watch Out for Jackboots and
        Swagger Sticks,
        http://www.acts2.com/thebibletruth/Fatherland_New_Powers.htm ("In
        America, 'Homeland' is a neuter word. In German, however, the word is
        translated as 'Vaterland' (Fatherland).")

7   See Amnesty Slams "Bankrupt" Vision of US in Damning Rights Report (May
        26, 2004) http://www.commondreams.org/headlines04/0526-02.htm. A
        google search will pull up other reports and statements by Amnesty from
        the past two years that provide further details and conclusions.

8   For a hard look at race politics relating to the U.S. and Haiti, see Stan
        Goff, Hideous Dream: A Soldier's Memoir of the US Invasion of Haiti (Soft
        Skull Press, 2000).

9   Jeff Jarvis, F*cked by the F*CC,
        http://www.thenation.com/doc.mhtml?i=20040517&s=jarvis.

10   Id.

11   Id.

12   Christopher S. Carson, An Unapologetic Apology (June 2, 2004),
        http://www.nationalreview.com/comment/carson200406020845.asp. For
        the Times self-critique, see, The Editors, The Times and Iraq (May 26,
        2004),
        http://www.nytimes.com/2004/05/26/international/middleeast/26FTE_NO
        TE.html?ex=1087185600&en=6822e66f3d4974f2&ei=5070.

13   Carson, id. (emphasis in original).

14   Richard A. Clarke, Against All Enemies: Inside American's War on Terror
        (Free Press, 2004) 245.

15   See Chapter 1, Down the Road to Fascism.

16   C. William Michaels, No Greater Threat: America After September 11 and
        the Rise of a National Security State (Algora Publishing, 2002) 129.

17   U.S. v. Sattar, et al, 02 Cr. 395, http://news.findlaw.com/hdocs/docs/terror-
        ism/ussattar72203opn.pdf. The court declared the PATRIOT Act provi-
        sion in question unconstitutional-as-applied and dismissed the charges.
        The government has since brought a superseding indictment renewing the
        charges under a related provision of the Act. See http://www.lynnestew-
        art.org/IndictmentSuperceding.pdf.

18   John O. Edwards, Gen. Franks Doubts Constitution Will Survive WMD
        Attack (November 21, 2003), http://www.newsmax.com/archives/arti-

cles/2003/11/20/185048.shtml.

19   *See*, William Glaberson, *Judges Question Detention of American* (November 18, 2003), www.nytimes.com/2003/11/18/national/18BOMB.html.

20   Ben Knight, *Claims of torture in Guantanamo Bay* (October 8, 2003, interview with Richard Bourke, an Australian lawyer working full time in the U.S. on the cases of detainees at Guantanamo Bay) www.abc.net.au/am/content/2003/s962052.htm; Editorial Staff, *Top UK judge slams Camp Delta* (November 26, 2003), http://news.bbc.co.uk/2/hi/uk_news/politics/3238624.stm; Seymour M. Hersh, *Torture at Abu Ghraib* (April 30, 2004), http://www.newyorker.com/fact/content/?040510fa_fact, and Editorial, *A System of Abuse* (May 5, 2004), http://www.washingtonpost.com/wp-dyn/articles/A2372-2004May4.html.

21   *See* Col. Daniel F. McCallum, *Why GTMO?*, 6, http://www.ndu.edu/nwc/writing/AY03/5603/5603G.pdf. All quotes used here from this paper are at this URL. McCallum noted: "As the planning for the war in Afghanistan continued, it became apparent a facility would be needed to detain captured personnel." There were seven factors taken into consideration in deciding the location of such a facility: impact on U.S. foreign relations, impact on domestic security, facility security, facility size, remoteness of location, litigation risks, and logistics.

22   Senator Edward M. Kennedy, *The Bush Doctrine of Pre-Emption* (October 7, 2002) http://www.drmomentum.com/aces/archives/000253.html. All Kennedy quotes in this section are from this speech.

23   Lizzie Rushing, *The International Criminal Court and American Exceptionalism* (May 5, 2003), http://www.sit-edu-geneva.ch/international_criminal_court_and.htm. ("Rushing, *ICC*")

24   Information for this section was obtained from (1) observations and interviews with persons in Haiti by myself and my colleagues on the Phase II National Lawyers Guild Haiti Delegation (April 12-19, 2004) (*see*, NLG, *Summary Report of Phase II of NLG Delegation to Haiti, April 12-19, 2004* (May 11, 2004), http://www.nlg.org/programs/international/Haiti_delegation_report_phaseII.pdf), (2) interview with Stan Goff (June 3, 2004), and (3) Marjorie Cohn, *The Kidnapping of President Jean-Bertrande Aristide from Haiti Violated International and United States Law* (ca. early May 2004), http://www.nlg.org/news/articles/cohn_haiti.htm. ("Cohn, *Kidnapping*")

25   Cohn, *Kidnapping*.

26   Much of the material here is taken from Rushing, ICC., *and* International Criminal Court (ICC), *[The]US and the ICC* (no date), http://www.icc-now.org/documents/usandtheicc.html.

27   *Id.*

28   Rome Statute of the International Criminal Court, U.N. Doc. A/CONF.183/9 (1998) (United Nations Diplomatic Conference of Plenipotentiaries on the Establishment of an International Criminal

Court, 17 July 1998, *reprinted in* 37 I.L.M. 998 (1998) [hereinafter Rome Statute]. The Rome Statute, as well as further information about the Statute and the ICC, may be found at www.un.org/law/icc and http://www.iccnow.org/romearchive/romestatute/rome-e.pdf.

29 Former Secretary Robert McNamara recently stated: "I don't agree that it's clear Clinton would not have submitted the treaty to the Senate. He didn't sign the treaty until one hour before the deadline. In fact he never had time to submit it. That signature has since been removed." These remarks were made in the context of a Q & A with ICC's President, Philippe Kirsch, before the Council on Foreign Relations, Washington, D.C. (January 16, 2004), archived at http://groups.yahoo.com/group/icc-info/message/3506.

30 Rushing, *ICC* (citing Rapport de Position n°8 : Cour Pénale Internationale. « NON A L'EXCEPTION AMERICAINE », Fédération Internationale des Ligues des Droits de l'Homme (FIDH), N°345 (novembre 2002)).

31 See William Blum, *Killing Hope: U.S. Military and CIA Interventions Since World War II* (Common Courage Press, 1995) and Colin A. Ross, M.D., *Bluebird: Deliberate Creation of Multiple Personality by Psychiatrists* (Manitou Communications, 2000).

32 Rebecca L. Sandlin, *NAFTA First Hand*, (August 14, 2003), http://www.thepostandmail.com/articles/2003/08/14/news/news/news01.txt .

33 *Id.*

34 Anthony Boadle, *Anti-FTAA Activists Plan Protests to Kill Pact* (January 29, 2004), http://www.forbes.com/business/newswire/2004/01/29/rtr1235153.htm.

35 Tamara Straus, *Trading Democracy,* (January 15, 2002), http://www.alternet.org/story.html?StoryID=12233.

36 *Id.*

37 Amy Chua, *World on Fire: How Exporting Free Market Democracy Breeds Ethnic Hatred and Global Instability* (Anchor Books, 2004), 16.

38 Charles A. Kupchan, *The End of the American Era: U.S. Foreign Policy and the Geopolitics of the TwentyFirst Century* (Vintage, 2002) 89.

39 Marjorie Kelly, *The Divine Right of Capital: Dethroning the Corporate Aristocracy* (Berrett-Koehler Publishers, Inc., 2001) 27.

40 *Id.*

41 *Id.* at 21.

42 *Id.* at 28.

43 Jerry Mander, *In the Absence of the Sacred: The Failure of Technology & the Survival of the Indian nations* (Sierra Club Books, 1991) 136.

44 *See* Mary (Beka) Economopoulos, *A Crisis in Democracy* (January 28, 2004), http://ftaaimc.org/or/2004/01/3563.shtml, *and* Jennifer Van Bergen, *Miami Police Admit Absolute Responsibility* (February 6, 2004), http://www.saveourcivilliberties.org/en/2004/02/234.shtml.

45   Catherine Wilson, *Greenpeace Challenges Prosecution in Mahogany Case*
      (December 12, 2003), *originally at*
      http://www.theledger.com/apps/pbcs.dll/article?AID=/20031212/APN/312
      120837 (no longer available on the internet, as of June 16, 2004), and
      Jonathan Turley, *Ashcroft's actions suggest selective prosecution* (October 23,
      2003),
      http://www.arbiteronline.com/vnews/display.v/ART/2003/10/23/3f975cfbe
      901e.

46   See Mark Hamblett, *Defense: Sheik's Lawyer Lacked Notice Her Actions
      Violated the Law* (April 12, 2004),
      http://www.law.com/jsp/article.jsp?id=1081348872998.

47   *U.S. v. Sattar, et al.*, http://news.findlaw.com/hdocs/docs/terrorism/ussat-
      tar72203opn.pdf.

48   *See also, Guantanamo lawyer quits after threat* (December 4, 2003),
      http://www.msnbc.com/news/1001354.asp?cp1=1.

49   *See* Heidi Boghosian, *NLG Fights Off Illegal Government Subpoenas*
      (February 11, 2004, Press Release),
      http://65.240.226.25/en/2004/02/36.shtml, *and* C. Clark Kissinger, *Just Say
      NO to Grand Jury Attack on the Anti-War Movement* (February 11, 2004),
      http://65.240.226.25/en/2004/02/37.shtm.

50   *See http://www.innocenceproject.org/.*

51   Email # 1 from activist [name withheld] to author, February, 2004.

52   Email # 2 from activist [name withheld] to author, February, 2004. *See*
      http://www.shacamerica.net/ for more information.

53   Daniel S. Levine, *Animal rights 'terror' rattles biotechs' cage* (February 8,
      2004), http://sanfrancisco.bizjournals.com/sanfrancisco/sto-
      ries/2004/02/09/story3.html.

54   Tom Regan, *Artist Falls Afoul of Patriot Act*,
      http://www.csmonitor.com/2004/0607/dailyUpdate.html.

55   *Id.*

56   National Lawyers Guild, *Press Release* (February 17, 2004),
      http://www.nlg.org/news/statements/UTexasLaw_pressrelease.htm.

57   *Id.*

58   *Id.*

59   MATRIX FAQs, www.matrix-at.org/faq.htm; Anita Ramasastry, *Why We
      Should Fear The Matrix: The "Multistate Anti-Terrorism Information
      Exchange" Program Threatens To Revive Total Information Awareness*
      (November 5, 2003),
      http://writ.news.findlaw.com/ramasastry/20031105.html.

60   *Olmstead v. United States*, 277 U.S. 438, 474 (1928) (J. Brandeis)

61   The (ACLU) National Technology & Liberty Program, [Barry
      Steinhardt], *White Paper on the MATRIX* (May 20, 2004),
      http://www.aclufl.org/PDFs/Whitepaper%20on%20new%20MATRIX%20
      docs%20-FINAL.pdf. ("ACLU, *White Paper*").

62   *Id.*

63   *Id.*

64   *Id.* (Emphasis in original.) This ominously resembles the mosaic theory
       discussed above in Chapter One, footnote 10.

65   *Id.*

66   ACLU, *Documents Acquired by ACLU Prove That MATRIX is a Data
       Mining Program* (January 21, 2004),
       www.aclu.org/Privacy/Privacy.cfm?ID=14763&c=130. *See also,* Bruce
       Glaser, *The Electronic Surveillance of America* (February 12, 2004),
       http://65.240.226.25/en/2004/02/38.shtml.

67   *Id.*

68   *Id.*

69   ACLU, *White Paper* (cited above).

70   Robert F. Kennedy, Jr., *Crimes Against Nature* (December 11, 2003),
       http://www.rollingstone.com/features/nationalaffairs/featuregen.asp?pid=21
       54.

71   *See* Jennifer Van Bergen, *Zalmay Khalilzad and the Bush Agenda* (January
       13, 2001), http://www.truthout.org/docs_01/01.14A.Zalmay.Oil.htm.

72   Earth Rights, *Unocal Can Be Held Liable For Human Rights Crimes in
       Burma,* Says Appeals Court (September 18, 2002), http://www.earth-
       rights.org/news/unocalsept19pr.shtml: John E. Howard, *The Alien Tort
       Claims Act: Is Our Litigation-Run-Amok Going Global?* (October 2002),
       http://www.uschamber.com/press/opeds/0210howarditigation.htm; *and*
       Earth Rights, *Defending the Alien Tort Claims Act* (last updated June 11,
       2004), http://www.earthrights.org/atca/index.shtml.

73   "The Federal Farmer," (Oct. 8, 1787), Ralph Ketchum, ed., *The Anti-
       Federalist Papers and the Constitutional Convention Debate* (Signet, 2003)
       259.

74   Vincent Bugliosi, *The Betrayal of America: How the Supreme Court
       Undermined the Constitution and Chose Our President* (Thunder's Mouth
       Press/Nation Books, 2001) 41-42. ("Bugliosi, *Betrayal*")

75   *Id.* at 42. There *were* voter suits brought in lower Florida courts that
       claimed the so-called butterfly ballots violated equal protection. These,
       however, had nothing to do with the case that made it to the Supreme
       Court. *See* Chronology of Lawsuits,
       http://news.findlaw.com/legalnews/us/elecction/election2000.html.

76   Quoted in *id.,* at 66.

77   Gary Rosen, *A Year Later: Reconsidering Bush v. Gore* (Nov. 2, 2001),
       http://www.opinionjournal.com/extra/?id=95001429.

78   Quoted in *id.,* without citation. (Emphasis added.)

79   Bugliosi, *Betrayal,* at 71.

80   *City of Mobile, Alabama v. Bolden,* 446 U.S. 55 (1980).

81   Bugliosi, *Betrayal,* at 72.

82   Editorial, *How to Hack an Election,* New York Times (January 31, 2004),
       http://www.nytimes.com/2004/01/31/opinion/31SAT1.html. Also archived
       at http://cryptome.org/hack-vote.htm. *See also, Jim's Diebold Page,*

     http://www.equalccw.com/voteprar.html.

83   67 Federal Register 54878 (August 26, 2002).

84   Bush is even secretive about environmental audits. *See The Privileged Class: Bush pushes secrecy for environmental audits*, http://txpeer.org/Bush/Privileged_Class.html.

85   James Hall, *Secrecy as a Principle of Government* (January 30, 2002), http://www.american-partisan.com/cols/2002/hall/qtr1/0130.htm

86   *Democracy Dies Behind Closed Doors: Throwing Out the Bush Secret Courts* (August 29, 2002), http://whiteplainscnr.com/article752.html. The case is *North Jersey Media Group v. Ashcroft*, 308 F.3d 198 (3d Cir. 2002).

87   Kyle F. Hence to Jennifer Van Bergen (e-mail) (February 6, 2004). Hence runs http://www.unansweredquestions.org/.

88   *See* Marie Cocco, *Bush Needs to Stop Gamesmanship on Probes* (February 5, 2004), http://www.newsday.com/news/columnists/ny-vpcoc033653618feb03,0,4825544.column?coll=ny-news-columnists, *and* Robert Cohen, *9/11 conspiracy theories abound, and inquiry takes* (January 1, 2004), notehttp://www.cleveland.com/news/plaindealer/index.ssf?/base/news/1072 954556323650.xml *See also*, Paul Thompson, *Notes on the Latest Timeline Update* (January 30, 2004), http://www.cooperativeresearch.org/timeline/updates/update18.html, and *September Outlines and Timelines*, http://www.cooperativeresearch.org/wot/sept11/default.html.

89   Hence email to JVB (Feb. 6, 2004).

90   *Id.*

91   Hall, *Secrecy as a Principle of Government*.

Chapter Seven

1   *Reid v. Covert*, 354 U.S. 1, 39-40 (1957) (J. Black, plurality op.) (quoting *Boyd v. United States*, 116 U.S. 616, 635 (1886)(J. Bradley)).

2   *See* Jennifer Van Bergen, *Repeal the PATRIOT Act*, http://www.truthout.org/docs_02/04.02A.JVB.Patriot.htm; Nancy Chang, *The USA PATRIOT Act: What's So Patriotic About Trampling on the Bill of Rights?*, http://www.ccr-ny.org/v2/reports/docs/USA_PATRIOT_ACT.pdf; Susan Herman, *The USA PATRIOT ACT and the US Department of Justice: Losing Our Balances?*, http://jurist.law.pitt.edu/forum/forumnew40.htm.

3   *See*, Nancy Chang, *Silencing Political Dissent: HowPost-September 11 Antiterrorism Measures Threaten Our Civil Liberties*, (Seven Stories Press, 2002); James X. Dempsey & David Cole, *Terrorism & the Constitution: Sacrificing Civil Liberties in the Name of Security* (First Amendment Foundation, 2002) ("Dempsey & Cole, *Terrorism & the Constitution*"); C. William Michaels, *No Greater Threat: America After September 11 and the Rise of a National Security State* (Algora Publishing, 2002) ("Michaels, *No*

Greater Threat").

4 I have chosen to keep the discussion relatively uncluttered by not discussing in detail other statutes such as the Model Health Emergency Powers Act (MEHPA), the No Child Left Behind Act, the Homeland Security Act, various DOJ regulations, Executive Orders (including the Military Commissions), and so on. Nor do I discuss many earlier administrations' enactments, such as the Federal Emergency Management Act, or FEMA, or the Antiterrorism and Effective Death Penalty Act, or AEDPA.

5 Michaels, *No Greater Threat*, at 129.

6 Neither this chapter nor the next is intended to be a comprehensive survey of the Act.

7 *See* Dempsey & Cole, *Terrorism & the Constitution, passim.* (Parts I and II discuss the history of FBI investigations back to the early 1980's. Part III discusses the more direct history of the 1996 and 2001 anti-terrorism laws.)

8 David Cole, *Enemy Aliens* (New Press, 2003) 188 ("Cole, *Enemy Aliens*").

9 Jason Burke, *Secret World of US Jails* (June 14, 2004), http://observer.guardian.co.uk/international/story/0,6903,1237589,00.html .

10 Cole, *Enemy Aliens*, at 5. *See also, id.* at 7-8 and 75-82 for examples.

11 *People's Mojahedin Organization of Iran v. U.S. Department of State*, 182 F.3d 17, 19 (D.C. Cir. 1999), http://laws.lp.findlaw.com/dc/011465a.html.

12 I would point out that this is another example of a reversal. Reversals were discussed above at the end of Chapter 3.

13 Cole, *Enemy Aliens*, at 190.

14 Cole, *Enemy Aliens*, at 76 (citing *Humanitarian Law Project v. Ashcroft*, a case in which a longstanding human rights organization was accused of providing material support to the Kurdistan Worker's Party, for training them in human rights advocacy and peace negotiation skills). Cole won this case before the 9th Circuit court, which declared that a part of the material support provision was unconstitutional. *Humanitarian Law Project v. Ashcroft*, No. CV 03-6107 (C.D. Cal. Jan. 22, 2004), http://news.findlaw.com/hdocs/docs/terrorism/hlpash12304ord.pdf. *See also*, Center for Constitutional Rights, *CCR Files Constitutional Challenge to Patriot Act* (August 2003), http://www.ccr-ny.org/v2/reports/report.asp?ObjID=FjMAeaTxLu&Content=278, and links to other documents.

15 In fact, federal courts are required to infer an intent element into federal statutes that do not explicitly state one. *See U.S. v. Morisette*, 342 U.S. 246 (1952).

16 James Bovard, *Terrorism and Tyranny: Trampling Freedom, Justice, and Peace to Rid the World of Evil* (Palgrave Macmillan, 2003) at 166.

17 Foreign Intelligence Surveillance Act, P.L. 95-511, Title I (October 25, 1978), 92 Stat. 1796, at 50 U.S.C. § 1801(e)(2).

18 The "relevance" standard is found in sections 214 (Pen register, trap &

trace taps), 216 (universal jurisdiction for pen register, trap & trace taps), & 217 (computer trespassers). Section 215 (third party records - contains a requirement that records may only be sought under that provision if they are sought "as part of an investigation to protect the U.S. from international terrorism or clandestine intelligence activities"). Section 218 applies the "significant purpose" standard to certification of any FISA surveillance order. Other provisions apply similar diluted standards: section 213 (delayed notice—"jeopardize an ongoing investigation or unduly delay a trial"), section 206 (roving wiretaps—ordering assistance from "other persons" [common carriers, landlords, etc.] if target may "thwart identification of a specified person"), section 203 (information sharing allowed if related to foreign intelligence). See Congressional Research Service (CRS), *Terrorism: Section by Section Analysis fo the USA PATRIOT Act* (December 10, 2001), http://fpc.state.gov/documents/organizatoin/7952.pdf. ("CRS, *Report*")

19   See, ACLU, *SAFE Act: Urge Congress to Reject Ashcroft's Veto Threat* (no date),
       http://www.aclu.org/NationalSecurity/NationalSecurity.cfm?ID=13907&c=24.

20   Intelligence Authorization Act (IAA) of 2004, HR 2417 (cleared November 21, 2003), http://thomas.loc.gov/cgi-bin/query/z?c108:H.R.2417.ENR:, *see* Kim Zetter, *Expansion of "National Security Letters" Gives Unaccountable Power to FBI* (January 6, 2004), http://reclaimdemocracy.org/articles_2004/national_security_letters.html.

21   See Jennifer Van Bergen, *Secret Court Decision Silently Overrules Provision of PATRIOT Act*, August 25, 2002,
       http://www.truthout.org/docs_02/08.26A.jvb.sec.crt.htm.

22   An excellent overview of the history of FISA is Nathan C. Henderson, *The PATRIOT Act's Implication on the Government's Ability to Conduct Electronic Surveillance of Ongoing Domestic Investigations* (no date)(52 Duke L. J. 179), http://www.law.duke.edu/shell/cite.pl?52+Duke+L.+J.+179.

23   [Bill_of_rights] *H.R. 3179 - Secret Evidence Bill Headed for Markup* (post by Hope Marston, June 4, 2004) *at* http://mailman.efn.org/pipermail/bill_of_rights/2004-June/000030.html. (The "lone wolf" provision is contained in section 4 of the bill.) *For further analysis, see, ACLU Letter to the House Judiciary Committee Expressing Opposition to H.R. 3179, the "Anti-Terrorism Intelligence Tools Improvement Act of 2003"* (May 14, 2004), http://www.aclu.org/SafeandFree/SafeandFree.cfm?ID=15763&c=282.

24   United States, Senate Select Committee to Study Governmental Operations with respect to Intelligence Activities, *Supplementary Staff Reports on Intelligence Activities and the Rights of Americans, Final Report, Book III*, Report 94-755, Ninety-fourth Congress, Second Session, April 23, 1976, *in* Whitfield Diffie & Susan Landau, *Privacy on the Line: The Politics of Wiretapping & Encryption* (MIT Press, 1998) 149.

Chapter Eight

1   For my analysis in this section, I have liberally drawn from Center for
     Democracy & Technology (CDT), *Setting the Record Straight: An Analysis
     of the Justice Department's PATRIOT Act Website* (October 27, 2003),
     http://www.cdt.org/security/usapatriot/031027cdt.shtml. ("CDT Analysis")

2   Viet Dinh, a law professor and former top aide to Attorney General John
     Ashcroft, is often identified as the primary architect of the PATRIOT
     Act. *See* Kim Zetter, *The Patriot Act is Your Friend* (February 24, 2004),
     http://www.wired.com/news/print/0,1294,62388,00.html. *But also see,*
     James X. Dempsey & David Cole, *Terrorism & the Constitution: Sacrificing
     Civil Liberties in the Name of National Security* (First Amendment
     Foundation, 2002), *passim* (showing a long history to the PATRIOT Act).
     Dinh has recently spoken out against Guantanamo. *See* Vanessa Blum,
     Tactics Shift on War on Terrorism (December 9, 2003),
     http://www.law.com/jsp/article.jsp?id=1069801699305.

3   Department of Justice (DOJ), *The USA PATRIOT Act: Preserving Life and
     Liberty,* www.lifeandliberty.gov. All discussion in this section refers to the
     home page of this web site.

4   *See* CDT Analysis for CDT's responses to Ashcroft's other two, unobjec-
     tionable points.

5   All topical headings are copied exactly from www.lifeandliberty.gov.

6   *Id.*

7   Cong. Rec. 10/25/01.

8   CDT Analysis.

9   To be blunt, these three phrases are not only synonyms but code words
     that the DOJ uses to mean "We are getting around the Constitution."

10   The interchangeable use of these three terms by Ashcroft, the DOJ, and
     other government officials and bodies, has been picked up by the media,
     but of course without a full understanding of their significance. The term
     "foreign intelligence information" is defined in the Foreign Intelligence
     Surveillance Act (FISA), P.L. 95-511, Title 1 (October 25, 1978), 92 Stat.
     1796, at 50 U.S.C. § 1801(e), as "possible hostile acts of a foreign power
     or an agent of a foreign power, sabotage or terrorism by a foreign power or
     agent, and clandestine intelligence activities by a foreign power or agent."
     It includes information with respect to a foreign power or foreign territory
     that "relates to" the national defense, national security, or conduct of for-
     eign affairs of the United States. § 1801(e)(2). Recently, and I don't know
     exactly when or who started it, the terms "terrorist investigation" and
     "national security investigation" began to be used in place of "foreign
     intelligence investigation." But they all mean the same thing. They all
     refer to FISA investigations, which were originally intended to apply only
     to foreign powers and agents thereof, not specifically to terrorists. Indeed,
     the term terrorist is simply a new term for spies and saboteurs, who have
     existed for all time. Alliance with a foreign government has never been

mandatory for a foreign intelligence investigation. (FISA stipulates "foreign power or agent," not foreign government official.)

11   CDT Analysis.

12   Congressional Research Service [Charles Doyle], *Terrorism: Section by Section Analysis of the USA PATRIOT Act* (December 10, 2001) 10, http://fpc.state.gov/documents/organization/7952.pdf. ("CRS Report")

13   See Chapter 1, footnote 10 on the "mosaic theory," and Chapter 6, Part Two, section on MATRIX, re. the "terrorism quotient."

14   ACLU, *How the USA-PATRIOT Act Expands Law Enforcement "Sneak and Peek" Warrants* (October 23, 2001), www.aclu.org/congress/l102301b.html, and ALCU, *Surveillance Under the "USA/Patriot" Act*, http://archive.aclu.org/issues/privacy/USAPA_surveillance.html.

15   *See* Chapter 6, Part Two, the section on prosecutions and legal processes for examples of abuses of the grand jury.

16   Intelligence Authorization Act of 2004, HR 2417 (cleared November 21, 2003), http://thomas.loc.gov/cgi-bin/query/z?c108:H.R.2417.ENR:

17   Kim Zetter, *Expansion of "National Security Letters" Gives Unaccountable Power to FBI* (January 6, 2004), http://reclaimdemocracy.org/articles_2004/national_security_letters.html.

18   *Id.*

19   Heather MacDonald, *Why the FBI Didn't Stop 9/11* (Autumn 2002), www.city-journal.org/html/12_4_why_the_fbi.html. (MacDonald, *Why*)

20   *Id.*

21   *Id.*

22   Congressional Research Service (CRS), *Terrorism: Section by Section Analysis of the USA PATRIOT Act* (December 10, 2001) 5. ("CRS, Report")

23   MacDonald, *Why.*

24   Electronic Privacy Information Center (EPIC), *Overview of FISA*, www.epic.org/privacy/terrorism/fisa/. ("EPIC, *Overview*")

25   *Id.*

26   Cole, *Enemy Aliens,* at 199.

27   *Id.*

28   Clarke was National Coordinator for Security, Protection, and Counterterrorism under Clinton and continued in that office under George W. Bush. He was a career member of the Senior Executive Service, having begun his federal service in 1973 in the office of the Secretary of Defense, as an analyst on nuclear weapons and European security issues. Under Reagan, Clarke was the Deputy Assistant Secretary of State for Intelligence and in the first Bush administration, he was the Assistant Secretary of State for Politico-Military Affairs.

29   Richard A. Clarke, *Against All Enemies: Inside America's War on Terror* (Free Press, 2004) 91.

30   *Id.* at 91-92.

31   *Id.* at 92.
32   *See also* Section 504 of the PATRIOT Act, *Coordination With Law Enforcement,* which states the combination of 203 and 218: "Section 504 confirms that the certification requirement does not preclude intelligence officers operating under FISA orders from coordinating their investigations with law enforcement officers in cases involved a foreign attack or other grave hostile attack, sabotage or international terrorism by a foreign power or agent, or foreign clandestine intelligence activities."
33   Cole, *Enemy Aliens,* at 231.
34   ACLU, *How the USA-PATRIOT Act Puts the CIA Back in the Business of Spying on Americans,* www.aclu.org/congress/l102301j.html.
35   *Id.* (all quotes in paragraph)
36   Cole, *Enemy Aliens,* at 201.
37   *Id.*
38   EPIC, *Overview.*
39   *Id.*
40   CRS *Report,* at 14. (emphasis added by CRS)
41   *Id.*
42   *Id. at* 15.
43   *Id.*
44   EPIC, *Overview.*
45   U.S. Constitution, Amendment V (Ratified 12/15/1791).
46   James X. Dempsey & David Cole, *Terrorism & the Constitution: Sacrificing Civil Liberties in the Name of National Security* (First Amendment Foundation, 2002) 163 (both quotes).
47   Jethro K. Leiberman, *A Practical Companion to the Constitution: How the Supreme Court Has ruled on Issues from Abortion to Zoning* (University of California Press, 1999) 217. (Leiberman, *Constitution*)
48   Dempsey & Cole, , *Terrorism & the Constitution,* at 163.
49   Lieberman, *Practical Companion to the Constitution,* at 217.
50   Dempsey & Cole, *Terrorism & the Constitution,* at 164.
51   *Id.*
52   *Id.*
53   *Id.*
54   *Id.* at 163 (the prohibition is codified at 50 U.S.C. §403-3(d)(1).
55   *Id.*
56   *Id.*
57   *Id.*
58   *Id.*

Chapter Nine

1   Boyd v. United States, 116 U.S. 616, 635 (1886).
2   David Armstrong, *Dick Cheney's Song of America: Drafting a Plan for Global Dominance* (October 2002),

http://www.thirdworldtraveler.com/American_Empire/Cheney's_Song_Am erica.html. All otherwise un-attributed quotes in this chapter are to this article.

3 Richard Clarke, *Against All Enemies: Inside America's War on Terror* (Free Press, 2004) 30.

4 *Id.* at 31.

5 Internal paragraph break removed.

6 Jonatha Brooke, *War*, from *Plumb*.

7 Stan Goff, *Full Spectrum Disorder: The Military in the New American Century* (Soft Skull Press, 2004) 18.

8 The phrase comes from, Thomas Jefferson, *Declaration of Independence*, para. 1.

Chapter Ten

1 This section is modified from Jennifer Van Bergen and Charles B. Gittings, *Bush War: Military Necessity or War Crimes?* (15 July 2003), in 3 parts, starting at: http://truthout.org/docs_03/071403D.shtml. *Also archived at* http://www.puzzle-element.org/bushwarmilitarynecessityorwarcrimes.doc.

2 Alexander Hamilton, *The Federalist Papers, No. 47*, http://memory.loc.gov/const/fed/fed_47.html.

3 William Cole, *UN Inspectors Say U.S. Relied on Forged Reports of Iraq Nucelar Efforts* (March 7, 2003), www.commondreams.org/head-lines03/0308-06.htm.

4 See the *Military Tribunal Order*, http://www.whitehouse.gov/news/releas-es/2001/11/20011113-27.html, and the *White House Fact Sheet on the Status of Detainees at Guantanamo*, http://www.whitehouse.gov/news/releas-es/2002/02/20020207-13.html.

5 U.S. Constitution, Article VI, para. 2.

6 See *Paquete Habana*, 175 U.S. 677 (1900) and *U.S. v. Belmont*, 301 U.S. 324 (1934).

7 Title 18, Section 2441, United States Code.

8 Geneva Common Article 3(1)(d), http://www.yale.edu/lawweb/avalon/lawofwar/geneva03.htm#art3, and Hague IV Annex (HR) Article 23, http://www.yale.edu/lawweb/avalon/lawofwar/hague04.htm#art23.

9 International Committee of the Red Cross (ICRC) (Jean S. Pictet, ed.), *Commentary to the Protocol Additional to the Geneva Conventions of 12 August 1949, and relating to the Protection of Victims of International Armed Conflicts*, 8 June 1977 (hereafter "*Geneva Commentary*"), vol. 3, pp. 75-76, http://www.yale.edu/lawweb/avalon/imt/proc/imtconst.htm#sec1.

10 International Military Tribunal Charter (London 1945).

11 Hague IV Annex (HR) Art. 23-28, supra footnote 41.

12 Fourth Geneva Convention (Civilians) Article 4. Other definitions

specifically include POW's. See Pietro Verri, Dictionary of the International Law of Armed Conflict, (ICRC, 1992), http://www.icrc.org/ihl.nsf/c525816bde96b7fd41256739003e636a/78eb50e ad6ee7aa1c12563cd0051b9d4?OpenDocument.

13   Both quotes from: International Committee of the Red Cross (ICRC), *Punishing Violations of International Humanitarian Law at the National Level: A Guide for Common Law States* (2001), pp. 9-10 (emphasis in the original).

14   All information in this paragraph is from: ICRC, *Geneva Commentary*, vol. 3, p. 27.

15   *See* footnote 16 for cite. This statute applies only to violations against U.S. citizens. *See* footnote 8 for the Hague Convention articles.

16   18 U.S.C. §2441 http://www4.law.cornell.edu/uscode/18/2441.html. The clause ends with "and which deals with non-international armed conflict." Thus, clause (1) and (2) apply to international conflicts, and clause (3) applies to non-international ones. The meaning of this is that there is no "sovereign immunity" for officials who commit war crimes against domestic rebels, criminals, or untermenschen. (Sub clause (4) relates to any person who willfully kills or causes serious injury to civilians under the Protocol on Prohibitions or Restrictions on the Use of Mines, Booby-Traps and Other Devices.)

17   Third Geneva Convention Article 130, http://www.yale.edu/lawweb/avalon/lawofwar/geneva03.htm#art130. (The spelling is so in the original.)

18   Hague IV Annex (HR) Article 23, *supra* footnote 41.

19   Burrus M. Carnahan, *Lincoln, Lieber and the Laws of War: The Origins and Limits of the Principle of Military Necessity*, 92 American Journal of Int'l Law, Vol. 92 (No. 2), 213 (April 1998).

20   Thomas P. Vincent, Esq., *Legal History and Philosophy* (last updated November 28, 2003), "A Few from Lieber's Code and the Law of War," www.commonlaw.com/Lieber.html. Lieber's *Code of War* was requisitioned by President Lincoln during the Civil War and became the foundation for other codifications of the law of nations.

21   ICRC, Geneva Commentary, pp. 681-82, http://www.icrc.org/ihl.nsf/b466ed681ddfcfd241256739003e6368/d80d14d 84bf36b92c12563cd00434fbd.

22   *See* Rebecca Grant, *In Search of Lawful Targets*, Air Force Magazine (February 2003), http://www.afa.org/magazine/feb2003/02targets03.pdf.

23   Francoise Hampson, *Military Necessity*, (From *Crimes of War Project*-The Book), (no date) http://www.crimesofwar.org/thebook/military-necessity.html.

24   Douglas P. Lackey, *The Ethics of War and Peace* (1989) p. 59, quoted in, Colonel J.G. Fleury, *Jus In Bello and Military Necessity*, Department of National Defence (Canada), Advanced Military Studies Course. (The author appended the following statement: "This paper was written by a student attending the Canadian Forces College in fulfillment of one of

the communication skills requirements of the Course of Studies. The paper is a scholastic document, and thus contains facts and opinions which the author alone considered appropriate and correct for the subject. It does not necessarily reflect the policy or the opinion of any agency, including the Government of Canada and the Canadian Department of National Defence [sic].").

Chapter 11

1   Stan Goff, *Full Spectrum Disorder: The Military in the New American Century* (Soft Skull Press, 2004), 49.
2   *Id.* at 175.
3   *Id.* at 177.
4   *Id.* at 172.
5   *Id.*
6   *Id.* at 175.
7   *Id.* at 183.
8   *Id.* at 177 (quoting Colin Gray, *Modern Strategy* (no cite)).
9   Robert Browning, *The Ring & the Book*, Book IV, *Tertium Quid*, line 10 (Penguin Books, 1971).
10 James Parton, *The Life and Times of Aaron Burr* (Johnson Reprint, 1967; original publication by Mason Brothers, 1858) 613.

Epilogue

1   Article I, section 9, para. 2, U.S. Constitution. The Writ of Habeas Corpus (Latin for *have the body*), also called "The Great Writ of Liberty" (or just "the Great Writ"), enables a detained person to challenge the grounds of his detention by demanding that his person be brought before a court of law. The Supreme Court held in *Ex Parte Milligan*, 4 Wallace 2 (1866), that only Congress may suspend the writ and only if civilian courts were closed.
2   Thomas Jefferson to James Madison (July 31, 1788), *in* Julius Boyd, ed., *Papers of Thomas Jefferson*, 13:442. (Spelling and punctuation modernized.) Jefferson, however, attempted to suspend the Writ of Habeas Corpus in 1807 during the so-called Burr Conspiracy. The measure failed to pass Congress.
3   This opinion was expressed by the unnamed person who compiled a find-law update I received by email.
4   Jennifer Van Bergen, *Repeal the Patriot Act, Part III: Civil Rights Violations and Torture* (April 3, 2002), http://truthout.com/docs_02/04.04E.JVB.Patriot.htm. ("JVB, *Repeal the Patriot Act, Part III*")
5   *Rasul v. Bush*, No. 03-334 (June 28, 2004),

http://supct.law.cornell.edu/supcit/html/03-334.ZS.html.

6   *Hamdi v. Rumsfeld*, No. 03-6696 (June 28, 2004),
    http://supct.law.cornell.edu/supcit/html/03-6696.ZO.html.

7   In a third case, *Rumsfeld v. Padilla*, involving another Bush-designated
    unlawful enemy combatant, the Court decided that it had been filed in
    the wrong jurisdiction. The Court thus reversed the Second Circuit deci-
    sion and remanded it to be re-filed in the District of South Carolina, the
    district in which Padilla is being held. *Rumsfeld v. Padilla*, No. 03-1027
    (June 28, 2004), http://supct.law.cornell.edu/supct/html/03-1027.ZO.html.

8   Jennifer Van Bergen, *The Detainees & the Bush Tyranny* (June 29, 2004),
    http://www.counterpunch.org/bergen06302004.html. ("JVB, *Bush
    Tyranny*")

9   Human Rights Watch, *The Road to Abu Ghraib* (June 2004) 1,
    http://www.hrw.org/reports/2004/usa0604/. ("HRW, *Abu Ghraib*")

10 Bush's grandfather did business with I.G. Farben, the Nazi war factory,
    well into World War II, and was finally ordered to stop by the U.S. gov-
    ernment, and G.W. Bush's own business history shows he did not comply
    with securities laws. There are abundant sources on the internet on these
    topics. *See, for example*, Robert Lederman, *The Corpocracy Uncovered —
    Bush family supported Third Reich (The GW Bush Gang, IG Farben)
    http://www.georgewalkerbush.net/bushgang.htm, and* Knut Royce, *Bush
    Violated Security Laws Four Times, SEC Report Says* (July 2, 2002),
    http://www.abusaleh.com/index.php?id=104.

11 HRW, *Abu Ghraib*.

12 *See* Duncan Campbell, *An Exquisite Danger* (June 2, 2004),
    http://www.soaw.org/new/newswire_detail.php?id=454.

13 I don't mean to say that the PATRIOT Act *caused* torture. That Act is, as
    I have made clear in this book, one component of an entire array of
    actions by those in power. It is merely one manifestation of a government
    gone awry, but it was obvious to me two years ago that the PATRIOT Act
    was a step down the road leading to torture and was, in fact, preparatory
    to such "regimes of tyranny." (I borrow this term from Jane Maslow
    Cohen, *Regimes of Private Tyranny: What Do They Mean to Morality and for
    the Criminal Law?*, 57 U. Pitt. L. Rev. 757 (1996). *See* JVB, *Bush Tyranny*.

14 JVB, *Repeal the Patriot Act, Part III*. (All references to my article are from
    this part.)

15 *For case highlights, see* Center for National Security Studies, *CNSS v. DOJ
    Case Highlights*, http://www.cnss.org/casehighlights.htm. *For March 18
    amended complaint, go to:* http://www.cnss.org/cnssmemoinsupport.htm.
    The D.C. Circuit ruled on July 15 2003, that the DOJ properly withheld
    names and information. On January 12, 2004, the Supreme Court
    declined to review the case.

16 The Star Chamber was a circa 16th century English court that sat in
    closed sessions on cases involving state security. The term "star chamber"
    to this day means "secret, harsh, and arbitrary." Hammurabi was a

Babylonian King from the 18th century B.C., who is best known for his code of nearly three hundred laws whose stated objective was "to cause justice to prevail in the land, to destroy the wicked and evil, to prevent the strong from oppressing the weak...and to further the welfare of the people." R. F. Harper, *The Code of Hammurabi* 3 (University of Chicago Press, 1904). Hammurabi has been called "an enlightened despot." *See* T. Walter Wallbank, *Civilization: Past and Present* 14 (HarperCollins Publishers, 1992). And Moses, of course, in the 13th century B.C. brought the Ten Commandments to the Jews.

17 Human Rights Watch notes: "Among the most disturbing cases, perhaps unprecedented in U.S. history, are the detainees who have simply been 'disappeared.'" HRW, *Abu Ghraib*, p. 12.

18 Foreign Policy Research Institute, *Orbis: A Journal of World Affairs* (*The New Protracted Conflict*, vol. 46, No. 2, Spring 2002). ("*Orbis, Protracted Conflict*")

19 Sam C. Sarkesian, *The U.S. Army Special Forces Then and Now*, *Orbis, Protracted Conflict* 247-58. ("Sarkesian, *Special Forces*")

20 18 U.S.C. §2331(5) (added by USA PATRIOT Act, Section 802) (defining domestic terrorism) and utilized in 18 U.S.C. §2332b(g)(5) (amended by PATRIOT Act, Section 808 (listing dozens of predicate offenses for the federal crime of terrorism)).

21 Sarkesian, *Special Forces*, at 256-57.

22 Bruce Berkowitz, *Intelligence and the War on Terrorism* (Foreign Policy Research Institute) *Orbis: A Journal of World Affairs* (*The New Protracted Conflict*, vol. 46, No. 2, Spring 2002) 289, 293.

23 Michael Radu, *Terrorism After the Cold War: Trends and Challenges* (Foreign Policy Research Institute) *Orbis: A Journal of World Affairs* (*The New Protracted Conflict*, vol. 46, No. 2, Spring 2002) 275, 283. ("Radu, *Terrorism*")

24 HRW, *Abu Ghraib*, at 1.

25 Maj. Gen. Archer Lerch, *The Army Reports on POWS*, The American Mercury, May, 1945, pp. 536-547. Quoted in a July 5, 2004 post to the American Society of International Lawyers (ASIL) forum list serve by the Honorable Evan J. Wallach, US Court of International Trade. Archived at: http://pegc.no-ip.info/_UPDATES_/PEGC_20040705_extra.txt. Of Lerch's comments, Judge Wallach noted: "Although they address the 1929 Geneva convention, I find them distinctly relevant to White House Counsel Alberto Gonzales and John Yoo's arguments about [the] obsolescence [of the 1949 Geneva Conventions]."

26 Radu, *Terrorism*, at 283, 287.

27 *Id.* at 275-6. Radu states: "Terrorism is any attack, or threat of attack, against unarmed targets, intended to influence, change, or divert major political decisions." This is indeed similar to the definition now in the U.S. Code (*see* footnote 10), as amended by the PATRIOT Act.

28 Joanne Mariner, *The EU, The FARC, The PKK, and the PFLP:*

Distinguishing Politics From Terror,
http://writ.news.findlaw.com/mariner/20020513.html, and Joanne
Mariner, *Make a List But Check It Twice: Prosecuting Supporters of Terrorist Groups,* http://writ.news.findlaw.com/mariner/20020902.html.

29   *Radu, Terrorism* at 285.

30   *See* Human Rights Watch, *Summary of International and U.S. Law Prohibiting Torture and Other Ill-treatment of Persons in Custody* (last updated May 24, 2004),
http://hrw.org/english/docs/2004/05/24/usint8614_txt.htm.

31   Jacques deLisle, *The Roles of Law in the Fight Against Terrorism, Orbis, Protracted War,* 301-319.

32   Mark Bowden, *The Dark Art of Interrogation* (October 2003)
http://www.theatlantic.com/issues/2003/10/bowden.htm. ("Bowden, *Interrogation*")

33   Radu, *Terrorism, at* 284.

34   Bowden, *Interrogation.*

35   Human Rights Watch, *Bush Administration Lawyers Greenlight Torture: Memo Suggests Intent to Commit War Crimes* (June 7, 2004),
http://hrw.org/english/docs/2044/06/07/usdom8778_txt.htm.

36   Johanna McGeary, *The Scandal's Growing Stain* (*Time,* May 17, 2004) 34. (Preview only available at http://www.time.com/time/archive/preview/0,10987,1101040517-634634,00.html.)

37   I intend a pun on the FBI/DOJ "mosaic theory." *See* Chapter One, footnote 10, for a brief discussion of this theory, the most recent excuse for invasion of privacy.

38   *Hamdi* (J. O'Connor), part III (D), para. 4.

39   The plurality opinion states that "it is notable that military regulations already provide for such process in related instances, dictating that tribunals be made available to determine the status of enemy detainees who assert prisoner-of-war status under the Geneva Conventions." *Hamdi v. Rumsfeld* (cite at footnote 5) (J. O'Connor, plurality op.), part III, D, para. 4.

40   *Hamdi* (O'Connor), part III, C, para.2.

41   *Id.*, part II, para. 16.

42   *See* Wayne R. LaFave & Jerold H. Israel, *Criminal Procedure* (Hornbook Series, 2d ed., West Publishing, 1992), §28.2(b). ("The King's Bench apparently accepted counsels' contention that the writ could be used to enforce the Magna Charta's guarantee [of due process], but responded that it could not look beyond the crown's return [e.g., reply, mandate] , which stated on its face that the detention was lawfully authorized. Dissatisfaction with this ruling eventually led to a 1641 Act that removed the power of the Crown to arrest *without probable cause* and granted to any arrested person immediate access by writ of habeas corpus to a judicial determination of the legality of his detention.") (Emphasis added.) *See also Rasul* (J. Kennedy, concurrence) para. 6. ("Indefinite detention with-

out trial or other proceeding" suggests "much greater alignment with the traditional function of habeas corpus.")

43   *Hamdi* (J. Souter, op.), intro.

44   *Id.* (J. O'Connor), part II, para. 3.

45   *Johnson v. Eisentrager*, 339 U.S. 763 (1950).

46   *Hamdi* (J. Scalia, dissent), part I, para. 1.

47   Sir William Blackstone, *Commentaries on the Laws of England*, 1:132-133 (1765), *quoted in Hamdi* (J. Scalia, dissent), *id.*, para. 2. (Spelling modernized.)

48   Joseph Story, *Commentaries on the Constitution of the United States* §1783, p. 661 (1833), *quoted in id.*, para. 5.

49   Alexander Hamilton, *Federalist No. 84* (G. Carey & J. McClellan eds. 2001) 444, *quoted in id.*, para. 9. (Spelling modernized.)

50   *Id.*, para. 6.

51   *Id.*, quoting *Kansas v. Hendricks*, 521 U.S. 346, 358 (1997).

52   *Id.*, part II, para. 1 & (A), para. 1.

53   Sir Michael Foster, *Discourse on High Treason* (1762), *quoted in id.*, part II (A), para. 4.

54   U.S. Constitution, Art. III, section 3.

55   *Hamdi* (J. Scalia, dissent), part II (A), para. 9.

56   *Id.*, part III, para. 2. (Emphasis in original.)

57   *Hamdi* (J. O'Connor, plurality op.) part III (C), para. 3, *quoting from Mathews v. Eldridge*, 424 U.S. 319, 335 (1976).

58   Andrew C. McCarthy, *A Mixed Bag* (June 30, 2004), www.nationalreview.com/mccarthy/mccarthy200406300915.asp.

59   *See* Anne-Marie Cusac, *Abu Ghraib, USA* (July 2004), http://www.progressive.org/july04/cusac0704.html.

60   *Id.*

61   Lynne Stewart, who has been accused of providing material support to terrorists, was Rahman's defense attorney and it is her post-trial representation of him that led to the indictment against her.

62   Andrew C. McCarthy, *Torture: Thinking About the Unthinkable* (July-August 2004), www.benadorassociates.com/article/5900. ("McCarthy, *Torture*")

63   Andrew C. McCarthy, *Abu Ghraib & Enemy Combatants* (May 11, 2004), www.nationalreview.com/mccarthy/mccarthy200405110832.asp. ("McCarthy, *Abu Ghraib*")

64   McCarthy, *Abu Ghraib*. (All quotes in this section are from this article, unless or until noted.)

65   McCarthy, *Torture*. All subsequent quotes are from this article, unless otherwise noted.

66   Bowden, *Interrogation*.

67   Oddly, despite this one and only example of the result of regulated torture, Bowden nonetheless concludes that torture should be permitted.

68   Bowden, *Interrogation*.

69   Id.
70   Anthony Lewis, *One Liberty at a Time* (May/June 2004) (p. 78 in print
      edition), http://www.motherjones.com/news/feature/2004/05/04_403.html.

About the Author

Jennifer Van Bergen, who resides in South Florida, is on the State Board and Legal Panel of the Florida ACLU and has written, spoken, and debated widely on the PATRIOT Act and other civil liberties concerns. She was co-chair of the Broward Bill of Rights Defense Coalition, which in early 2003 obtained the passage by the Broward County Commission of a Resolution protesting the PATRIOT Act and reaffirming official commitment to the Bill of Rights. Broward was the 100th and, at the time, most populous (1.6 million people) community to pass such a resolution in the United States.

Jennifer is a graduate of Benjamin N. Cardozo School of Law in New York City. During law school, she worked on the appellate brief in one of the World Trade Center bombing cases and did an internship at Immigration Court in New York. Her main interests are criminal law, immigration, civil liberties, and the effects of trauma on memory.

Professionally, Jennifer is a journalist, legal analyst, and a non-practicing attorney who does criminal appellate research and writing for practicing attorneys. She has recently published two articles with the *Cardozo Public, Law, Policy & Ethics Journal*: one on the electoral tie of 1801 between Thomas Jefferson and Aaron Burr (Spring 2003) and another on the designation and material support provisions of the USA PATRIOT Act (Spring 2004).

She was an adjunct faculty member of the New School for Social Research in New York, where she taught in the Writing Program from 1993-2003. Her last semester there, she also taught "The Anti-terrorism Laws, the Constitution, and Civil Rights" in the Social Sciences Dept.

She has been involved occasionally with the Project to Enforce the Geneva Conventions (PEGC), a one-man project based in California, which is working on holding top U.S. officials accountable for violations of international law (on such issues as Guantanamo detentions, unlawful enE-Epilogemy combatant detentions, etc.).

In addition to the ACLU, Jennifer is a supporter and member of Amnesty Int'l, the Sierra Club, and Mensa, and an active member of the National Lawyers Guild (NLG). She is on the NLG's Military Law Task Force and International Committee. She joined Phase II of the NLG's fact-finding human rights delegation to Haiti in April 2004 and co-authored the delegation's report, which is at www.nlg.org.

Jennifer works frequently with numerous South Florida peace and justice groups to organize events, forums, debates, and rallies.

Back in the 1980's, she worked with the U.S. Raoul Wallenberg Committee and subsequently founded the Wallenberg Committee of Holland (where she was living at the time).

Jennifer, who was raised in the theater, is a trained Shakespearean actress and singer/songwriter. Although she no longer performs, some of her songs can be heard at www.puzzle-element.org. Jennifer also enjoys reading books about quantum physics and she practices astrology. She studies Egyptian heiroglyphs for relaxation. For Jennifer, law, science the arts, spirituality, and esoterica, all go hand in hand.